World Trade and Investment Law Reimagined

THE ANTHEM IGLP RETHINKING GLOBAL LAW AND POLICY SERIES

In today's world, poverty, conflict, injustice and inequality are also legal and institutional regimes. **The Anthem IGLP Rethinking Global Law and Policy Series** explores the ways in which they are reproduced and what might be done in response. The series seeks contributions mapping the levers of global political, economic and legal authority, and which bring new and critical perspectives to international legal research and policy. We aim to encourage innovative approaches to global policy in the face of a legal and institutional architecture manifestly ill-equipped to address our most urgent global challenges. The series is particularly interested in contributions that highlight voices from and issues of concern to the Global South. Proposals that cross disciplinary lines and draw upon heterodox intellectual and political traditions are encouraged.

This series is undertaken by Anthem in collaboration with Harvard's Institute for Global Law and Policy.

Series Editor

David Kennedy—Harvard Law School, USA

Editorial Board

The editorial board is comprised of members of the
Academic/Advisory Councils of IGLP.

World Trade and Investment Law Reimagined

A Progressive Agenda for an Inclusive Globalization

Edited by

Alvaro Santos, Chantal Thomas and David Trubek

ANTHEM PRESS

Anthem Press
An imprint of Wimbledon Publishing Company
www.anthempress.com

This edition first published in UK and USA 2020
by ANTHEM PRESS
75–76 Blackfriars Road, London SE1 8HA, UK
or PO Box 9779, London SW19 7ZG, UK
and
244 Madison Ave #116, New York, NY 10016, USA

First published in the UK and USA by Anthem Press 2019

British Library Cataloguing-in-Publication Data
A catalogue record for this book is available from the British Library.

ISBN-13: 978-1-78527-452-7 (Pbk)
ISBN-10: 1-78527-452-X (Pbk)

This title is also available as an e-book.

CONTENTS

Section 5 Reinforcing Social Protection: Spreading the Benefits of Trade, Dealing with Losses and Exploring the Trade–Immigration Nexus

ACKNOWLEDGMENTS

This volume was produced by the project on Rethinking Trade and Investment Law (ReTAIL) sponsored by Harvard Law School's Institute for Global Law and Policy (IGLP) and Georgetown Law's Center for the Advancement of the Rule of Law in the Americas (CAROLA) with additional assistance from Cornell Law School. IGLP's director, David Kennedy, enthusiastically supported ReTAIL and helped at all stages. The editors are grateful for financial and staff support from both IGLP, CAROLA and Cornell, and we acknowledge outstanding editorial assistance by Kelly Messier. The essays were initially presented at a workshop at IGLP in April 2018. We thank the contributions of Lucie White, Daniela Caruso and other discussants in that workshop. In October 2018, IGLP held an "Incubator" at which a draft of the introductory overview essay was discussed. We are grateful for comments and suggestions at that event from Joel Trachtman, Mark Wu, David Kennedy, Love Ronnelid and others.

—*Alvaro Santos, Chantal Thomas and David Trubek*

CONTRIBUTORS

Dan Danielsen is a professor of law and the faculty director of the Program on the Corporation, Law and Global Society at Northeastern University School of Law. His research explores the complex role of the business firm in global governance and economic development, most recently through the study of global supply chains. Prior to joining the Northeastern faculty, Danielsen was executive vice president and general counsel of Europe Online Networks S.A., a pioneer in the provision of broadband internet and interactive multimedia services to consumers across Europe. He was also a partner at Foley Hoag LLP, where his practice focused on the representation of US and European public and privately held businesses with respect to corporate finance, mergers and acquisitions, strategic partnerships and joint ventures, content and technology licensing, and corporate strategy.

Dennis M. Davis is a judge and president of the Competition Appeal Court of South Africa and a professor of law at the University of Cape Town and has taught as a visiting professor at Melbourne, Georgetown, New York and Harvard universities. His latest book, with Michelle Le Roux, is *Lawfare: Judging Politics in South Africa* (2019).

Antonia Eliason received her BS in cell and molecular biology and computer science from the University of Michigan, her MA in European and Eurasian studies from George Washington University, and her JD from the University of Michigan. Eliason joined the University of Mississippi School of Law faculty in 2013. She previously worked as an associate at Allen & Overy in London and Hong Kong in the area of debt and equity securities. Her research focuses on trade and investment law as well as critical legal theory. She has written extensively on the WTO and regional trade agreements. Her recent articles include works on trade facilitation, the role of the WTO in addressing climate change and sustainable development, and the judicial review of international investment awards.

Kevin P. Gallagher is a professor of global development policy at Boston University's Frederick S. Pardee School of Global Studies, where he directs the Global Development Policy Center. Gallagher is the author or coauthor of six books, including *The China Triangle: Latin America's China Boom and the Fate of the Washington Consensus* (2016); *Ruling Capital: Emerging Markets and the Reregulation of Cross-Border Finance* (2014); and *The Clash of Globalizations: Essays on the Political Economy of Trade and Development Policy* (2013). He serves on the United Nations' Committee for Development Policy and cochairs the T-20 Task Force on an International Financial Architecture for Stability and Development at the

G-20. He previously served on the investment subcommittee of the Advisory Committee on International Economic Policy at the US Department of State.

Frank J. Garcia is a professor of law and a Dean's Distinguished Scholar at the Boston College Law School. A Fulbright Scholar, he has lectured widely on globalization and international economic law in Europe, South America and the Asia-Pacific region. Garcia has held various leadership positions within the American Society of International Law and currently sits on the editorial board of the *Journal of International Economic Law*, where he is chief book review editor. He is the author of *Consent and Trade: Trading Freely in a Global Market* (2019) and *Global Justice and International Economic Law: Three Takes* (2013).

Rob Howse is the Lloyd C. Nelson Professor of International Law at New York University School of Law. He has been a visiting professor at, among other institutions, Harvard Law School, Tel Aviv University, the Hebrew University of Jerusalem and the University of Paris 1 (Pantheon-Sorbonne). Howse has been a frequent consultant or adviser to government agencies and international organizations such as the OECD, UNCTAD and the Inter-American Development Bank. He is a member of the Board of Advisers of the NYU Center for Law and Philosophy.

Pasha L. Hsieh is an associate professor of law and Lee Kong Chian Fellow at the Singapore Management University School of Law. He has written on ASEAN law, Asia-Pacific free trade agreements, and the roles of China and Taiwan in international legal order. His work has been cited by the Federal Supreme Court of Switzerland, the Brookings Institution and the Organisation for Economic Co-operation and Development. Hsieh has been invited by various institutions, such as the European Parliament and the Singapore Judicial College, to present on trade law issues. Recently, he was elected to serve as the cochair of the Law in the Pacific Rim Region Interest Group of the American Society of International Law and an executive council member of the Society of International Economic Law.

Jason Jackson is the Ford Career Development Assistant Professor in Political Economy and Urban Planning and a member of the Task Force on Work of the Future at MIT. He received his PhD in political economy at MIT and has won fellowships from the Social Sciences Research Council and the UK-based Overseas Development Institute. Jackson has also worked with a variety of private, nongovernmental and multilateral organizations in the Caribbean, South Africa and the United States.

Poul F. Kjaer is a professor of governance and sociology of law at the Department of Management, Politics and Philosophy, Copenhagen Business School. He holds degrees in law (European University Institute, Florence), sociology (Goethe University, Frankfurt) and political science (Aarhus University, Aarhus, Denmark). He has been a visiting scholar at, among others, Harvard University, London School of Economics and Political Science, and Sciences Po in Paris, as well as a fellow at the Institut d'études Avancées de Paris. Kjaer is the author of *Between Governing and Governance: On the Emergence, Function and Form of Europe's Post-national Constellation* (2010) and *Constitutionalism in the*

Global Realm—A Sociological Approach (2014). Recent publications include *Critical Theories of Crises in Europe: From Weimar to the Euro*, with Niklas Olsen (2016) and "The Status of Authority in the Globalizing Economy: Beyond the Public/Private Distinction," with Eva Hartmann, *Indiana Journal of Global Legal Studies* 25, no. 1 (2018).

Andrew Lang is a professor of law and the chair of International Law and Global Governance at Edinburgh Law School. He has a combined BA/LLB from the University of Sydney, and his PhD is from the University of Cambridge. From 2004 to 2006, Lang was a junior research fellow at Trinity Hall, University of Cambridge, before teaching at the London School of Economics from 2006 to 2017. He is a cofounder, with Colin Picker, of the Society of International Economic Law. He sits on the editorial committee of *Modern Law Review* and the editorial boards of the *London Review of International Law* and the *Journal of International Economic Law*, and has been a book review editor for the *International and Comparative Law Quarterly*. Lang has taught at Harvard's Institute for Global Law and Policy, the University Melbourne LLM program, the World Trade Institute's Master of Advanced Studies in International Law and Economics (MILE) program, the University of Barcelona's IELPO course, as well as the IIEM Academy of International Trade Law in Macau. He has been a visiting scholar at Harvard Law School, visiting fellow at the Institute of International Economic Law at Georgetown University Law Center, visiting faculty at the University of Michigan and an International Visiting Research Fellow at the University of Sydney.

Fabio Morosini is an associate professor at the Federal University of Rio Grande do Sul School of Law. He is a research fellow at the National Council of Scientific and Technological Development (CNPq, Ministry of Science and Technology, Brazil) and a State of São Paulo Research Foundation (FAPESP) Research Fellow at FGV School of Law (2018–19). During the 2015–16 academic year, he was a Global Hauser Research Fellow at NYU School of Law. Morosini holds a PhD and an LLM from the University of Texas at Austin and a master's, with honors, from the University of Paris 1/Paris Institute of Political Sciences. Upon completion of his PhD, he was a postdoctoral fellow at the World Trade Organization. Morosini has taught at the UN's Regional Courses in International Law. He is the coeditor of *Reconceptualizing International Investment Law from the Global South* (2018).

Nicolás M. Perrone is an assistant professor of international law at Durham Law School. His main research interests are in international economic law, particularly in international investment law and policy. Perrone has been a faculty member of the Institute for Global Law and Policy (Harvard Law School) and a visiting professor at the Universidad Nacional de San Martín, the International University College of Turin, the University of Eastern Piedmont and the Externado University of Colombia. He has worked and consulted for the governments of Argentina, Ecuador and Colombia; the Organisation for Economic Co-operation and Development, United Nations Conference on Trade and Development; the International Institute for Sustainable Development and the Friedrich Ebert Stiftung. He is a member of the Editorial Committee of the Yearbook on International Investment Law and Policy, and his research has been published in journals such as *Transnational Legal Theory*, the *Journal of International Dispute Settlement* and the *Journal of World Investment and Trade*.

Kerry Rittich is a professor of law, women and gender studies, and public policy and governance at the University of Toronto. She writes in the areas of labor law, global governance, law and development, and gender and critical theory. Her publications include "Black Sites: Locating the Family and Family Law in Development" (2010), with Guy Mundlak; "The Challenge to Comparative Labor Law in a Globalized Era," (2015); and "Theorizing International Law and Development" (2016). She has been a fellow at the European University Institute, the Mackenzie King Visiting Professor of Canadian Studies at Harvard University, a visiting professor at the Watson Institute for International Studies at Brown University, and a professor and academic director of the Center for Transnational Legal Studies, London.

Dani Rodrik is the Ford Foundation Professor of International Political Economy at the Harvard Kennedy School. He has published widely in the areas of economic development, international economics and political economy. His current research focuses on the political economy of liberal democracy and economic growth in developing countries. He is the recipient of the inaugural Albert O. Hirschman Prize of the Social Sciences Research Council and the Leontief Award for Advancing the Frontiers of Economic Thought. Rodrik is currently president-elect of the International Economic Association. His newest book is *Straight Talk on Trade: Ideas for a Sane World Economy* (2017). He is also the author of *Economics Rules: The Rights and Wrongs of the Dismal Science* (2015), *The Globalization Paradox: Democracy and the Future of the World Economy* (2011) and *One Economics, Many Recipes: Globalization, Institutions, and Economic Growth* (2007).

Sonia E. Rolland is a professor of law at Northeastern University School of Law. Rolland's writings focus on the legal framework for sustainable and socioeconomic development in international economic law, international environmental law and energy regulation. Through the exploration of different subject matters, she examines the intersection of legal regimes to improve the understanding of an increasingly multi-layered international and transnational legal order. Rolland publishes widely in French and English. Her work has appeared in the *Journal of International Economic Law*, *Harvard International Law Journal*, *Georgetown Immigration Law Journal*, *Global Community Yearbook* and *European Journal of International Law*, among others. She has taught and guest lectured at a number of institutions in the United States, Europe, Asia and the Pacific. She has served on expert groups and provided consulting services for governments and think tanks.

Alvaro Santos is a professor of law and director of the Center for the Advancement of the Rule of Law in the Americas at Georgetown University. He recently served as deputy chief negotiator of the USMCA Agreement for the newly elected government of Mexico. He writes in the areas of international trade, economic development, transnational labor law and drug policy. Santos is a coeditor of *Law and the New Developmental State: The Brazilian Experience in Latin America* (2013) and *The New Law and Economic Development: A Critical Appraisal* (2006) and the author of numerous articles including "Carving Out Policy Autonomy for Developing Countries in the World Trade Organization: The

Experience of Brazil and Mexico" in the *Virginia Journal of International Law* (2012). Santos serves on the editorial boards of the *American Journal of Comparative Law*, the *Journal of International Economic Law* and the *Law and Development Review*. He served as codirector of the Center for Transnational Legal Studies (CTLS) in London in 2014–15. He regularly teaches at Georgetown's Global Trade Academy and Harvard's Institute for Global Law and Policy (IGLP) and has also taught at the University of Texas, Centro de Investigación y Docencia Económicas (CIDE), Melbourne Law School, Tufts University and the University of Turin. Santos received an LL.B. with high honors from Universidad Nacional Autonóma de México and an LL.M. and S.J.D. from Harvard Law School.

Gregory Shaffer is Chancellor's Professor and director of the Center on Globalization, Law and Society at the University of California, Irvine. His publications include seven books and more than 100 articles and book chapters, including *Constitution-Making and Transnational Legal Order*, with Tom Ginsburg and Terence Halliday (2019); *Transnational Legal Orders*, with Terence Halliday (2015); *Transnational Legal Ordering and State Change* (2013); *Dispute Settlement at the WTO: The Developing Country Experience*, with Ricardo Meléndez-Ortiz (2011); *When Cooperation Fails: The International Law and Politics of Genetically Modified Foods*, with Mark A. Pollack (2009); *Defending Interests: Public-Private Partnerships in WTO Litigation* (2003); and *Transatlantic Governance in the Global Economy*, with Mark A. Pollack (2001).

Thomas Streinz is an adjunct professor of law, executive director of Guarini Global Law & Tech and a fellow of the Institute for International Law and Justice at New York University School of Law where he teaches the Guarini Colloquium: International Law of Global Digital Corporations (with Benedict Kingsbury and Joseph H. H. Weiler) and the Global Tech Law: Selected Topics Seminar. He is one of the editors of *Megaregulation Contested: Global Economic Ordering after TPP* (2019). His current research interests include global economic governance, the governance of digital infrastructures, the regulation of the global data economy, and global law and technology.

Chantal Thomas is the Radice Family Professor of Law at Cornell Law School, where she also directs the Clarke Initiative for Law and Development in the Middle East and North Africa and coedits the Savannah Dialogues Platform of the Institute for African Development. Thomas has consulted for the UN Economic Commission for Africa and the US Agency for International Development and the World Bank, and has served on the US State Department's Advisory Committee on International Law. She writes on the relationship between international law, political economy and global social justice in a variety of contexts, with a focus on international trade and international migration. Her writings include *Disorderly Borders: How International Law Shapes Irregular Migration* (Oxford University Press, forthcoming, 2019), and she is the coeditor of *Developing Countries in the WTO Legal System* (2009).

David Trubek is the Voss-Bascom Professor of Law and dean of International Studies Emeritus at the University of Wisconsin-Madison. He has written extensively on the role of law in development. His recent books include *The Brazilian Legal Profession in the Age of Globalization: The Rise of the Corporate Legal Sector and Its Impact on Lawyers and Society* (coeditor) (2018); *Law and the New Developmental State: The Brazilian Experience in Latin*

American Context (coeditor) (2013); *Direito, Planejamento e Desenvolvimento do Mercado de Capitais Brasileiro 1965–70*, 2nd edition, with Gouveia Viera and Sa (2011); and *The New Law and Economic Development: A Critical Appraisal*, with Alvaro Santos (2006). Trubek taught at Yale and Harvard law schools, the Catholic University Law School in Rio de Janeiro and the FGV Law School in São Paulo and has been a visiting scholar in residence at the European University Institute in Florence, the Fundacão Joaquim Nabuco in Recife, the London School of Economics and the Maison des Sciences de L'Homme in Paris.

Robert Wai has been a faculty member of Osgoode Hall Law School, York University, Toronto, since 1998. He teaches and researches in various areas of transnational economic law including international business transactions, private international law and international trade regulation. He has been a Fernand Braudel Senior Fellow and Jean Monnet Fellow at the European University Institute at Florence, a visiting senior fellow at the LSE Department of Law and a visiting professor at Brown University, Sciences Po Law School and, in 2019, the University of Hong Kong.

Introduction

WORLD TRADE AND INVESTMENT LAW IN A TIME OF CRISIS: DISTRIBUTION, DEVELOPMENT AND SOCIAL PROTECTION

David Trubek, Alvaro Santos and Chantal Thomas

We are witnessing a major crisis in world trade and investment relations. The system that operated for decades and facilitated global integration is under attack from many sides. While economic globalization has helped billions emerge from poverty and facilitated the growing geopolitical importance of emerging economies, it has come at a cost. In both rich and poor countries, many have felt the brunt of globalization in the form of job loss, stagnant wages, displacement, economic insecurity and a closing down of opportunities open to the previous generation. Those who have lost are often left without recourse while being admonished on the wonders of the global market. A simmering discontent has finally given way to a backlash against globalization, which has revealed serious flaws in the international economic regime.

Two voices dominate the public debate right now. On the one hand, there are the nationalists who blame trade for job loss and community decline, propose protectionism and global disintegration as the solution and are willing to walk away from the rule-based system that was consolidated with the founding of the World Trade Organization (WTO). On the other hand are those who defend the current global trade institutions and rules, blaming domestic policy for any maldistribution, and are bent on preserving the status quo.

Our view is that this binary is too limited. We recognize that the existing framework has generated some benefits in the North and the South, but also point out that it has created winners without compensating losers. We can see that there are benefits to multi-lateralism and a rule-based institutional framework while highlighting that the current system imposes constraints on domestic policy choices that restrict strategic choices and limit economic growth. And we can indicate that it provides windfalls and rents for corporate interests, exacerbates inequality within and between nations, contributes to societal fragmentation and feeds reactionary politics—all without concluding that either nationalism and protectionism or total global deregulation provide the only correctives.

Our quest, then, is for a different type of global economic regime, one that recognizes and confronts the many pitfalls that have fueled the current backlash. *World Trade and*

Investment Law Reimagined: A Progressive Agenda for an Inclusive Globalization seeks to move beyond the dominant debate by proposing ideas, policies and institutional reforms for a progressive reshaping of globalization.

Our approach assumes that globalization has been driven by legal changes in the late 1980s and 1990s that were inspired by a particular vision of world order and development. It has many dimensions, but two central pillars are the global trade regime that was formed by the WTO and numerous preferential trade agreements, and the less centralized investment regime structured by bilateral investment treaties (BITs) and designed primarily to protect foreign investors in developing-country markets.

We look in this volume at these and related systems, building on decades of analysis and critique to explore new directions. We assembled 21 experts from 10 countries to write short essays analyzing specific problems of the current system and proposing solutions. We met and discussed these essays under the rubric "Rethinking Trade and Investment Law."[1] As part of these discussions, we also convened an exchange on Dani Rodrik's book *Straight Talk on Trade*, one of the earliest, and most fully fledged and nuanced, critiques of globalization in the so-called post-Brexit period. The exchange around *Straight Talk on Trade* also provided a fulcrum for bringing together heterodox perspectives from economics and from law. As we hope to show here, this kind of exchange between disciplines can sharpen the contributions of each, and perhaps even push our collective analysis further than it might otherwise go.

In this introduction, we identify the main ideas in the book. The next section, "Cross-Cutting Themes," sets out major themes that cut across the substantive topics and individual essays. "Rethinking the Political Economy of Trade" reconsiders the political economy of global trade through an assessment of *Straight Talk on Trade*. "Setting the Stage for a Progressive Vision" reviews important issues in world trade and investment law today. And "Toward a Progressive Agenda" lists some concrete measures for inclusion in the progressive agenda.

Cross-Cutting Themes

The book deals with a wide range of issues, from the rise of China to measures to improve local community participation in decisions over foreign investment. But four overarching themes can be seen throughout the volume: distribution, policy flexibility, the changing role of the state and the role of law and legal institutions.

The question of distribution

An overarching theme is economic distribution and international economic law (IEL): how economic gains and losses are shaped by international institutions. The globalization backlash has been fueled by a sense of disappointment and frustration with the economic results. Job losses and displacement are in fact predicted by trade theory

---

[1]   Hosted by the Institute for Global Law and Policy, Harvard Law School, April 2018.

as a consequence of liberalization, but governments have not done much either to compensate those who have lost or to find ways to share the gains more widely. In fact, in some countries, globalization has coincided with the hollowing out of social protection mechanisms designed to compensate losers and provide insurance in hard times.

Two major distributional issues emerge from the discussion: the distribution of resources between labor and capital and the effect of globalization on income distribution between and within nations. Trade and investment law agreements create benefits for capital by protecting property, placing limits on regulation and expanding the available pool of labor. At the same time, critics argue, the regime has done little to protect labor or enhance its condition globally. And, if we look at this from the perspective of income distribution, we see negative effects of globalization in the period from the late 1980s onward, but also some positive ones that need to be preserved. The book addresses both issues.

Branko Milanovic offers a useful diagnosis of the income distribution effects of globalization.[2] Three conclusions stand out. First, income inequality between countries, when accounting for population size, has been reduced, thanks in large part to the spectacular income growth of China and India. However, the difference in average incomes among countries, if population size is not factored in, has increased. This experience makes clear that one of the strategies to reduce inequality among countries is to promote conditions for rapid economic growth in developing countries. That requires a global trade and investment system that can encourage—or at the very least accommodate—pro-growth strategies like the ones followed by successful countries, which often diverged from the reigning model. This lesson should bring into focus the laws and institutions, both at the international and domestic level, that made this growth possible.

Second, if we consider global income, the winners of globalization were the very rich everywhere, the middle classes of some emerging countries and much of the bottom third in global income distribution. It is because globalization has been beneficial for many in the developing world that we seek to reimagine, not reverse it. The big losers were the bottom 5 percent—including the populations of many least developed countries in Asia and Africa—and those at the 75th to 90th percentile of global income distribution: neither saw any increase in income. The group in the 75th to 90th percentile globally mainly consists of the middle class in rich industrial democracies whose incomes stagnated while the rich in these countries moved ahead: these relative losses are a major source of the ongoing globalization backlash. Politicians in Europe and the United States have responded to the grievances—real and imagined—of this demographic to ascend to power while challenging the international regime that produced this result. A crucial part of a powerful response to these ills, largely overlooked in these same industrialized countries, is the compensatory and social insurance mechanisms that would allow people to confront the adversities of globalization, and we address this need in the volume.

---

[2]　See Branko Milanovic, "Global Income Inequality in Numbers: In History and Now," *Global Policy* 4, issue 2 (May 2013), and Branko Milanovic, *Global Inequality: A New Approach for the Age of Globalization* (Cambridge, MA: Harvard University Press, 2016).

The most striking feature of global income distribution, however, is the importance of location as a prediction of individuals' income in their lifetime. Country of origin largely continues to determine a person's economic prospects in life: "[M]ore than 50 per cent of one's income depends on the average income of the country where a person lives or was born (the two things being the same for 97 per cent of world population)."[3] Compared to the nineteenth century, Milanovic argues, we have moved from a class-based world to a location-based world. In the nineteenth century, national average incomes among countries varied less than did incomes within countries, which differed greatly. Workers' experience, income and life conditions were similar in much of the world. Solidarity among workers everywhere made sense, and it could inspire revolutionary movements. Not so today, Milanovic argues, since the poor in a rich country like the United States would still be high up in the global income distribution scale. A sense of shared experience among workers—or the poor—in rich and poor countries is hard to come by. "Around 1870, class explained more than two-thirds of global inequality. And now? The proportions have exactly flipped: more than two-thirds of total inequality is due to location."[4] Given large differentials in national incomes, and given how much distribution of global income depends on location, powerful incentives for people to move will continue to exist. That is why Milanovic proposes that, in addition to promoting higher rates of growth in poor countries, we should consider freer migration from poorer to richer countries as one way to reduce income equality.

The recognition of the distributional impact of trade and investment agreements has created a new narrative that we engage with. Critiques of economic insecurity and precarious jobs in the developing world associated with globalization have long been familiar. What seems new in the current moment is that these critiques, and the opposition to the international economic regime, are now also coming from rich countries. More strikingly, those critiquing globalization are now in power in the United States and the United Kingdom and are on the rise in Europe. This may provide an opening to reform a system that had looked very resilient to change. The direction and potential effects of the change, however, remain unclear. In this volume, we seek ways to ensure that any changes will ensure that trade and investment law promotes growth and global equality and helps the have-nots in the world. That is the progressive agenda!

The maldistribution effects of the trade and investment regime mark the starting point for many of the essays in this volume. The authors overwhelmingly reject the mainstream economics argument that the international economic regime serves only to enhance overall efficiency or increase aggregate welfare, just as they question the mainstream notion that concern with societal distribution should remain exclusively a national question. In any given setting, there are many possible efficient outcomes, and legal rules set at the international level directly affect how the gains are distributed. The global legal architecture shapes the global market, creating different entitlements for governments,

---

[3] Milanovic, "Global Income Inequality in Numbers: In History and Now," 204.
[4] Ibid.

firms, workers and consumers, defining how they can operate and decidedly affecting the distribution of power and wealth.

If the current distributional landscape is socially unacceptable, then the global agreements and institutions that underpin it can and should be reformed. None of this precludes national obligations to establish policies for compensating losers from global economic reallocation or creating economic opportunities for those who have fallen behind. In the end, however, the goal is to make globalization work for those who have been hardest hit or have remained excluded, not to revert to a narrow self-regarding economic nationalism. To that end, we have suggested ways to strengthen labor versus capital, improve income distribution globally by reducing obstacles to policies for growth with equity in the developing world, capture some of the gains from trade for those who may be negatively available by it and allow people affected by trade some access to higher-income locations through trade-migration linkages.

Policy flexibility versus locking in the social agenda in trade agreements

Some essays advocate for policy flexibility and autonomy, while others propose new rules and restrictions on labor and social policy. For some authors, the main problem of liberal globalization is that it is too restrictive on countries' economic policies. Authors like Dennis M. Davis and Fabio Morosini on investment and Kevin P. Gallagher on cross-border financial flows conclude that the regime has impinged on states' rights to regulate and that states need to reclaim their space by either exiting from or reforming the system. Other authors, such as Frank J. Garcia and Thomas Streinz, would like trade agreements to tax economic transactions for purposes of social compensation. They point out that states have failed to compensate losers domestically, either because they are unwilling or because of competitive pressures. Locking in tax and compensation at the treaty level would make the project of redistribution more effective by helping to ensure that states can make good on such promises.

This tension is probably best captured in Gregory Shaffer's essay, where he proposes a bargain: developing countries get policy space for pursuing industrial policies, such as exceptions to the subsidies rules, while rich countries get a new mechanism for countering social dumping. One may think about this as a rebalancing that loosens restrictions in one domain and tightens up space in another. Shaffer is explicitly trying to operationalize some of Dani Rodrik's proposals. In response to the potential objection that social dumping remedies would harm developing countries' competitive advantage, Rodrik has argued that the best strategy for developing countries would be to expand their policy space and experiment with pro-growth programs. In the end, nothing would improve labor conditions more than domestic economic growth.

At one level these proposals seem to be in conflict, with one group of authors arguing for fewer international restrictions and another for more. To be sure, these ideas are in tension but do not necessarily represent a fundamental contradiction. The authors as a whole continue to believe in the importance of regulation at the global level; they just disagree with the current balance between global restraint and national autonomy. They believe that rebalancing globalization requires a more nuanced and pragmatic approach that expands flexibility in some domains but shrinks it in others, depending on the desired consequences.

Rethinking the role of the nation-state: Neoliberalism, value chains and all that

A question running throughout this book is what role the nation-state should play in this new era. Many of the authors argue that we need to rethink the role of the state. This is a major issue in *Straight Talk on Trade*. Rodrik believes that global governance has weakened the nation-state's capacity to manage the economy and provide social protection. The essays commenting on Rodrik in "Rethinking the Political Economy of Trade" and others in the volume echo this concern. They note that under the pressures of neoliberal doctrines that promoted the idea of a single global market and a limited role for the state, a whole system of BITs and free trade agreements (FTAs) has been created that curtail national policy space, thus facilitating unrestricted globalization. This has generated resistance among those negatively affected by global trade and investment and fueled the current backlash. Several essays document these effects and call for measures to increase the power of nation-states in economic and social policy.

In drawing attention to the law-created nature of the current globalization and urging a stronger role of the national state, many authors clash with some of the prevailing wisdom about the world economy. Take, for example, the well-known work of Richard Baldwin, whose challenge to the role of the nation-state is raised in the exchange between Rodrik and Thomas in this volume. Baldwin argues that the world is changing ever so fast and, driven by technological innovation and changes in the modes of production, countries are converging in the same model of globalization.[5] We are, according to Baldwin, in a new globalization, marked by lower costs of trade and of information and communication technology. Baldwin argues that "the new globalization should change how governments think about their policies."[6] Comparative advantage has been denationalized, he claims. Accordingly, developing countries are not building the entire supply chain domestically but instead joining international supply chains to industrialize. In this view, nations are no longer, or will not be for long, the relevant unit of policy analysis. Rather, firms are crucial entities. Economic changes are increasingly unpredictable. Winners can't be grouped only by sectors and skills. There are winners and losers even within the same sectors and skills groups, depending on production stages and occupations. One corollary of Baldwin's views is that it would be practically impossible for nations to pursue an industrial policy to create comparative advantages in specific national sectors.

While our authors accept Baldwin's description of the importance of global value chains (GVCs) and their effects on development strategy, they take a very different

---

[5] See Richard Baldwin, *The Great Convergence: Information Technology and the New Globalization* (Cambridge, MA: Harvard University Press, 2016).

[6] Ibid., 13

approach to how we got here and where we should go. First, Baldwin's account places economic change, and particularly technological innovation, in the driver's seat, while in this book we stress the role of law in motivating or enabling those changes. We show that the lower transportation costs and more rapid movement of ideas that Baldwin notes were the result of new rules and institutions. It is not a coincidence that his "second unbundling," whose origin he locates in the 1990s, happened during a time of a momentous change in the rules of the international economic order, associated with the rise of the Washington Consensus. Baldwin seems oblivious to both the social and political forces that made this globalization possible and the importance of the rule changes that established it.

Not only does the conventional wisdom overlook the extent to which this new global economy is constituted through law, but it also fails to recognize the way this new market has become "disembedded" and does not autonomously take into account social and political concerns. Neoliberal governance has helped create markets that are distant from society's norms and values. Our authors propose policies to re-embed the liberal market with societal commitments regarding the distribution of opportunity and wealth. But to do that, they recognize, we must restore some of the nation-state's capacity lost through globalization.

The nation-state, our authors argue, must continue to play a leading role in creating the kinds of institutions needed for an international market that both facilitates trade and investment and preserves social integration. Of course, if states have more policy space, they must calibrate their policies to the changing features of the global market. In addition, while both the argument for increased policy space, in the section above, and the argument on behalf of the nation-state here support national institutions insofar as they can be used to address local social imperatives, it is important to note that this does not happen automatically. States can, of course, be subject to corruption and capture in both the Global North and Global South. The phenomenon of the so-called strong states that appeal to nationalistic considerations, while in fact marginalizing and subordinating the less advantaged within their societies, is well understood. Indeed, this is one reason the authors' interventions as a whole refrain from any call to populism or nationalism. They recognize that decisions of national governments are not sacrosanct and can be limited by global provisions. But states remain key players and can reshape the existing international order in ways that will both facilitate growth and ensure that globalization is fairer and more politically acceptable.

Background conditions: Focus on the right law

An important critical insight, going back all the way to legal realism, is that the most relevant legal regimes for questions of distribution may not be the most apparent. Often, it is the background norms of property, contracts or torts—those we take for granted as constituting the market—and not those foreground norms specifically intervening in the market or regulating it (such as labor, the environment or health) where the most promising interventions may lie. This insight helps identify the interaction of different normative orders and see how they may influence one another. Given the concern with jobs and labor conditions, much of which has fueled the globalization backlash, one may think that labor chapters in trade agreements are vital and need to be perfected and better enforced. But Kerry Rittich and Alvaro Santos both conclude that if one is concerned about labor conditions, such labor chapters are not where the real action may lie.

They each contend that labor chapters could disappear from trade agreements and little would happen. Rittich notes the importance of background laws and institutions that structure the workplace and help determine the consequences of trade liberalization. The most powerful responses to redressing the effects of trade on labor, then, may lie in identifying what changes to background laws might improve the resilience of the social benefits of work. One answer lies in delinking health insurance and other Social Security provisions from work, making them universal. This would reduce incentives to cut labor costs or hire informally and would give workers flexibility without insecurity. Another answer lies in linking firms' responsibility for labor conditions in their contractors' and subcontractors' facilities along the global supply chain. Santos also suggests looking beyond trade agreements to areas like government procurement, investment and social dumping remedies and supports including more robust pressure for labor law reform in trade agreements, citing the recent agreement between the United States, Canada and Mexico.

Dan Danielsen and Robert Wai echo the concern for a broader understanding of the legal orders that affect transnational flows of goods and people. Danielsen notes that trade and investment law as we know it has little purchase on the legal institutions that shape global value chains and affect the distribution of rents from these chains. Wai tells us we need to think of normal trade law as incorporating a wide range of legal orders, not just those thought of as IEL.

Rethinking the Political Economy of Trade

Globalization has been driven—or at least supported—by a political economy vision that advocated for open markets, private enterprise and limited state intervention while assuming that the resulting policies driven by this vision would benefit all and be compatible with democracy. To develop new approaches to trade and investment law, we need to challenge this vision and work toward a new one. Few sources are more valuable for such an endeavor than *Straight Talk on Trade*. This volume, which synthesizes Rodrik's work, outlines the type of political economy approach that must undergird a progressive agenda. What follows is the result of an exchange between Rodrik and four of our contributors from whom we solicited comments on the book's relevance for the field of IEL and policy.[7] We summarize their interventions and Rodrik's response in the following section.

The commentators identified several key ideas set out by Rodrik that deserve consideration as we craft a new approach to IEL.

---

[7]   The initial dialogue occurred at the workshop on Rethinking Trade and Investment Law, referenced above (see n. 1).

You can have too much globalization: Excessive globalization has undermined democracy

"Elites," notes Thomas, "have pushed economic integration far past the point where political institutions have been able to keep up. The imbalance must be corrected in one of two directions: 'expand governance beyond the nation-state or restrict the reach of markets.' The tendency of 'polite company' among cosmopolitan elites is to speak only of the former, but Rodrik makes a strong argument that the second option should be considered, consciously going against the conventional tendencies of his cohort of international economists." Shaffer notes that Rodrik believes "we need to place the requirements of liberal democracy ahead of those of international trade and investment." If, despite the gains from trade, economic globalization puts liberal democracy at risk, Shaffer adds, then we need to readjust the balance in favor of more domestic policy space and less economic integration facilitated by IEL. Santos takes up the same theme but more cautiously. Looking at Rodrik's principles for fair trade, which would allow a nation to ban imports that affected core social values, Santos notes that such rules are useful, but they could, at the same time, affect core social values in the exporting nation. Santos argues that the tension between two countries' standards needs to be addressed deliberately, preferably by a global institution, considering the economic and social consequences of the available options.

Loosen the ties that bind: Trade and investment law has constrained policy experimentation

Rodrik parts company with many economists and development agencies that mention a single formula for growth. He notes that economic policy must be based on local conditions and the only way to find the optimal growth path is through experimentation. He sees current trade and investment law as insensitive to context and restrictive of experimentation. Shaffer notes that Rodrik "believes that countries must experiment to find the optimal development path"; Shaffer argues that IEL should facilitate such experimentation.

Regulation starts at home: The nation-state remains the key institution for regulating the economy

Noting that "markets require rules to facilitate economic exchange, create stability and provide a sense of legitimacy," Shaffer quotes Rodrik's argument that the nation-state is "the only game in town when it comes to providing the regulatory and legitimizing arrangements on which markets rely." Economically, Shaffer concludes, "the state enables the mobility of resources, enhancing efficiency and increasing productivity essential for economic growth and social welfare. Politically, the state fosters the spread of participatory, representative institutions, giving rise to liberal democracy. Legally, the state creates public order through laws and institutions that reduce violence and uphold the social contract." Santos agrees that the state remains a central institution but notes that nations can be the source of inequality and oppression. He suggests that Rodrik's enthusiastic embrace of the nation may entail risks and that other dimensions of governance must play a role. Echoing Santos's concerns about relying too much on the nation-state, Thomas asks whether the growth of GVCs and the resulting deterritorialization of production may require more, not less, regulation beyond the national level.

No more tigers? The threat of premature deindustrialization

Rodrik fears that changes in the world economy may make it hard for developing nations to follow the path of the Asian Tigers and China. These regions relied on growth for exports of manufactured goods to advanced markets. Rodrik worries that the opportunities for such strategies have declined due to technological advances and China's first-mover advantage in many industries. Thomas summarizes this argument:

> The obstacles to growth through conventional industrialization lie both in contemporary technology and in contemporary trade. With respect to technology, because manufacturing is now much more knowledge- and capital-intensive, barriers to entry are higher and less available to countries further down the economic ladder. With respect to trade, not only does the sheer formidability and market dominance of current competitors like China reduce the possibilities for market share gains for smaller economies, but also international trade rules have now reduced the amount of protection countries can introduce to attenuate that market dominance by locking in commitments to market openness.

While acknowledging the importance of Rodrik's concerns, Thomas notes that trade law is not as restrictive as Rodrik suggests. And she thinks that the clustering effect might help some developing regions overcome premature deindustrialization. She wonders "whether it really is the end of industrialization or whether alternatively a place remains for localized industrial production among today's low-income countries if they can amend and manage trade rules to be supportive and can operate with reasonable governance, effective institutions and sound 'targeting' of promising industries and firms."

It's the economists, stupid: We need a new approach to trade in economics and other social sciences

The commentators welcome Rodrik's critique of trade economics and its use in policy debates. Rodrik has questioned the standard models, and Gallagher echoes that critique, though he also argues for a systemic view of these academic failures, seeing them not only as the fault of trade economists but as pervasive in the social sciences more generally. Gallagher notes that standard models fail to take into account the effects of trade agreements and make unrealistic assumptions. He states that "[t]he modeling exercises that dominate trade policymaking take the form of computable general equilibrium (CGR) models that 'work' only if good trade is modeled and if there is perfect competition, fixed employment, no externalities, no international investment and no technological change." Gallagher also points out that models do not take distribution into account and fail to measure the impact on losers:

> While the gains from trade are small relative to entire economies, they are highly concentrated into the hands of a few in a small number of key sectors (pharma, finance and factory food). The losers from trade are also small relative to entire economies but highly concentrated in a few sectors (manufacturing, of course). In addition, the losses may be small relative to economies but overwhelming relative to the budget constraints of the losers themselves and the alternative opportunities they may have.

As Santos points out, Rodrik recognizes indeterminacy in the models, stating that "[e]conomics is really a toolkit with multiple models—each a different, stylized representation of some aspect of reality." There are competing models that lead to different explanations and policy recommendations. Rodrik celebrates this pluralism. The key, and this is what Rodrik is after, is to learn how to choose between competing models.

While Rodrik believes this to be possible apparently without injecting normative preferences, Santos is "more skeptical of the project of developing a method to choose the 'right' model." Santos refers to Rodrik's own "war of trade models" blog post concerning the effects of the Trans-Pacific Partnership (TPP) where Rodrik argues that "neither side's models generate numbers reliable enough on which a case for or against the TPP could be made. Just about the only thing we can say with some certainty is that there would have been gainers and losers." Santos is not convinced that there is a meta model that can be employed to select the right model to adjudicate important policy debates.

Gallagher summarizes what he takes from the book: "[T]he winners of globalization are writing the rules of globalization, economists are cheerleading, other social scientists are out to lunch, and the working class in the North and future entrepreneurs of the South have had enough."

Rodrik's rejoinder

Acknowledging the comments, Rodrik welcomed the observations regarding the limitations of standard modeling as complementary to the overall viewpoint put forward in *Straight Talk on Trade*. Rodrik accepted Gallagher's corrective critique of the social sciences more broadly. He replied to Santos's suggestions that there is no value-free meta stance from which models can be chosen by noting that, while this is true, the methodological focus on data gathering does force a certain "discipline in the process" that is nonideological. "Objective facts do exist," Rodrik writes, "and they do matter." And he welcomed Shaffer's reference to the employment of insights from legal realism refining economists' analyses of law.

With respect to specific types of policy reform, Rodrik also agreed that there are limits to the capacities of the nation to manage global trade but felt that any move to the global level for governance and efforts at international harmonization tend to empower business interests to the detriment of other concerns. And he met Thomas's queries regarding challenges to national governance from the contemporary economic landscape, such as whether the importance of GVCs might require regulation to move to regional or global levels, by observing that the GVCs are far less important than generally thought.

Setting the Stage for a Progressive Vision

The terrain in IEL is shifting. New geopolitical alliances are forming, resistance to some aspects of the regime have emerged, economic structures are changing and the costs of globalization have become more apparent and more troubling. In this part, we summarize how the authors in the book view these and other developments, which form the context in which we must develop a progressive vision.

Mapping the new context for trade and investment law

The trade and investment law regimes took their current shape in the 1990s. Almost three decades later, there have been major changes that must be taken into account in the progressive agenda. These include the rise of China, the proliferation of preferential FTAs, the persistence of heterodox models and the resistance of emerging economies to some of the constraints of the regime. Poul F. Kjaer paints these developments in stark terms: he sees them as the result of the decline of the West and the world order created after World War II:

> The breakdown of the Eurocentric world is now being followed by the breakdown of the Western-centric world. The Eurocentric world started to collapse in the late nineteenth century with the rise of the United States, and later Japan and the Soviet Union, and became manifested in the mid-twentieth-century decolonization processes. Today the concept of the West is disintegrating, with Europe and the United States moving steadily apart in political, economic, social and cultural terms and becoming strangers. Furthermore, this development unfolds with the rise of non-Western powers, most notably China, greatly exacerbating the consequences.

The emergence of this new context presents both challenges and opportunities for a progressive agenda.

Cometh the dragon: The rise of China

China's rise to economic predominance, and the West's reaction to it, arguably constitutes the most important development affecting trade and investment law today. China has benefited greatly from globalization. Moreover, although current trade and investment law tilts heavily toward convergence on market models of political economy, thus creating pressures on China's heterodox economic organization and strategy, China has resisted much of this pressure and has recently doubled down on its commitment to state capitalism. While these deviations from the liberal market model were tolerated when China was weak, its industries posed no threat to those in advanced economies, and there were hopes for gradual convergence, everything has changed now that China is the second largest economy in the world. Chinese companies are already globally competitive, and China aspires toward even greater leadership in many key industries. The flood of exports from China and China-centered value chains that drove China's remarkable rise have caused serious dislocation in industries and regions in both advanced and developing economies.

Faced with this challenge to their economic predominance, countries North and South are scrambling to figure out how to deal with China. In the North, leaders are asking whether they should double down on pressures on China to liberalize or look for new forms of accommodation with an economy that is now closely linked to their own and slated to become the world's largest in the not-too-distant future. Should they pressure China to reform its labor market or seek to delink their economies from China through tariffs and other barriers? In the South, countries are both attracted by Chinese investment and trade opportunities and concerned about Chinese dominance. China has embarked on a major global initiative both through investments everywhere and through the massive Belt and Road Initiative, which offers infrastructure assistance to countries in many parts of the world. China is seeking closer integration in Asia through the Regional Comprehensive Economic Partnership (RCEP). Countries North and South are trying to take advantage of these developments, and these new relationships reverberate through the whole field of trade and investment law, generating many of the issues taken up in the book.

Coping with the continued diversity of economic models

When the current regime took form, many thought that the world would gradually converge on a model of regulated market capitalism. Andrew Lang notes,

> [T]he years following the collapse of communism seemed to herald a radical reduction in the global economy's degree of institutional diversity as states throughout the former "second" and "third" worlds converged toward a single model of market capitalism. But the reality has proved more complicated: the national marketization projects initiated during this period have each evolved according to different dynamics, resulting in the emergence of a variety of new and heterodox market forms in different countries and regions of the world.

This new pluralism and heterodoxy have presented a major challenge to the regime and led to resistance by emerging economies that have challenged existing rules and blocked new ones. Sonia E. Rolland and David Trubek describe this tension and note that until recently it seemed to lead to a fragile equilibrium in which developed countries tolerated some diversity while emerging economies accepted some restrictions to gain access to developed country markets. They observe that

> despite tensions between the current international economic law (IEL) system and the policy preferences of many emerging economies, countries of the Global South have managed to achieve some kind of balance between the neoliberal thrust of the system and their desire to pursue strategies that—from a neoliberal viewpoint—are heterodox. The result is a system they can use to further their own ends and one that only intrudes on their policy space to

a tolerable degree. Think of it as a "truce" between a radical liberalization campaign and strong resistance in the name of state-led growth and sovereignty.

The authors think the truce has offered benefits to both developed and developing countries. They do not consider it an ideal situation for developing countries but rather the best they could get in the context of the time. However, they fear that even these partial victories may be at risk due to recent actions, especially those initiated by the Trump administration, which may be destabilizing the truce. This fear is echoed by Lang, who notes that from the beginning of the General Agreement on Tariffs and Trade (GATT), the regime has dealt with institutional diversity and heterodox policies in two ways: sometimes serving as an interface to mediate tensions between competing economic systems and sometimes as a force for convergence along free market lines. During much of the post–World War II period these two tendencies remained in tension, and an unsteady compromise between them prevailed. However, Lang notes, during the last decades of the twentieth century, in part as a result of the disruptions to existing patterns of comparative advantage caused by the rise of new capitalist forms in East Asia, the balance shifted toward convergence, and this trend has continued to this day. "It is now perfectly apparent," he states, "that a large part of the new agenda of rulemaking in international trade agreements is designed specifically to place additional constraints on new institutional forms emerging in China and elsewhere. The development of new rules on state-owned and state-controlled enterprises, alongside the concerted use of existing subsidies rules to challenge the practices of Chinese state-owned enterprises, is the best example."

Echoing a Rodrikian theme, Lang points out that institutional diversity can be a positive force in the world economy as it encourages the kind of experimentation that can lead to faster and more sustainable growth. For that reason, he urges us to think beyond the compromise,

> imagining the present system not just as a mechanism for managing the interface among different economic systems or as a force for reducing institutional frictions, encouraging institutional convergence and leveling the international competitive playing field, but also as a system for encouraging democratically driven institutional experimentation.

Many of the essays, such as those of Kjaer and Wai, share Lang's sympathy for the idea of trade law as an interface between countries' different institutional preferences and values, rather than a tool to create global homogeneity. In addition, *Straight Talk on Trade* offers a great example of this position as Rodrik argues that we should allow regulatory diversity up to a point and unlock the straitjacket—real and imagined—of globalization in favor of greater policy autonomy. In this concept, trade law would serve as a neutral link between disparate economic systems and provide results that would allow maximum feasible diversity while facilitating trade relations.

Although showing support for a system that avoids imposing one country's economic system on another, several authors question whether such an interface can really be neutral and doubt that the system in action could really weigh each country's interests equally when there is conflict. The asymmetry of power plays an important role in trade law outcomes and often is reflected in notions of what the normal baseline ought to be; for example, what counts as a distortion in the normal market or protectionism. Similarly, the interface position relies heavily on the nation-state as the agent that could effect change and improve the conditions of work and of life that have led to the globalization backlash. While the authors believe that nations should be given more leeway to experiment with different development strategies, they also recognize that states may not take into account the needs of all within their territory and believe that even an interface system must have some global level standards to protect domestic interests that may not be taken into account in national policymaking. This concern is seen in calls for ensuring that workers in emerging economies are not exploited in the race for growth and that local communities are not ignored or overlooked by the promise of greater national welfare: dealing with these issues may require international-level governance.

Nonetheless, the authors tend to favor an approach that exhibits maximum feasible tolerance for policy divergence in areas like economic organization and strategy, including state-owned enterprises (SOEs) and industrial policy, while calling for more robust global standards in areas like labor markets. This approach would apply to China as well as other emerging economies and is at odds with current US trade policy, which is designed to force China to modify its state capitalist model in favor of a normal market orientation—or punish it if it does not.

Learning from the fragmentation of world trade law

In addition to the need to recognize a variety of economic strategies and models, the progressive agenda must take into account the growth of preferential trade agreements, each with its own set of rules, and the resulting fragmentation of IEL. There are many such agreements, including agreements that have recently entered into force or are pending as of this writing, such as the Comprehensive and Progressive Agreement for Trans-Pacific Partnership (CPTPP), the EU–Canada Comprehensive Economic and Trade Agreement (CETA) and the United States–Mexico–Canada Agreement (USMCA). They introduce new rules, many of which may differ from the global rules established by the WTO. The result is a different trade law for different parts of the world—some call it a "spaghetti bowl" of rules.

To test the range and scope of such agreements and their relevance for the progressive agenda, we looked at the RCEP. Pasha L. Hsieh describes the RCEP,

The [RCEP] represents a new era of regionalism and offers a distinct paradigm for world trade law. When it is launched, the RCEP will be the world's largest free trade agreement (FTA) and a clear alternative to the extant neoliberal trade regime. Built upon the Association of Southeast Asian Nations (ASEAN) free trade areas, the 16-party RCEP covers half of the global population and 30 percent of global gross domestic product (GDP). It also encompasses the world's most vigorous economies, such as China, India and Indonesia. [...] It also exhibits the Global South's contemporary normative vision, which challenges the dominant neoliberal approach and the Indo-Pacific strategy of the Trump administration.

Hsieh lists several features of the RCEP that distinguish it from the CPTPP and other Western-led preferential FTAs. These are features that should be taken account of in crafting the progressive agenda. Whereas recent agreements like the CPTPP include provisions that force SOEs to act like commercial actors, the RCEP will have no restrictions on SOEs. In addition, rather than asking all members to enter into a single undertaking, the RCEP follows an evolutionary approach that recognizes different levels of development among members, which range from Australia to Myanmar. Finally, unlike most FTAs, the RCEP does provide for some labor mobility, although, unlike the EU's free movement provision, it is limited to skilled professionals. While in some regards, the RCEP (which is still being negotiated) represents an alternative to current FTAs, which are more restrictive of policy space, in others, like intellectual property, it may turn out to be less innovative.

Kjaer sees regional trade agreements like the RCEP as a harbinger of a more general fragmentation of IEL:

> The paradox of globalization is that it is producing global disintegration and increased diversity rather than increased integration and uniformity. The world is likely to be made up by a number of centers with overlapping political, economic, social and cultural regimes, with none of them acting as a singular global anchor.

He sees this as creating both an opportunity and a duty for progressives, urging a rethinking of IEL as an "exercise of reconnection, developing models that match the cultural universes, economic structures and political worldviews of the world's different regions."

Expanding the notion of normal trade law

In his essay, Wai takes the analysis even further. He favors the interface approach to trade law but argues that this approach requires us to expand our idea of normal trade law to include a wider range of legal orders and approaches. He envisions a multidimensional transnational law that includes public and private law, domestic and international law. He sees such an approach as necessary to dealing with institutional diversity and fragmentation:

> Finding the normal role of law in trade may therefore require a broader sense of the legal orders that help structure not just particular legal claims but also the political and economic bargaining of trade relations.

Dealing with major changes in the world economy

Whereas the section of the book addressed above focuses on world trade and investment law, the next section of the book deals with adjacent transformations in the world economy that shape world trade and investment law and so must also be taken into account. This is not a comprehensive survey of all relevant changes. Rather, we have selected a few recent changes—supply chains, platform firms and the legalization of formerly illicit products—to show how legal rules shape global markets, allocate rents and affect development possibilities. These chapters underscore the crucial roles of legal institutions of all types, not just trade and investment law. They show that progressives must both understand fast-changing economic structures and processes and craft new forms of intervention to promote values of equality and fairness.

The progressive agenda for world trade and investment law seeks to revise the rules of the game in ways that will foster growth with equity, particularly including social protection for workers, in both the Global North and Global South. Two authors suggest that changes in the operation of capitalism make that task incredibly difficult. Danielsen's analysis of supply chain capitalism and Jason Jackson's study of platform firms show why existing regulatory tools are inadequate and demonstrate the need for new approaches.

Restructuring of capitalism and the limits of regulation: The supply chain revolution

Danielsen, like other authors, stresses the significance of the rise of GVCs for the future of globalization. He sees that this development radically alters the way we have to think about global governance. While some think this development makes national policy almost irrelevant, Danielsen believes the state continues to be a primary agent in creating the norms of the international markets on which firms rely for structuring GVCs. To make these fairer and ensure maximum gains for developing countries, he asserts, these nations must confront the power of buyer firms and the legal institutions that support them.

Danielsen notes that the power of buyer firms and the competitive pressures on suppliers mean that the buyers secure most of the rents from these industries, while firms in developing countries are squeezed by competitive pressures. Unless they can deal directly with these conditions, developing countries may be limited in their ability to use exports as a tool of sustained growth. While progressive trade lawyers have argued that reforms in the trade regime could empower developing countries to maximize gains from exports, Danielsen argues that such changes will have little or no impact on growth or poverty alleviation in the developing world unless new tools are fashioned to address inequalities of power in the GVC context. Trade law reform may be necessary to improve the situation, but it is far from sufficient. Danielsen calls for better maps to

> illuminate new legal tools and policy strategies beyond the traditional tools of trade law and policy for disrupting the current configuration of power and distribution of resources under supply chain capitalism and enabling more equitable patterns of trade and distribution to emerge.

Platform firms: A new global phenomenon

Jackson's analysis of platform firms like Uber and Lyft represents a similar challenge for regulation at all levels. These and similar firms represent a novel organizational form that has been called a "Nikeficated" networked firm. In principle, they serve as intermediaries that match buyers and sellers and thus claim to simply facilitate transactions between willing parties. In this conception, they hope to avoid most costs of conventional Fordist-era firms and not even take on the more limited responsibilities multinational firms assume in their governance of GVCs. Many platform firms exploit the weak condition of labor in both developed and developing markets to squeeze the workforce. Their rise is fueled by new forms of finance that are willing to bet on strategies designed to secure monopoly rents in markets through the use of disruptive tools provided by technology and big data. Jackson notes,

> This approach is not directed toward supporting steady profit growth and relatively egali-tarian distribution between capital and labor, as in the Fordist era (or the European welfare state model), nor does it seek short-term profits, as in the shareholder value model. Instead the strategic objective is monopoly control of horizontally related markets through "winner-take-all market strategies."

Platform firms like Uber are global actors that operate in local markets. Jackson notes that these firms have been skillful in avoiding the kind of regulation at national and local levels that might ensure for labor a fairer share of the gains from their innovations. Like buyer firms in supply chains, the small core platform firms get most of the rents. Jackson concludes that we need more attention to regulation at local, national and global levels if we want to ensure that these innovations contribute to global growth with equity.

Ensuring new products contribute to sustainable growth with equity: The case of cannabis

In addition to learning to deal with new forms of production and new kinds of firms, progressive trade law must learn to cope with shifts resulting from the emergence of new products into the domain of legal trade. We take the partial legalization of cannabis as an example. In their essay, Antonia Eliason and Rob Howse assess the legal and eco-nomic implications of the gradual legalization of cannabis, showing how various legal regimes including international trade law affect the development of this industry. Among other things, they discuss how the legal regime might be mobilized to avoid developing an industry dominated by Big Pharma and Big Tobacco and harmful to disadvantaged classes of users.

Framing a more equitable investment law regime

Globalization is not a natural phenomenon. It was created in part by legal institutions at the global and national levels. Chief among these are BITs. These agreements give foreign investors rights to challenge the actions of host governments in international arbitral tribunals. Many developing countries signed such treaties in the 1990s, while a few were skeptical and never joined the system. Today, some of the original enthusiasts, chafing under restrictions that BITs imposed, are reconsidering these commitments. To get insights for the progressive agenda, we looked at Brazil, which never signed on to the

BIT system, and South Africa, which has recently reconsidered its commitment to BITs. We also look at how BITs can lead to investments that disproportionally impact local communities and explore ways to minimize such damage.

Enthusiasm, skepticism and withdrawal: South Africa and Brazil

In his study of South Africa's history of engagement and disengagement, Davis notes that behind the movement toward BITs was a vision, articulated by the World Bank during the 1990s, that imagined "a fully integrated global economic order in which investment would be unfettered by national regulation designed to promote indigenous objectives and would inevitably be located where significant returns could be obtained." By guaranteeing protection for foreign investors against adverse actions by national governments, BITs helped create such an order.

South Africa's embrace of BITs is illustrative of what made developing countries sign on to a system that limited their sovereignty and displaced their judiciary. This decision came after the African National Congress (ANC) came to power. The new government sought to rectify the wrongs created by the apartheid regime while stimulating economic growth. To that end, the government hoped to attract foreign investment. But, Davis notes,

> Foreign investors were concerned about the legacy of the history of postcolonial African states, which had embarked on a course of economic nationalization together with a proclamation of redistribution of economic growth. With this history in mind, the British government, under the leadership of then prime minister John Major, who was concerned that the ANC might expropriate British assets in South Africa, was the first to approach the newly installed South African government with a BIT proposal.

The BITs South Africa signed were designed to have a twofold effect. On the one hand, they would deter the country from adopting regulatory policies and nationalization plans that were inconsistent with the interests of foreign investors; on the other, they would guarantee to investors compensation should deterrence fail and investor interests be threatened.

While South Africa signed numerous BITs, initially little attention was paid to the potential tension between the commitments made to investors and the goal of redressing wrongs created by the apartheid regime. But in 2006, South Africa was faced by a claim that its recently passed mining law amounted to a direct or indirect expropriation in violation of a BIT because it both required mine owners to get a license to continue exercising common-law rights and required that 26 percent of company stock be held by historically disadvantaged South Africans. Although eventually settled, the case drew attention to the conflict between treaty obligations and important social policies. The result was that the country has withdrawn from some existing BITs and passed new legislation providing that future investor-state disputes should be handled by its domestic courts. So far, there does not seem to be a decline in foreign investment resulting from this change.

In his study of Brazil, Morosini also recounts the South African experience, in the course of explaining that Brazil never entered into a standard BIT. Initially, Brazil avoided any kind of investment treaty, but recently it has started signing a very different kind of agreement that stresses dispute prevention, has more limited rights for investors than has been the norm in BITs and does not allow for investor-state arbitration. He notes that, despite its reluctance to agree to BIT-type protections, Brazil has been a major recipient of foreign direct investment. Drawing on these two experiences, Morosini suggests that investment law should include an expanded right to regulate, explicitly allowing states policy space for goals like redistributive justice and industrial policy experimentation.

Protecting local communities impacted by foreign investment

Nicolás M. Perrone adds another dimension to the critique of investment law. Noting that the literature on international investment law and policy has consistently avoided the role and interests of local communities, he points out that, especially in natural resource and infrastructure projects, local communities are often the most affected, while national governments, eager to attract foreign investment, may overlook these impacts. The solution, he suggests, is to require local participation at every stage of the investment approval process:

> Local participation should begin as early as possible and continue throughout the project. [...] The scope of participation, on the other hand, should vary depending on the stage of the project. Before establishment, local actors should be protagonists of the human and environmental impact assessment. [...] During and after the investment, local communities should also have an important role in the governance of the project.

Needless to say, ensuring such participation would require a major change in investment law. Perrone notes that it "would imply a shift from a regime based on the rule of law and dispute settlement to a more relational and participatory model."

While much of the critique of investment agreements has come from developing countries, voices in the North have also been heard. For example, as Santos points out in his essay on labor, labor advocates in the United States have criticized BITs because they may encourage offshoring of jobs: this position has found some favor with the Trump administration.

Supporting development

Many of the essays in the book deal with conflict between trade and investment law and development strategies in emerging economies. Two of our authors, Gallagher and Shaffer, home in on specific issues and suggest reforms.

Facilitating heterodox approaches

A dominant theme in the volume is the need for a more pluralist approach to economic models and development strategies. As discussed above, many of our authors, from Rodrik to Lang to Morosini, contend that standard trade and investment law no longer takes an interface approach that tolerates heterogeneity and increasingly pressures states to converge toward a free market system. Intolerant of heterodox strategies, this approach deters the kind of experimentation that they believe is essential for sustainable growth with equity. Shaffer pays special attention to this problem and suggests specific policies that could reverse the trend toward convergence. In a two-pronged essay that deals with industrial policy, social dumping and their interrelation, Shaffer stresses the importance of allowing policy space for experimentation:

> Considerable policy experimentation is needed to catalyze economic development since no one knows in advance what works. This is particularly the case given the vastly differing contexts that countries face. Rodrik and others critique WTO rules for taking industrial policy options off the table for developing countries. Industrial policy experimentation for development could be expressly authorized by amending existing WTO agreements, which already provide a framework.

Shaffer outlines reforms of WTO law needed to make this work. They would include general principles, substantive criteria, time limits, and reporting and transparency obligations. Industrial policies that would otherwise be WTO-inconsistent would be allowed if their aim is greater productivity. Only developing countries would be eligible, and exceptions might be time limited or designed to fade away once an industry became globally competitive. As a check on the potential impact of such rules, Shaffer proposes to allow other WTO member states to impose countervailing duties in some cases. He notes,

> This proposal would represent a return to the trade policies under the GATT where developing countries could subsidize infant industries, but their products could be countervailed when imported into a developed country where the subsidies caused, or threatened to cause, significant injury to a domestic industry.

While Shaffer's carefully circumscribed reforms would allow some heterodox experiments to proceed, others might call for even more freedom from market-oriented constraints. Whereas Shaffer would allow deviations from the market model on a temporary basis, and even allow countervailing duties during that period, some might argue that countries should be free to maintain alternative models indefinitely without being penalized.

Limiting the effects of capital flows

Developing countries can benefit from inward flows of investment in stocks and bonds. These funds bolster domestic savings. Gallagher observes,

> Cross-border financial investments that are not foreign direct investment—such as bonds, stocks, derivatives and other instruments—can be essential parts of government, banking and corporate finance. Indeed, many developing countries may lack the savings or financial

institutions that can help finance business activity. Capital from abroad can fill that gap. Therefore, under normal circumstances, the more capital flowing into a developing country, the more the country benefits.

However, this kind of money is highly volatile and can flow out easily if risks look too great or the gap between the return on such investments and safer opportunities in developed markets narrows. Such counterflows can seriously destabilize an economy. Recognizing that these destabilization effects can undermine development efforts, the International Monetary Fund (IMF) has approved the use of capital controls by developing countries. The problem, Gallagher notes, is that clauses in many trade and investment agreements limit or rule out such controls, thus overriding the IMF:

> [T]he trade and investment treaty regime has largely closed the opening in the Articles of Agreement of the International Monetary Fund (IMF) that allow nations to regulate cross-border capital flows. The lack of policy space for regulating cross-border capital flows conflicts with prevailing economic theory and new policy at the IMF that encourages nation-states to regulate cross-border capital flows in certain circumstances.

Gallagher states that many existing trade and investment treaties do have exceptions that would permit capital controls under limited circumstances. But this is not the case with US agreements, which ban controls altogether:

> [T]he template for US trade and investment treaties does not leave adequate flexibility for nations to regulate capital flows to prevent and mitigate financial crises. At their core, US treaties see restrictions on the movement of speculative capital as a violation of their terms. Moreover, the safeguards in US treaties were not intended to cover the regulation of capital flows.

Because US treaties and others with similar restrictions cover a great deal of the world, this means that the IMF policy has been effectively undermined. Gallagher calls for a reversal of these policies and suggests amendments to treaty language.

Reinforcing social protection: Spreading the benefits of trade, dealing with losses and exploring the trade–immigration nexus

One of the most important issues the project looked at was the social effects of trade and investment law, and central among these has been the effect on workers. Law has played a major role in constituting globalization, which has led to many changes in the conditions of work worldwide. Jobs have been created and jobs have been lost in both the North and the South. Trade has facilitated the growth of new industries in the South, creating jobs for many, but eliminating others as new imports undermine traditional agriculture and small-scale production. Trade has lowered the cost of many items for consumers in the North and fostered certain high value-added export industries but has also led to the closure of companies unable to compete with low-cost imports. This has led to a loss of jobs and, in some cases, the devastation of cities and regions.

Trade and investment law has done a lot to facilitate the upside of trade but failed to deal with the downside in both the North and the South. The most prominent efforts to deal with costs and distributive impacts of trade in trade and investment law have been the inclusion of labor clauses in trade agreements and the provision of trade adjustment assistance (TAA) for those losing jobs due to trade. The first deals with labor conditions in the South; the second with those who lost jobs in the North. The authors in this volume see both efforts largely as failures. They think that the whole analysis of the social impact of trade has been too narrowly conceived, and they call for a new approach. Rittich concludes,

> At the end of the day, trade liberalization is a social as well as an economic project. The form and substance of trade agreements have profound implications for questions of equality, solidarity, citizenship and justice at the domestic as well as transnational levels. We can continue to focus on labor standards and social clauses hoping they will address, if not entirely fix, the complex distributive problems in which trade regimes as a whole are implicated. But if we move beyond imagining trade regimes simply as devices to set the ground rules of economic competition and begin to view them instead as mechanisms for allocating risks and immunities, powers and disabilities, including among workers and those that employ them, we might well start to make some different choices about their design and content. We will certainly argue more clearly about what trade regimes are for and how they work.

With this in mind, our authors explored five issues:

The limits of labor clauses in trade agreements

"Cross-Cutting Themes" (above) noted that labor clauses in trade agreements may prove less effective than many other background rules affecting the workplace. This critical tack runs against some of the conventional wisdom among progressive scholars, who have advocated in favor of labor clauses even while conceding their flaws. That view reflects a long-standing strategy to improve the conditions of workers in the South and protect labor in the North against social dumping by insisting that trade agreements include requirements for the maintenance of existing labor standards (nonderogation) and recognition of certain basic labor rights. Rittich points out that such labor clauses may be of some use but are woefully inadequate to deal with the impact of trade on labor. Nonderogation clauses and basic rights requirements may have little impact on actual labor conditions on the ground. The existing standards that must be maintained under these clauses may be specific, but they are often very low, while the basic rights that these clauses name, however aspirational they appear, are vague and can easily be interpreted away. Moreover, even if these clauses did have some effect in the designated territory, they may not reach the labor conditions in GVCs. Rittich notes,

> The changing, often-transitory contractual relations that organize the operation of supply chains provide well-documented mechanisms to destandardize the terms under which workers labor. Insulating lead firms from the costs and legal responsibilities associated with employment, they exacerbate distributional inequities.

Rittich concludes, "It is simply magical thinking to imagine that adding labor standards and workers' rights to trade agreements will fix, or even dent, the complex problems at work." She urges a broader approach, one followed by Santos, who argues that if the now revised TPP less the US (now called the CPTPP) and its labor chapter represent the gold standard of globalization as some claimed, then there is good reason to abandon it, just as countries dropped the gold standard in monetary policy in the twentieth century. Pinning our hopes of improving labor conditions on a chapter that relies entirely on adjudication, and whose claims would have to be taken up by states and take years to reach a resolution, is illusory at best. Santos notes that, as pointed out by the US labor movement, reform in other areas of trade agreements may be more promising, including government procurement, investment and social dumping remedies. Santos argues that an overlooked contribution of the TPP was the use of the trade negotiation to put pressure on domestic reform of labor laws and institutions. Consistent with the lessons of the TPP, changes in several of these areas did end up taking place in the new USMCA, beyond the labor chapter. Most important of all was the Labor Annex, whereby Mexico committed to enacting legislation guaranteeing freedom of association and collective bargaining rights.

Prospects for bans on social dumping

One proposal that would put pressure on developing countries to respect basic labor rights would be to treat low labor standards and weak enforcement as a form of dumping, thus justifying domestic trade remedies. As noted above, Shaffer outlines a proposal to deal with "social dumping of products—that is, products produced under exploitative labor conditions—that sell for less than domestically produced products, thus leading to concerns over wage suppression and reductions of labor protections in the North." The norms, he suggests, should address only labor rights violations and thus not undercut developing countries' comparative advantage in producing goods with lower-skilled labor in the reflection of differences in productivity. Shaffer provides a list of labor norms:

> rights against forced labor, child labor, hazardous work and discrimination; establishment of maximum working hours and a minimum wage; and most fundamentally, rights to freedom of association and collective bargaining.

A country deciding to impose duties would need to show sustained violations, and the process should include all the procedural protections available in standard antidumping cases. Rittich agrees that such a remedy might have some use. But she cautions that the standards that are universally acceptable are low and will not help many workers, problems of proof of violation are serious and the rise of such actions could trigger fears of protectionism.

The need to regulate GVCs

Neither labor clauses nor social dumping actions are likely to reach abuses embedded in GVCs—to deal with those, special rules will be needed. Rittich comments,

Because so much production and service delivery is now transnationally organized, finding ways to reallocate costs and risks, benefits and burdens, across GVCs is also a central challenge. Along with more effective taxation of worldwide corporate income, what is needed are legal rules that more effectively bind lead firms to the debts and obligations of their contractors and subcontractors, as well as rules and regimes that permit workers to organize more easily across borders and thereby capture more of the gains of their labor.

Better ways to compensate losers: Overcoming the flaws in trade adjustment assistance

Trade agreements bring about economic adjustment as some industries wax under new conditions and others wane. The goal is to ensure that net gains exceed net losses. The problem is that while the gains come automatically as industries expand under the stimulus of an expanded market, compensating losers requires explicit action by government. While many countries have created mechanisms to provide such compensation, they have often proven inadequate. This is especially true in the United States, writes Garcia. The US system, called trade adjustment assistance (TAA), is too narrow in scope. Moreover, funding is both uncertain and inadequate. TAA is often promised as an inducement to get labor support for trade agreements. But dependent as it is on annual congressional appropriations, TAA can be, and usually is, scaled back once agreements have been signed. To avoid this, Garcia proposes that the funding to support those most vulnerable to trade come from trade itself.

Streinz echoes this idea and argues that we need to rethink what trade agreements are all about. He notes that agreements like the TPP create a more open space for private actors to expand their business operations free of restrictions. While multinational corporations (MNCs) are the beneficiaries of the agreements, they are not seen as part of the deal. He notes,

> FTAs are better understood as tools to expand firms' freedom to operate transnationally. Take the revived Trans-Pacific Partnership agreement, which creates a transoceanic economic megaregion in which tariffs are to be gradually phased out, multicountry production networks benefit from cumulative rules of origin, states' interference with the market is disciplined and domestic rule- and decision-making has to comply with common (global) administrative law standards of transparency, participation, reason giving and review.

Streinz and Garcia agree on the need for mechanisms that would tap the gains from trade and earmark them for TAA and other social programs that would benefit those whose jobs have been lost due to trade. They differ on the best way to do it, with Streinz proposing a passport fee to be levied on all companies that want to enjoy the benefits created by a trade agreement, and Garcia proposing a tax on all financial transactions within the new region. In either case, the revenues raised would go directly into a reformed and expanded TAA, bypassing the process of annual budgets and congressional appropriation. While Rittich does not reject such proposals, she notes the difficulty of separating the effect of trade from all the other drivers of job loss and suggests that more robust measures to protect against job loss of any kind might be more effective.

Addressing the social cost implications of the trade–immigration nexus
in both the North and the South

Well-funded and expanded versions of TAA should help provide compensation for trade losers and help them return to the labor market. But domestic economies may adjust too slowly to fully absorb those whose livelihoods have been affected by a trade agreement. Using the example of Mexican farmworkers displaced by NAFTA, Thomas argues for explicitly linking trade-opening policies to concomitant policies on immigration, not only to reflect conceptual consistency but also to reflect norms of equality and equity as well as awareness of the social cost implications of trade in both the Global North and Global South.

Toward a Progressive Agenda

Here, we outline some elements for a progressive agenda and discuss ways that these ideas might be brought into the policy area.

Measures for a progressive agenda

Integrate trade and social policy

The first priority is to ensure that changes from trade create net benefits for society. To achieve that, we need to ensure that the disruption created by expanded trade will lead to significant gains, develop ways to minimize the negative social impact of trade agreements and provide adequate compensation for those who suffer losses. This would include measures to strengthen the rights of labor in exporting countries, impose penalties on countries that seek to gain market share by exploiting labor and ensure that losses in importing countries are adequately compensated. But progressives need to go further to ensure not only that losses in the North are compensated and labor conditions in the South improved but also that gains from trade are widely shared. We need to develop policies that will ensure not only that there are net gains but that they are widely shared in a rising tide that lifts all boats. Measures could include the following:

- Requiring a social impact statement for trade agreements, including the views of groups that stand to lose
- Taxing trade winners and earmark receipts to compensate losers and redistribute gains, and create these mechanisms in international trade agreements
- Linking immigration and trade by including migration in trade agreements. Examples might include expanding commitments on Mode 4 (movement of natural persons) in services chapters, and reinforcing capacities for sector-by-sector reciprocal liberalization over time.
- Deterring races to the bottom by strengthening labor rights clauses and enabling social dumping remedies

- Focusing on other areas of trade law that affect workers beyond labor chapters, such as rules of origin, government procurement and investment chapters
- Using leverage during FTA negotiations to trigger domestic labor reform in both poor *and* rich countries

Tolerate diversity in economic models and facilitate economic development

Trade law functions best when it manages tensions between different ways to organize economies. Increased pressure for convergence erodes national sovereignty, deters experimentation and threatens democracy. At the most basic level, trade law should not penalize different economic models unless trade frictions cause serious harm. Further, it should facilitate, not deter, the search for better ways to achieve growth in the context of specific economies. Finally, trade law should not force changes that are deeply undemocratic: popular approval, if not the process for adopting such laws, at least should create an outer boundary for them. In the last three decades, trade law has tilted toward convergence to a single model of market economy, which has been presented as the only viable path to development despite strongly held views in many countries and solid evidence to the contrary. We need fewer restrictions on policy experimentation. Broadly speaking, challenges to alternative economic models and strategies should bear the burden of proof. Other measures could include

- A stronger concept of subsidiarity in WTO law in which national decisions are given priority
- A new concept of fair trade that tolerates diversity
- A less restrictive subsidies agreement
- A revamped use of the industrial policy exemption
- Fewer limits on the operation of SOEs
- Fewer limits on capital controls
- Positive incentives for policy experimentation

Create a system for regulation of GVCs

Changes in the world economy render some traditional legal strategies obsolete. In GVCs, traditional labor law may have little effect. Buyer firms exercise disproportionate power. They secure most of the gains from exporting, thus limiting the growth potential for developing countries. Private governance systems fail to protect workers. Measures to deal with these conditions include

- A tax regime that ensures that the exporting countries get a fair share of rents
- Passport fees for firms that want to participate in the benefits of a FTA
- Trade law measures that impose responsibilities on buyer firms to ensure that fair labor standards are followed down the chain

- Meta regulation in trade agreements requiring national governments to deal more effectively with GVCs by creating rules that affect buyer firms and hold them responsible for fair labor practices
- Global, regional and bilateral monitoring of buyer firm and national government compliance

Make investment protection development friendly and socially progressive

Resistance to the BIT regime is growing as countries begin to realize its potential impact on important social policies and development objectives. Especially in the hands of arbitrators with pro-business approaches, protections like indirect expropriation can be used to limit policy space. Some FTAs have included a right to regulate covering environment, health and safety, but this does not go far enough. Investments, especially in infrastructure and mining, can have a disproportionate impact on local communities powerless to affect decisions. Measures could include

- Eliminating or severely circumscribing indirect expropriation
- Limiting the scope of the full protection and security guarantee
- Including an expansive Right to Regulate in treaties covering redistributive and industrial policy as well as environment, health and safety
- Providing protection in national foreign direct investment legislation instead of treaties
- Relying on state-to-state arbitration instead of investor-state dispute settlement

Engaging with emergent progressive forces

The goal of this book is threefold. We seek to elaborate a framework that can undergird a new and progressive approach to world trade and investment law, provide analysis of some of the more important issues now under discussion and make tentative suggestions for new policy initiatives. However, this book is just a beginning, and further steps need to be taken to fashion tools for action. These ideas should be elaborated in dialogue with other progressive forces. Real change will require engagement by interest groups, social movements, think tanks and policymakers in both the North and the South. We need to find ways to engage at those levels. We see that groups committed to work for a better and fairer globalization are emerging: we look forward to engaging with them.[8]

---

[8]   In the political world, the newly formed Progressive International, led by Bernie Sanders and Yannis Varoufakis, offers promise. In the academic world, the Law and Political Economy Blog and Network (https://lpeblog.org/) and the *Journal of Law and Political Economy* (https://escholarship.org/uc/lawandpoliticaleconomy) share many of the views set forth in this volume.

PART I

RETHINKING THE POLITICAL ECONOMY OF TRADE: COMMENTS ON DANI RODRIK'S *STRAIGHT TALK ON TRADE*

Chapter One

COMMENTS ON *STRAIGHT TALK ON TRADE*

Chantal Thomas

Dani Rodrik's *Straight Talk on Trade: Ideas for a Sane World Economy* ably synthesizes complex ideas and distills them into clear and common sense—in other words, straight talk. Rodrik's writing warrants high admiration both for this synthetic quality as well as for some of the counterintuitive or provocative arguments (from an orthodox economist's perspective) that he makes: the talk offered by this book seeks to upend much conventional wisdom in economics and politics. These analytic qualities will be familiar to fans of Rodrik's extensive body of earlier work. Here, as well as in earlier work, they span with seeming effortlessness a vast geographic range, moving across countries and regions in both the Global North and the Global South.

It would be difficult to do justice to the rich and variegated insights in *Straight Talk on Trade*. I will comment on only two of the many arguments Rodrik presents in the book, focusing on developed and developing countries, respectively. The first of Rodrik's arguments that I want to address is the assertion that developed states should privilege national policy space over hyperglobalization; I will ask about the significance of the turn to global value chains. The second argument is that industrialization may no longer be possible for developing countries; I will ask whether flexibility in both the law (General Agreement on Tariffs and Trade/World Trade Organization (GATT/WTO)) and the economics (the effects of localization) warrants a reexamination of the possibility.

Straight Talk for Developed States: National Policy Space Should Prevail Over Cosmopolitan Fantasies

Rodrik bracingly upbraids contemporary "elites and technocrats" for what he deems an obsession with "hyperglobalization"[1] at the expense of economic policy that is more flexible, and therefore more sensible and more sustainable. He writes, "We—the world's financial, political and technocratic elite—distanced ourselves from our compatriots and lost their trust."[2] This lament expresses the core of the allegations of political and ideological irresponsibility that Rodrik lays at the feet of the governors of today's global

---

[1] Dani Rodrik, *Straight Talk on Trade: Ideas for a Sane World Economy* (Princeton, NJ: Princeton University Press, 2018), 13.

[2] Ibid., 16.

economy. Rodrik's reference to "compatriots" is by no means incidental: this book in many ways offers a full-throated defense of the nation-state. As one of its more salient themes, it calls for a return to the national scale as the basis for economic policymaking. Rodrik argues for prioritizing national economic and social priorities and for making full use of the range of trade and other economic instruments to do so.

Several avenues for such reform, and for innovation in ways of balancing economic and social concerns, are elucidated; for example, through antidumping duties for "social dumping." Such measures, he wagers, are often much more effective than austerity or structural reforms have proven, despite the "amnesia" Rodrik describes that allows such guidance to rise from the ashes of each of its previous failures (Africa, Latin America, the Asian financial crisis and, most recently, Greece).

Conversely, for both empirical and normative reasons, Rodrik argues that the tendency of cosmopolitan peers to "think of national borders as a hindrance"[3] and to celebrate globalization both as an economic phenomenon and as a normative project is wrongheaded. He marshals both normative and empirical evidence for this proposition. First, as an empirical matter, according to the sociodemographic evidence Rodrik presents here, the *idea of a nation-state* remains very much the focus of people's "imagined communities" (to cite my Cornell colleague Benedict Anderson). National attachment is much more closely linked to personal identity—for example, people are overwhelmingly more likely to agree with the statement that they are citizens of a particular country than that they are world citizens.[4] Moreover, even in the age of globalization, the reality of economic life seems to remain significantly localized. Studies of "distance elasticity"—the degree to which geographical distance negatively affects trade—show that the penalty of distance has actually increased since the 1960s.[5]

The locality of globalization that Rodrik describes is surprising, or perhaps even paradoxical, given that, as Richard Baldwin has recently elucidated, the removal of transportation and communication barriers has both greatly increased international trade and, as Baldwin argues, reoriented production toward *denationalized* value chains.[6] Baldwin's empirical analysis is not, however, actually inconsistent with the data that Rodrik offers. Notwithstanding the "unbundling" of production into global value chains, Baldwin's analysis takes localization effects into account, arguing that this explains why offshoring from the industrialized world has tended to cluster in a few sites in the developing world (Baldwin calls them the "industrializing six" developing nations).[7]

Yet on another level, Baldwin's analysis may seriously challenge Rodrik's perspective, particularly when it comes to the normative reasons to return to the nation-state as a site of policymaking. Baldwin seems to suggest that denationalization has rendered somewhat archaic and effectively obsolete the notion that nations can be identified with particular

---

[3]   Ibid., 17.

[4]   Ibid., 21–23.

[5]   Ibid., 38–39.

[6]   Richard Baldwin, *The Great Convergence: Information Technology and the New Globalization* (Cambridge, MA: Belknap Press, 2016), 12.

[7]   Ibid., 2–7.

trade interests. It has killed the nation-state as a site for policy, both for developing countries in forming development strategies and for developed countries in following nationalistic industrial policies. My central question to Rodrik with respect to this aspect of his analysis, therefore, is how he would respond to the argument that the deterritorialization of economic production has made nationalized economic governance, however ideal from some perspectives, no longer realistically possible or effective.

Of course, Baldwin's analysis came out in 2016 and undoubtedly was finished before Great Britain's decision to exit the European Union, the election of President Trump in the United States and other clear reassertions of nationalism in economic space. Such events arguably point to the continued cultural and ideational relevance of nation-states that Rodrik identifies with his sociodemographic discussion, even if the empirical reality is now more complex.

This observation further underscores the second, normative set of reasons that Rodrik marshals in defense of the nation-state—that nations not only can but also should be the locus for policy. One major reason Rodrik gives picks up on a theme of his writing through many different works, which is the possibility of local variation and heterogeneity in economic policy, and the importance of ensuring sufficient flexibility to enable such differentiation. Because conditions vary locally, there is no "single ideal point along [the] trade-off"[8] between market openness and market stability, no one answer to the question of how a particular society should balance its social concerns with a market orientation. Rodrik also points to the continued salience of the nation-state as the "lender of last resort" and the place where the buck stops. It is national governments that do, and are best positioned to, step forward in moments of social crisis.

All this I largely agree with, but to raise a second and perhaps more far-flung question of this analytical line, I didn't see anything that would necessarily disqualify quintessentially cosmopolitan visions of global governance, such as the foundational cosmopolitan Immanuel Kant's argument for a global federation in his *Perpetual Peace*. Such a federation would continue to delegate primary responsibility to localities. In other words, is the nation-state really necessary, even within Rodrik's normative framework emphasizing local governance, or is it just the result of path dependence?

Rodrik alludes in *Straight Talk on Trade* to the famous trilemma he developed in earlier work: the proposition that, across democracy, sovereignty and globalization, only two of these three can coexist. (To achieve globalization, nations have to ignore their citizenries at the peril of their democratic processes; socially responsible globalization could occur, but it would have to dismantle sovereignty to have democracy be effective at the global scale or follow the traditional model, which has sovereignty and democracy without globalization.)

Rodrik is clear that we have gotten ourselves stuck on the horns of this trilemma. Elites have pushed economic integration far past the point where political institutions have been able to keep up. The imbalance must be corrected in one of two directions: "expand governance beyond the nation-state or restrict the reach of markets."[9] The tendency of

---

[8] Rodrik, *Straight Talk on Trade*, 34
[9] Ibid., 30.

polite company among cosmopolitan elites is to speak only of the former, but Rodrik makes a strong argument that the second option should be considered, consciously going against the conventional tendencies of his cohort of international economists.

Straight Talk for Developing States: Conventional Industrialization Is No Longer Possible

Whereas the aforementioned sections of the book focus largely on economic policy debates in the developed world, other portions are devoted primarily to policy for developing countries. Here again, Rodrik bucks the orthodoxy of international economists upholding market openness as the path to development. As he has done elsewhere (e.g., *One Economics, Many Recipes*),[10] Rodrik argues forcefully that available evidence seriously problematizes the orthodox belief. For example, in studies of the correlation between economic growth and liberalization, the impact was statistically insignificant in one direction or another,[11] meaning that there was no clear association between liberalizing national economic policy and increasing national economic growth. In many countries that *did* adopt liberalization reform, such as India in the 1990s, the takeoff in growth well preceded the reforms.[12] Moreover, many countries, such as China and Vietnam, have *not* hewed to the conventional economic wisdom and instead have mixed market-oriented export promotion with protective measures that would violate liberal trade norms and even some of the current trade rules.[13] By contrast, some countries that went much more by the book of economic orthodoxy in "rely[ing] on free trade alone," like Mexico, have "languished."[14] Rodrik suggests that countries that have succeeded seem to have done so by targeting particular businesses and sectors for growth rather than introducing broad, economy-wide reforms. In other words, a mix of market orientation and industrial protection, applied in an informed and effective way, seems to have prevailed among developing-country success stories.[15]

Notwithstanding the track record of the emerging economies, one of the notable assertions that arises in these passages of the book questions whether smaller countries in today's environment can even reproduce those economies' success records. Rodrik here introduces the phenomenon of "premature deindustrialization."[16] It may no longer be possible, according to this argument, for a developing country to follow a model of industrialization through traditional goods manufacturing, with subsequent shifts to services and information sectors. Developing countries are now, like the rest of the world, seeing more growth and more employment in their services sectors than in traditional manufacturing.

---

[10] Dani Rodrik, *One Economics, Many Recipes: Globalization, Institutions, and Economic Growth* (Princeton, NJ: Princeton University Press, 2007).

[11] Rodrik, *Straight Talk on Trade*, 53.

[12] Ibid., 56.

[13] Ibid., 3.

[14] Ibid.

[15] Ibid., 57.

[16] Ibid., 90.

The obstacles to growth through conventional industrialization lie both in contemporary technology and in contemporary trade.[17] With respect to technology, because manufacturing is now much more knowledge- and capital-intensive, barriers to entry are higher and less available to countries further down the economic ladder. With respect to trade, not only does the sheer formidability and market dominance of current competitors like China reduce the possibilities for market share gains for smaller economies, but also international trade rules have now reduced the amount of protection countries can introduce to attenuate that market dominance by locking in commitments to market openness.

If manufacturing no longer provides a clear path toward industrialization, the services path is also challenging in terms of achieving development, because so far it does not seem to generate the same kinds of mass wealth creation and transfer as conventional manufacturing-based industrialization did. Services firms are smaller, more likely to be informal and tend toward lower productivity. Higher employment in services also correlates with higher economic inequality in the studies that Rodrik cites here.

On the other hand, Rodrik says this could be a "blessing in disguise" because, to achieve high growth in the age of the service economy, developing countries will have to invest much more in broad social infrastructure such as education, and this should redound to the benefit of their populations.[18] This argument is persuasive, but my major question to Rodrik with respect to this part of his argument is whether he may have counted out industrialization as a strategy too quickly. Certainly, manufacturing remains a central part of the industrialization strategies of many developing countries, many of whom are now integrating their regional markets with the hope of boosting trade in both manufacturing and services sectors.

First, the "trade rules," meaning greater disciplines under international trade agreements that enforce greater market openness, are perhaps not as rigid as is portrayed here. Even with bound tariffs, the GATT provides the opportunity to modify tariff schedules (Article XVIII). It does say that the acting government must notify the adversely affected WTO members, who then can enter into negotiations with the acting member and, if no agreement can be reached, can withdraw "substantially equivalent" concessions. In other words, this is not a cost-free measure—the acting countries may lose access to most-favored-nation (MFN) tariffs in other markets—but the choice does exist within the rules.

Moreover, in many cases, if not all, the international trade rules still provide for special and differential treatment of smaller economies. Several trade protocols contain an exception for the least developed countries (e.g., the Trade-Related Investment Measures (TRIMs) and Trade-Related Aspects of Intellectual Property Rights (TRIPS) agreements) that would benefit many—even if not all—developing countries (e.g., about three-quarters of the countries in sub-Saharan Africa).

With respect specifically to trade in goods, since the focus is on goods manufacture, the GATT also includes generalized language in Article XVIII that was adopted to

---

[17] Ibid., 91.
[18] Ibid., 91–92.

provide a series of flexibilities for developing countries. The most commonly invoked one, less frequent now, was the rule for balance of payments (Article XVIII (B)), but there are also more general provisions (e.g., Article XVIII (C)). The reasons these provisions are not often used have to do with the larger political and strategic environment. For example, in 2017, the East African Community (EAC) banned secondhand clothing to encourage local textiles—a measure that arguably could be brought into compliance with the GATT/WTO law given its provisions on special and differential treatment. However, EAC countries were pressured to drop the ban by the United States, which exports large amounts of secondhand clothing to Africa each year. The United States threatened to withdraw its unilateral trade preferences to the EAC countries (under the US African Growth and Opportunity Act) if the ban was not dropped. (The question of whether countries *can* adopt these sorts of measures, of course, does not definitely answer the question of whether they should: there is always the danger of unintended consequences, such as an overall drop in economic activity due to the inability of domestic industries to ramp up to cost-effectively meet domestic supply—in other words, whether this measure follows the effective playbook of targeted market protection of scalable industries described above with respect to other developing-country success stories—but this is a separate question from whether it is legally permitted.)

Another consideration here arises from the very evidence that Rodrik discusses elsewhere on the locality of globalization—for example, that that economic integration remains significantly localized. If this is the case, this fact arguably provides further ballast to the proposition that developing economies should be able to generate effective local industrial growth even in today's highly open and competitive global environment. The relative advantages of clustering production might at some point outweigh the cost advantages that might come from China or other competitors.

An obstacle that these economies have faced in moving up the industrial economic ladder has been their orientation toward primary products so that the infrastructure of these countries follows a center–periphery organization. Yet South–South regional integration efforts, such as the current African Continental Free Trade Agreement, are trying to modulate that by reducing costs regionally to help bolster an internal market that would be diversified across agriculture, services and manufacturing. So the question here for Rodrik is whether it really is the end of industrialization or whether alternatively a place remains for localized industrial production among today's low-income countries if they can amend and manage trade rules to be supportive and can operate with reasonable governance, effective institutions and sound targeting of promising industries and firms.

Chapter Two

THOUGHTS ON *STRAIGHT TALK ON TRADE*

Kevin P. Gallagher

Straight Talk on Trade is an incredible collection and interweaving of many of Professor Dani Rodrik's accessible discussions on globalization and the world economy. While the book addresses issues of financial crises, trade policy and democratization, I will focus my comments on the issues most directly related to trade policy.

One of Rodrik's statements reflects his motivation for the book: "Globalization, at least as presently construed, tilts the balance of political power toward those with the skills and assets to benefit from the global economy, undermining whatever organized influence the losers might have had in the first place."[1] Implicit in this statement (though less so in his other writings) is the notion that the rules of the world economy are accentuating global inequities. Thus, the rules need fundamental reform to make the world economy work more efficiently and more equitably.

Like some of his other works, this book does not solely take aim at the major powers, and the interest groups that sway those powers, for these global inequities. Rodrik also blames economists.

It's the Economists

Riffing a bit from the book, one could argue that there are two major problems with the way most Western-trained economists engage with trade. First, they fail to acknowledge the content of trade and investment agreements and have consistent quantitative models for only a small part of what constitutes contemporary treaty-making. Second, they overstate—especially in public—the "gains" from their limited modeling exercises and understate the "losses."

The modeling exercises that dominate trade policymaking take the form of computable general equilibrium (CGE) models that "work" only if good trade is modeled and if there is perfect competition, fixed employment, no externalities, no international investment and no technological change. Once one introduces economies of scale, services and investment, unemployment and so forth, the models will give spurious results,

---

[1] Dani Rodrik, *Straight Talk on Trade: Ideas for a Sane World Economy* (Princeton, NJ: Princeton University Press, 2018), 206.

which, while important to study in seminars, should not be used by policymakers to make decisions.

As Rodrik discusses, the gains from trade, according to these modeling exercises, are minuscule relative to the size of the economies. The North American Free Trade Agreement (NAFTA), one of the largest trade deals, benefited the US economy by 0.08 of 1 percent. This brings us to the second flaw, explicitly outlined by Rodrik: economists in public tend to emphasize and exaggerate the gains from trade without acknowledging the Stolper–Samuelson aspects of their models. For instance, the Peterson Institute for International Economics predicted that the Trans-Pacific Partnership (TPP) would bring billions of dollars of benefits to the US economy. In press releases and briefings, these economists forgot to put the denominator in place, which showed that the TPP would actually bring much less than 1 percent in benefits to the US economy.

Another key problem is the blind eye toward the distributional aspects of trade, which are built right into our theories via Stolper–Samuelson. While the gains from trade are small relative to entire economies, they are highly concentrated into the hands of a few in a small number of key sectors (pharma, finance and factory food). The losers from trade are also small relative to entire economies but highly concentrated in a few sectors (manufacturing, of course). In addition, the losses may be small relative to economies but overwhelming relative to the budget constraints of the losers themselves and the alternative opportunities they may have.

To summarize, economists have put very little time into modeling investment flows, globalization of intellectual property rules, subsidies reductions and a host of other regulations in their formal quantitative models of trade and growth. They pretend that trade treaties resemble those previous to the Kennedy Rounds and lead only with the numerator, ignoring that those benefits are net of a winner–loser equation and ignoring the denominator.

This is dangerous because it locks in an inherently unequal rules system—so much so that those powerful "winners" have now been able to insert investor-state dispute systems into treaties that effectively let private interests govern the treaties' meatiest parts.

Blame Other Social Scientists, Too

The blame should be extended to political scientists and lightened a bit on economists.

Political scientists tend to see trade as fairly boring and easy to explain, given that Mancur Olson summed it all up decades ago. Trade deals are seen as optimal (because the economists tell them so) and as a political contest between the winners and the losers. When a deal falters, it is because of the "logic of collective action" whereby those consumers with the biggest gains (the sum of the consumer surplus across an economy—for example, those that will get lower prices and therefore implicit welfare increases) are so dissipated and unorganized that the losers overpower the winners.

The very models show that the net benefits are hardly positive, and perhaps the signs would change if other parts of treaties (especially intellectual property rights, or IPRs) were included in the modeling exercise. If political scientists read Rodrik's book and took it seriously, 1,000 dissertations with real research on trade politics might bloom.

Rodrik says that political economic analysis is very weak given that there "is no well-defined mapping from interests to outcomes."[2] That work has been left to the press. In 2015, the *Washington Post* did an investigative report titled "Industry Voices Dominate the Trade Advisory System." The *Post* found that there are 566 advisory group members who can look at US trade proposals and comment on them. (Congress members or their staff cannot.) According to the *Post*, though, 480 of those advisers, or 85 percent, represent industry or trade association groups. Those academics, unions and civil society members that can take part are most often relegated to small subcommittees that don't get access to the meat of the deal.

With this in mind, let me defend economists a bit. Very few economists at the best universities are doing work on trade, and of those, hardly any would be caught doing CGE models. Indeed, at the best universities, trade economists are trying to model the nuances of the world economy and not just snapping off crude estimates of the latest trade deal. Granted, trade economists are a smaller and smaller breed. Financial follies have attracted more international economists into finance these days. Of course, more emphasis and reward should go into breeding more trade economists and making sure that they are studying the trading systems' real complexities and are not afraid to discuss those complexities in public.

The economists who dominate the policy discourse are usually from government agencies, international financial institutions and think tanks that are fully financed by the winners. The bias and shortcomings of economists in international institutions and governments were exposed in the Evaluation of World Bank Research 1998–2005 panel chaired by Angus Deaton but largely ignored outside of academia. I am unaware of any study linking the positions of think tank economists and the interest groups that fund their research.

While this is not spelled out in Rodrik's book, one can connect the dots to say that the winners of globalization are writing the rules of globalization, economists are cheer-leading, other social scientists are out to lunch, and the working class in the North and future entrepreneurs of the South have had enough.

The question is, can we get a set of rules that will balance this power, or does the power have to be balanced before we get more equal rules?

---

[2]   Rodrik, *Straight Talk on Trade*, 165.

Chapter Three

READING RODRIK: A CALL FOR A NEW LAW AND ECONOMICS FOR INTERNATIONAL LAW

Gregory Shaffer

Dani Rodrik's *Straight Talk on Trade: Ideas for a Sane World Economy* is a model of how to combine theory, empirics and pragmatic and innovative proposals in a sophisticated but accessible way.[1] The result is a series of insights that are important for anyone wishing to develop a progressive agenda for international trade and investment law. In this essay, I highlight five insights that international economic law scholars should take into account as we rethink trade and investment law.

Globalization Has Gone Too Far

Rodrik's core argument is that international trade and economic integration agreements in support of globalization have excessively constrained national policy space.[2] They have done so through a web of multilateral, regional, plurilateral and bilateral trade, investment and economic integration agreements. The World Trade Organization (WTO) lies at the pinnacle of trade governance, but it is just the big meatball in a spaghetti bowl of agreements. The loss of balance between economic globalization and compensating domestic policy became politically salient following the 2008 financial crisis.

International Economic Law Should Respect Democracy and Empower Nation-State Regulation of the Global Economy

Rodrik's diagnosis is that the relation of domestic law and politics, on the one hand, and economic globalization (or "hyperglobalization"[3]), on the other, has become imbalanced.

---

[1] Dani Rodrik, *Straight Talk on Trade: Ideas for a Sane World Economy* (Princeton, NJ: Princeton University Press, 2018).

[2] Ibid., 13–14.

[3] Rodrik, *Straight Talk on Trade*, 13–14.

While economies globalize, politics remain local. International economic law, Rodrik argues, needs to *empower* nation-states to regulate the global economy, not disempower them. Prudence dictates a more modest approach, one in which international law does not aim to restructure states but rather to complement and support their policies under a guiding principle of nondiscrimination.

Rodrik argues that "we need to place the requirements of liberal democracy ahead of those of international trade and investment."[4] If, despite the gains from trade, economic globalization puts liberal democracy at risk, then we need to readjust the balance in favor of more domestic policy space and less economic integration facilitated by international economic law.

This calls for a law and economics that takes account of social and political context and thus the relation of international law and institutions to the nation-state. One can then adopt pragmatic policies to spur economic growth while maintaining economic stability and cooperative trade relations supported by law, all of which requires a balance of national and international rules and authority.

The Nation-State Is the Institution That Can Most Effectively Regulate and Legitimize Markets

Markets require rules to facilitate economic exchange, create stability and provide a sense of legitimacy. Rodrik makes the case for the nation-state as "the only game in town when it comes to providing the regulatory and legitimizing arrangements on which markets rely."[5] Economically, the state enables the mobility of resources, enhancing efficiency and increasing productivity essential for economic growth and social welfare. Politically, the state fosters the spread of participatory, representative institutions, giving rise to liberal democracy. Legally, the state creates public order through laws and institutions that reduce violence and uphold the social contract.[6]

When it comes to market regulation, global governance is no substitute for the state but is best viewed as a complement. State institutions more likely reflect preferences of national stakeholders and are thus more attentive to national and local contexts. Moreover, national diversity creates benefits in terms of experimentation (from which learning occurs) and resilience for the global economy (when things go wrong in any one jurisdiction).

Trade agreements should be retooled to provide policy space for countries to ensure social inclusion, such as by integrating policies to combat harmful tax avoidance and deter social dumping.[7] Investment treaties should be modified so that the fundamental guiding principle is enhancing the rule of law for foreign and domestic stakeholders alike (rather than privileging foreign investors), which will depend on strengthening domestic

---

4   Ibid., 12.
5   Rodrik, *Straight Talk on Trade*, 13.
6   Ibid., 24.
7   For a series of proposals, see Gregory Shaffer, "Retooling Trade Agreements for Social Inclusion," *University of Illinois Law Review* (forthcoming).

institutions and should be tailored to different national contexts.[8] In the area of capital regulation, states should be granted significant discretion to take prudential measures involving capital controls.

Rodrik illustrates this lesson with a discussion of the European Union (EU). The challenge for the EU, he says, is not to see economic integration as a one-way street, requiring ever more policymaking at the European level. Rather, the EU needs to find complementary ways of leaving policy to diverse EU members in light of their citizens' demands, contexts and experience. With the increase in EU membership, the EU needed to provide more, not less, space for national economic and regulatory governance but often went the other way, most significantly with the creation of the euro.

International Law Must Facilitate Experimentation in Development Policy

Rodrik rejects the one-size-fits-all approach to development adopted by many economists and followed by many development agencies. He believes that countries must experiment to find the optimal development path and argues that international economic law should facilitate such experimentation. Rodrik stresses that economic development is not just about the creation of property rights but fundamentally about institutions. Focusing on property rights is not enough, as exemplified when elites profit from state privatization programs, embedding crony capitalism. Economic transformation rather depends on institutions and experimentation in light of the economic context.

Applying this approach to China, Rodrik suggests a different response than many defenders of the current international economic legal order.[9] Trade liberals traditionally lambast China as "mercantilist" because of the strong role of the state in the economy, which they attest leads to losses in consumer welfare. Trade liberals believe that China must be pressured to abandon state-led development strategies. They argue that if China does not become "more like us,"[10] the whole trading system capped by the WTO will not work.

For Rodrik, the problem with this analysis is that there is no one way to structure economies to enhance their development. The proper relation of the state and the market for development will always be uncertain and contentious. Traditionally, US policymakers trumpeted a US model in which the state plays a minimal role. China, in contrast, adopted a developmental state model in which capitalism thrives but the state remains prominent.[11] China does not need to become "like us" in terms of its regulatory

---

[8] See Sergio Puig and Gregory Shaffer, "Imperfect Alternatives: Institutional Choice and the Reform of Investment Law," *American Journal of International Law* 112, no. 3 (2018): 361 (on the role of "complementarity," focusing first on domestic institutions, combined with institutional choice in light of context).

[9] Rodrik, *Straight Talk on Trade*, 135–36.

[10] Kurt M. Campbell and Ely Ratner, "The China Reckoning," *Foreign Affairs*, March/April 2018.

[11] Cf. Mark Wu, "The 'China Inc.' Challenge to Global Trade Governance," *Harvard International Law Journal* 57, no. 2 (2016): 261–324; and Nicolas R. Lardy, *Markets over Mao: The Rise of Private Business in China* (Washington, DC: Peterson Institute for International Economics, 2014).

model, nor us like them. What is needed is a diversity of models in competition with one another, with variation occurring in relation to different preferences, development contexts and experimental strategies.[12] There is no one development model. And a plurality of models will make for a more resilient global economy. As a counterfactual, just think if China had been "just like us" at the time of the 2008 global financial crisis, rather than providing a market of last resort when US-style capitalism imploded. The key question thus becomes managing the interface between different economic systems to protect domestic social bargains.

We Need a New Law and Economics to Deal with Economic Globalization

Rodrik castigates the economics profession for too frequently expressing unabashed support in the media for globalization and trade agreements without necessary caveats and thus constituting bad economics. He calls for a methodology that builds conditional theory from context.[13] Applying the famous trope of Isaiah Berlin, he distinguishes hedgehogs from foxes in economics.[14] Hedgehogs search for a single economic model that explains everything. Foxes develop and choose among a plurality of models applicable to differing contexts. In economics, more foxes are needed, just as they are in international economic law. Rodrik stresses that useful economic analysis requires choices among models that involves both science and craft. The science involves the creation and application of models based on differing assumptions. The craft lies in choosing among the models in light of the suitability of the assumptions and the question and context at issue.[15]

To develop a pragmatic international economic law, Rodrik's insight should be combined with the parallel ideas of the legal realists concerning the dangers of simple economic models that have been embedded in legal doctrine. The analogue to a hedgehog in law is a single norm (such as freedom of contract) and a single theory (such as a simple rational actor model) that is applied equally regardless of context. Legal realists like Karl Llewellyn and neorealists like Arthur Leff warned against these errors.[16]

---

12 Rodrik, *Straight Talk on Trade*, 131–32. With irony, Rodrik notes Milton Friedman's characterization of the government as "the enemy" when proclaiming the magic of the market, pointing to what goes into the making of a pencil. Today, that pencil would be produced in China with its complex hybrid of state-led and market form of capitalism.

13 Ibid., 115, 128. This important part of *Straight Talk* is further developed in Rodrik's earlier book, *Economic Rules: The Rights and Wrongs of the Dismal Science* (New York: W. W. Norton, 2015).

14 Ibid., 157.

15 Rodrik, *Straight Talk on Trade*, 118, 144.

16 See Karl N. Llewellyn, "Some Realism about Realism: Responding to Dean Pound," *Harvard Law Review* 44 (1931): 1222, 1233–34 (on breaking down categories); Arthur Allen Leff, "Commentary Economic Analysis of Law: Some Realism about Nominalism," *Virginia Law Review* 60 (1974): 451.

Legal realists stress the need for imagination and emergent analytics grounded in empirics.[17] Just as pragmatic economists engage with the world to improve it, help stabilize economies and help policymakers identify means to break through structural barriers impeding development, so with legal realists. As Benjamin Cardozo wrote, law is subject to an "endless process of testing and retesting."[18] As new experimentalist-governance legal scholars highlight, problems are solved through iterative processes encouraging learning through which new emergent analytics can arise.

Conclusion

Intelligent policymaking, in law as in economics, should be grounded in empirics and pragmatic responses to them. It demands modesty, in which one does not purport to have *the* model but instead uses judgment in selecting among various models. It requires understanding that the national and international spheres are linked with each other, and it recognizes the need to assess their reciprocal and recursive relationship. It calls for understanding trade-offs and assuming responsibility for pragmatic action in light of them. A close reading of *Straight Talk on Trade* will take international economic law scholars a long way toward such a goal.

---

[17] Victoria Nourse and Gregory Shaffer, "Empiricism, Experimentalism and Conditional Theory," *SMU Law Review* 67 (2014): 101, 145–46, 152 (on emergent analytics).

[18] Benjamin Cardozo, *The Nature of the Judicial Process* (New Haven, CT: Yale University Press, 1921), 179.

Chapter Four

REFLECTING ON *STRAIGHT TALK ON TRADE*

Alvaro Santos

It has been a treat to read Dani Rodrik's book. I have been an avid reader of his work for a while, and it has been influential in my own thinking, teaching and research. For some time, I have been interested in how critiques of mainstream economics can dialogue with critical legal thinking, and how they might benefit each other.[1] The goal is to explore how economic and legal thought can join forces to imagine alternatives to the existing institutional form globalization has taken. I offer my comments in the spirit of that exploration. A question that motivates this essay is: What insights can we offer from legal scholarship that Rodrik could take on board and put to good use?

Rodrik is an economist, but he might as well have been a lawyer in the way he builds his argument and anticipates counterarguments. I mean that as a compliment. As a bonus, he delivers the punch line with humor and grace. In his book, I recognized several of the many contributions Rodrik has made: his argument for policy space and revitalization of industrial policy, the globalization trilemma, the idea and process of growth diagnostics and the idea of premature deindustrialization and the powerful challenge it presents to developing countries.

I also recognized familiar characters: hyperglobalization, the globalization cheerleaders, the economics professor who speaks with nuance and qualifications when talking about the benefits of trade to graduate students in the classroom but is completely simplistic and even disingenuous when talking to the media. Let's call this character the "two-faced" economist. The book has many valuable ideas, but I want to focus on three themes: (1) the plurality of models, (2) fair trade and (3) the agenda for the nation-state.

A World of Many Models

Reading the chapters "Economists and Their Models" and "The Perils of Economic Consensus," I thought they could be called "Saving Economics from Economists." Rodrik takes the two-faced economists to task for contributing to a decrease in the credibility of the discipline and even to the globalization backlash. Arguing for trade liberalization as

---

[1] See, e.g., Alvaro Santos, "Carving Out Policy Autonomy for Developing Countries in the World Trade Organization: The Experience of Brazil and Mexico," *Virginia Journal of International Law* 52 (2012): 551–632.

an unqualified policy program had begun to tarnish the discipline that so uncondition-ally promoted it in the face of economic malaise and unfulfilled expectations. Instead of recognizing that the case for trade was complex and that there were good reasons to allow for trade barriers in some cases, and for slowing down in others, trade economists generally peddled for ever-increasing liberalization as if it was going to benefit all.[2]

Furthermore, by dismissing the critiques of trade liberalization, economists reduced the scope of the public debate and made globalization look more coherent and institu-tionally fixed than was warranted, thus contributing to the backlash. Economists shaded their arguments, afraid of giving ammunition to the protectionist "barbarians," but by doing so, they reinforced the idea that there was a binary of trade liberalization versus protectionism and that the trade regime could not accommodate important concerns about fairness and distribution.[3]

Now that the political backlash against globalization is set on rolling back trade liberalization and retrenching to economic nationalism, trade economists are less equipped and have less credibility to defend global trade. This becomes evident when the response to the policies of the Trump administration or of the United Kingdom's Brexit seems to focus on defending the global arrangements that existed before this crisis of legitimacy.

Rodrik's rendition of the pluralism of models in economics was fascinating and, again, advanced in the service of highlighting the sophistication, nuance and robust debates in the economics discipline, much of which gets lost when translated to public policy or to the public. His description very much reminded me of the condition of law as a discipline: there is no reigning model or method, but a plurality of them, which are often in competition, sometimes quite vigorously, which makes for a plural legal academy.

In the legal academy, this doesn't necessarily mean robust debate. There is that, to be sure. But sometimes it leads to silos or factions and to insecurity about not having a robust methodology so that we legal scholars often borrow from other social sciences. The freedom of this pluralism can sometimes lead to experimentation and originality that would be difficult to imagine if there was a dominant method. So plurality comes with ambivalence and, I think, is carried both with a certain insecurity and as a badge of honor.

Rodrik makes clear that there is often indeterminacy in the models, stating that "economics is really a toolkit with multiple models—each a different, stylized, represen-tation of some aspect of reality."[4] There are competing models that lead to different explanations and policy recommendations. Rodrik celebrates this pluralism. The key, and this is what Rodrik is after, is to learn how to choose between competing models. "One's skill as an economic analyst depends on the ability to pick and choose the right model for the situation,"[5] something that, he bemoans, economists are not taught to

---

[2] See Dani Rodrik, *Straight Talk on Trade: Ideas for a Sane World Economy* (Princeton, NJ: Princeton University Press, 2018), 114.

[3] Ibid., 138.

[4] Ibid., 143.

[5] Ibid.

do and the profession doesn't invest much research in. This part of economics is more "craft" than "science."[6] It requires judgment. And he seems to want to push in this direction, perhaps to build a method about how to choose the right model.

As appealing as the project sounds, I am skeptical of the project of developing a method to choose the "right" model. That, it seems to me, presupposes that there is a meta-level standpoint, free from the influence of method, from where we can choose. Reading Rodrik's own account about the situation of his discipline, it seemed to me that there is no neutral perch from which to pick and choose which model would be more useful. No high hill from which to see with clarity which road to follow. The view of the utility of one or another model will be colored by one's own assumptions, that is, by one's own implicit or explicit meta model. And at that level, too, there will be competition and uncertainty.

The parallel experience in legal scholarship might be illustrative. There are also a variety of "models" or approaches to "law," including formalism, legal realism, originalism, law and economics, legal process, critical legal thought, feminist legal theory, critical race theory and so on. These different models or approaches rely on different assumptions and provide a different diagnosis and prescription to a legal problem. The most sophisticated legal actors can deploy different arguments from this or that school to win a case or advocate for a policy proposal. But it would be hard for any lawyer or legal scholar to argue, in all candor, that he or she has chosen the "right" approach for a particular setting. Right for whom? Or for what purpose? It becomes an argument for policy preference and expected outcomes, based on normative assumptions.

In the face of indeterminacy in the legal materials[7]—of rules, rights, general principles and doctrines—legal scholars and lawyers often seek to ground their position on a higher plane, a constitutional right, for instance. But the US Constitution is often vague, and there are competing rights and principles at the constitutional level, too. So scholars have resorted to moral and political theory to ground their position. Only there are competing moral and political theories, too. The point is not to show a hopeless condition of infinite regression but rather to recognize that the choice of method for a given situation is that: a choice. Often a choice between equally plausible options, driven not by what is right but by what the chooser prefers or believes.[8]

Rodrik provides a powerful example of indeterminacy and the existence of competing models in his account of the debate about the Trans-Pacific Partnership (TPP), which he called the "trade numbers game"[9] or "war of trade models."[10] He argues

---

[6] Ibid., 143–44.

[7] See, e.g., Karl N. Llewellyn, "A Realistic Jurisprudence: The Next Step," *Columbia Law Review* 30, no. 4 (1930): 431; Karl N. Llewellyn, "Remarks on the Theory of Appellate Decision and the Rules or Canons about How Statutes Are to Be Construed," *Vanderbilt Law Review* 3 (1950): 395.

[8] See, e.g., Duncan Kennedy, "The Critique of Rights in Critical Legal Studies," in *Left Legalism/Left Critique*, ed. Janet Halley and Wendy Brown (Durham, NC: Duke University Press Books, 2002).

[9] Rodrik, *Straight Talk on Trade*, 123.

[10] http://rodrik.typepad.com/dani_rodriks_weblog/2015/05/the-war-of-trade-models.html.

that "neither side's models generate numbers reliable enough on which a case for or against the TPP could be made. Just about the only thing we can say with some certainty is that there would have been gainers and losers."[11] Undoubtedly, there is value in debate, and Rodrik argues that competition between models can help clarify where disagreement lies. It can help narrow the space between authors of different ideological bents, as illustrated by Robert Barro and Jason Furman's paper on the potential effects of the recent US tax reform.[12] This seems entirely plausible but still a long way from coming up with a method that helps one apply the "right" model to a particular context.

What I find most appealing about Rodrik's analysis in this regard, clearly stated in his critique of the trade liberalization cheerleaders, is his call for nuance and modesty, his insistence on the importance of stating assumptions and recognizing qualifications in the analysis, the courage to recognize uncertainty and tentativeness when pressured to give confident and bold answers. So Rodrik invites us to admit the terrain of uncertainty and not knowing, to recognize when we do not know and to admit public responsibility for our decisions and recommendations. Rodrik gives us a powerful image: "It is the neglect of the craft element—aiming to elevate economics' status as science—that occasionally turns it into snake oil."[13]

Rodrik's description of the two-faced economist fits nicely with the two-faced lawyer. Despite the experience of pluralism in legal methods, ask any lawyer involved in a case or a regulatory decision and he or she will speak in public with absolute certainty about the existence of this or that right solution. Everybody knows, however, that there is likely a plausible counter. Think about the hearings in the nomination ritual for justices in the US Supreme Court. The nominees are selected by a president who expects they will vote according to the ruling party preferences on a range of issues. Nominees go through this rite of passage in a completely predictable way, saying that they will only apply the law, not make it; that their role is that of an umpire, not a player; that they will follow precedent and so on.

First-year law students and the informed lay public can tell that what the nominees profess to do is just not possible in the types of cases that reach the Supreme Court. The reason a given nominee is selected is precisely so that he or she can decide cases, according to a liberal or conservative philosophy, with vast implications for the country. Everybody knows, but no one will admit it publicly, least of all the nominee, for whom it would be confirmation hara-kiri. Nobody speaks candidly, perhaps out of fear of the potential damage such overt admission of perspectivism would inflict on the legitimacy of the legal profession.

I perceive a similar, perhaps unstated, preoccupation with the legitimacy of the economics profession, and of its authority, if it admits not knowing. If it recognizes its uncertainty. If it acknowledges that there is no "right" answer or model. Rodrik presents us

---

[11] Rodrik, *Straight Talk on Trade*, 126.

[12] https://twitter.com/rodrikdani/status/971731300351700992.

[13] Rodrik, *Straight Talk on Trade*, 145.

with an intriguing paradox here in that the more confident and "right" the discipline has pretended to be, the weaker it becomes. If we take this insight seriously, we would need to conclude that this is true, too, for the project of building "an empirical method that helps us apply the *right* model to the particular context"[14] at hand.

Fair Trade and the New Rules for the Global Economy

One of the most enduring critiques in Rodrik's work has been that trade can undermine the social values and norms that a nation has worked hard to establish. The problem, he argues, is not that trade heightens competition and cheaper imports may displace domestic producers. That is expected of trade. The problem arises when those imports are produced under conditions that would be prohibited or simply not tolerated in the importing country because they go against its fundamental values. Think of basic labor rights, or environmental and health standards. When those imports threaten the viability of domestic norms by creating incentives to water these norms down or else push domestic producers out of business, that competition, Rodrik concludes, is unfair. Thus, he argues that trade barriers are entirely justified to prevent this affront to domestic social norms. In fact, he has proposed the design of trade remedies against social dumping, such as the increase of tariffs against imports, modeled after antidumping remedies.[15]

Rodrik enshrines these ideas in a set of seven principles or rights to guide the reshaping of globalization. Principle 4 states, "Countries have the right to protect their own regulations and institutions."[16] So countries should be allowed to impose barriers at the border if imports threaten to undermine their social norms, such as labor rights, financial regulation, environmental protection and so on. This, Rodrik tells us, will, in fact, strengthen rather than weaken the legitimacy of the trading system. Principle 5 reads, "Countries do not have the right to impose their institutions on others."[17] Rodrik explains that using trade restrictions to "uphold values and regulations at home must be sharply distinguished" from imposing those values on other countries.[18]

Each of these rights sounds great on its own and in the abstract. But from a legal perspective, they are hardly useful guidance once one tries to operationalize them. Why? Because these rights are relational.[19] Having a right to protect your domestic standard in international trade often does mean imposing it on others. Conversely, having someone else's standard prevail on your market makes your right to protect your own regulation rather hortatory. If two countries have competing rights, one will prevail.

In fact, a lot of the WTO (World Trade Organization) Appellate Body work has centered on trying to adjudicate between different national standards. Consider the

---

[14] Ibid., 143 (emphasis added).
[15] Ibid., 231–32.
[16] Ibid., 224.
[17] Ibid.
[18] Ibid.
[19] See, e.g., Wesley Hohfeld, "Some Fundamental Legal Conceptions as Applied in Legal Reasoning," *Yale Law Journal* 23, no. 1 (1913).

Shrimp-Turtle case.[20] The United States put in place a measure that conditioned market access of shrimp imports to foreign producers adopting essentially the same standard required of US producers, a technology called TED, or turtle excluder device. One may ask, why isn't the United States free to require other countries who want to export to the US market to follow the same standard it requires domestically for its own producers? That is exactly the argument the United States made in that and similar cases. Once again, the United States has the right to protect its own standard. But that means that Malaysia will have to adopt the US standard if it wants to sell in the United States, the biggest shrimp market. And that would probably mean, in practice, that it would change its shrimp-fishing practices overall.

Moreover, it is tempting to try to explain this tension away by referring to choice. In this case, Malaysia is free to decide whether it wants to sell shrimp to the US market or not. There is no imposition: Malaysia has the choice to sell or not to sell. While this is formally true, market conditions can be quite coercive so that the idea that there is no imposition is problematic in practice. There is a long tradition in legal scholarship, going back to the legal realists, of pointing to the coercive nature of market relations in contrast to the notion of free markets and free choice by market actors.[21] If the market was never free from the state, because it was always built on state-sanctioned law, and if it enabled coercive relations, the relevant question was not whether it was free or coercive but what effects did it deliver and whether those results were socially acceptable. Whether a country chooses to adopt another country's standard or lets the standard be imposed on it will depend on its alternatives and fallback position. It will depend on how costly it would be to adapt, how important that market is for the exporter and whether it can withstand its loss.

From the point of view of fairness, which animates Rodrik's work in this regard, one may ask: Is the United States imposing a cost on other countries by requiring them to adopt its own standard (Malaysia's point of view)? Or is Malaysia giving a subsidy to its producers or dumping by not requiring a higher environmental standard (the United States' point of view)? If producers in each country sold only in their own market, there would be no conflict. But as soon as they trade, a conflict may arise. It seems that we cannot resolve this conflict by resorting to the two general rights, or first principles, that Rodrik formulated above.

The idea here is that there is no normal baseline, no neutral way of deciding which should prevail.[22] From a policy perspective, the decision would depend on what one thinks of the protection of turtles from shrimp trawlers, the incidence of turtle deaths,

---

[20] Appellate Body Report, *United States—Import Prohibition of Certain Shrimp and Shrimp Products*, WT/DS58/AB/R (October 12, 1998).

[21] Robert L. Hale, "Coercion and Distribution in a Supposedly Non-coercive State," *Political Science Quarterly* 38 (1923): 470, 471–74, 492–94.

[22] See, e.g., Daniel K. Tarullo, "Beyond Normalcy in the Regulation of International Trade," *Harvard Law Review* 100 (1987): 546; Robert Howse, "From Politics to Technocracy and Back Again: The Fate of the Multilateral Trading System," *American Journal of International Law* 96 (2002): 94.

how altering the standard would affect Malaysian shrimp producers, US shrimp producers, consumers and so on—the kinds of questions Rodrik asks incisively at the domestic
level but that may be avoided at the global level by referring to these general principles,
which can't provide concrete answers.

Cases like this now abound in the WTO. They are not limited to conflicts between big
and small economies. In the *Beef-Hormones* case,[23] the European Union (EU) banned beef
meat produced with hormones, a common practice in the United States, from being sold
in its market, alleging potential risks to human health. So the EU has the right to protect
its no-beef-hormones standard but does not have the right to impose it on others. But if
the trading partner willing to sell to the EU does not choose to adopt that standard, there
will be no trade between them. The United States sued the EU claiming a violation of
the Agreement on the Application of Sanitary and Phytosanitary (SPS) measures. The
EU lost the case as it failed to demonstrate, according to the WTO Appellate Body, that
the risk assessment, based on scientific evidence concerning the effect of beef hormones
on human health, warranted the ban. It became a protracted and acrimonious dispute,
involving retaliatory measures by the United States and an ultimate settlement. The
result is nothing we could have predicted, or resolved, from reference to Rodrik's two
general rights.

Our sense of how those two rights may be balanced when there is conflict would often
depend on what is the standard at stake: for example, an environmental standard that
protects dolphins from being killed when catching tuna, a labor standard that bans goods
produced under slavery-like conditions, an intellectual property standard that protects a
lifesaving but expensive drug from being copied, a warning label on cigarette packages
and so on. Developing countries have often been suspicious of arguments to enable trade
barriers for not conforming to a given standard. They see it as an excuse by rich countries
to protect their own producers and undermine poor countries' competitive advantage.
This is why they resisted the link between trade and labor standards back in the WTO
Singapore Ministerial meeting in 1996.[24] Perhaps this mistrust, and this resistance, has
been a mistake and, in the case of labor rights, a type of self-inflicted harm. For even if
the motives of rich countries were self-interested, this may have helped improve labor
standards in poor countries in ways that could have been beneficial to them, too. But
again, this is a judgment based on the consequences of adopting those standards, not on
whether a country has the right to impose its standards on others.

Finally, an important question is: Who decides? Given the relational character of
rights, even if we wanted to take Rodrik's rights as guiding stars, there will inevitably be
conflict. Who will decide these conflicts and how? That's just as important a question
as what the rights are. Astute commentators of the WTO have noted the effort of its
Appellate Body to grapple with these questions, trying to balance the goal of national

---

[23] Appellate Body Report, *EC Measures Concerning Meat and Meat Products (Hormones)*, WT/DS26/
AB/R, WT/DS48/AB/R (February 13, 1998).

[24] See WTO Singapore Ministerial Declaration, WT/MIN(96)/DEC, 36 ILM 218 (December
13, 1996).

regulatory autonomy (preserving one's standard) with the goal to prevent discriminatory trade measures (imposing one's standard), moving gradually away from the deep integration, neoliberal ethos behind the founding of the WTO.[25] One may rightly quarrel with the current balance struck by the Appellate Body or with the criteria used, perhaps still too lopsided in favor of trade liberalization. But it is an effort to try to reconcile competing rights or interests between states and consider the consequences. No doubt the system is a far cry from inclusiveness, political deliberation and participation of relevant actors, something Howse and Nikolaidis have pushed for in their argument for "global subsidiarity" or "global trade ethics."[26] The point here is that we may need to spend considerable effort in redesigning the global institutions for decision making, be it the WTO or elsewhere, as an alternative to devolution to the nation-state.

The Return of the Nation-State

Rodrik turns his analysis to the nation-state as the key agent in globalization. He notes that "political communities are organized largely within nation-states and are likely to remain so for the foreseeable future."[27] His work has laid down a program for both rich countries (fair trade, measures to address inequality and distribution) and for developing countries (policy space for growth policies). I am very sympathetic to this project. But I also see some costs of this frame or "model" that would be worth considering.

I found his discussion in chapter 7, "Economists, Politics and Ideas," fascinating. It presents a challenge to "determinism," often expressed in the role that interests play in the analysis of political economists. "In truth," he claims, "we don't have 'interests.' We have *ideas* about what our interests are."[28] We have ideas about our preferences, our selves and how we optimize those preferences. But those ideas are not fixed. They are not necessary. Our interests, how we, or any group—the ruling class, the rich—see what our interests are is a construction based on ideas. And these ideas are subject to change. This insight opens up the door for reimagining. For plasticity rather than determinacy. For understanding the contingency of our interests and their ability to change. For realizing, too, that the institutional expression of those mutable interests is equally amenable to change. This is a very valuable insight.

But so is the nation-state: an *idea*. Rodrik seems to acknowledge this when he proposes a "normative case for the nation-state."[29] His is a refreshing and thoughtful counter to the global governance mantra.[30] Rodrik argues that the nation-state "remains the main

---

[25] See, e.g., Robert Howse, "The World Trade Organization 20 Years On: Global Governance by Judiciary," *European Journal of International Law* 27, no. 1 (2016): 9; Andrew Lang, *World Trade Law after Neoliberalism: Reimagining the Global Economic Order* (Oxford: Oxford University Press, 2011).

[26] Robert Howse and Kalypso Nikolaidis, "Toward a Global Ethics of Trade Governance: Subsidiarity Writ Large," *Law and Contemporary Problems* 79 (2016): 259.

[27] Rodrik, *Straight Talk on Trade*, 223.

[28] Ibid., 163 (emphasis in the original).

[29] Ibid., 24.

[30] Ibid., 16.

determinant of the global distribution of income, the primary locus of market-supporting institutions, and the chief repository of personal attachments and affiliations."[31] It is an argument for heterogeneity, and for experimentation and competition in institutional arrangements that respond to the particular context of each nation-state. Yet, Rodrik's support for the nation-state sometimes seems descriptive and practical, based on geography and space, on the convenience of already demarcated administrative and political jurisdictions called states.[32] On the expediency of reality as we know it rather than in the normative desirability of his project.

Rodrik's narrative of the inescapability of the nation-state is a powerful one, important for the normative project he has in mind. His advocacy for the nation-state anticipates the achievement of greater economic prosperity at the national and thus global level. But it also seems informed by an anti-elitist sensibility based on a hope for a more democratic distribution of income and opportunity. In *Has Globalization Gone Too Far?*,[33] Rodrik was already pointing to the widening cleavage within nation-states between a mobile, highly skilled professional class and the rest; an elite that increasingly saw its interests detached from the fortune of its nation-state; a class of people that saved and invested their money abroad, sent their children to study overseas, traveled and vacationed elsewhere. In sum, a well-off, cosmopolitan, mobile class that had benefited from globalization and did not see their future and their lot aligned with the interests of their nation-state, or that even perceived their own interests to be in conflict with their nation's economic efforts—in short, an economic integration that was engendering social disintegration and an unwillingness to cooperate and solve conflicts through the political process.

We have become used to thinking of big multinational corporations as stateless and unmoored. So are the wealthy and many highly skilled professionals. They often move around and change allegiance, depending on their interests or, I should say, the ideas they have about their interests. And this can be true, too, of a country's political elite. Consider criticisms of the Greek policy elite in charge of negotiating the bailout, seemingly more interested in pleasing and appeasing the European technocrats than their own people. Or the increasing number of Mexico's policy, economic and cultural elite, for whom the United States is a second home. Rodrik's project reads as a push for closing that widening gap and reasserting the power and autonomy of the state so that the economic elites, once again, see their interests as coinciding with their nation's to promote greater welfare at home.

Rodrik's project is a plea to reassert the nation-state as the main site for governance and political deliberation. The state is, or is becoming again, the most powerful idea of an organized political community today. No doubt about that. Why not take advantage of its gears and levers to advance greater welfare? Rodrik is, of course, aware of the horrors of the nation-state, past and present. Indeed, the current backlash against

---

[31] Ibid., 19.

[32] Ibid., 24.

[33] Dani Rodrik, *Has Globalization Gone Too Far?* (Washington, DC: Peterson Institute for International Economics, 1999), 69–70.

globalization has been fueled by nationalist movements, discontent with economic dis-location, and the erosion of national identity. So far, that nationalist project, be it in the United States or any of the EU countries, has shown an ugly face.

So the point is not that the nation-state is a factum, but that Rodrik thinks it is desir-able. That he thinks the greater promise for economic prosperity and meaningful polit-ical engagement lies within the nation-state. And that a globalization that is predicated on the welfare of these various political communities, accepting their varied choices and speed, would be a better one. The autonomy he would like to carve out for nation-states from hyperglobalization is also one designed exclusively for nation-states with democratic processes and values. There, he is not shy of value imposition on national autonomy.[34] It is an ambitious normative project, and it would be better to fully recognize it as such. Not because the state exists; many other ideas about organizing political communities exist (and others can be imagined). But because Rodrik probably thinks that the risks of emboldening the nation-state, of which there are many, are outweighed by the economic and social benefits it can bring about. Or because the types of lives we can lead under a more autonomous state would be more thriving and fulfilling, shielded from the fast winds of economic insecurity and more engaged in the decisions that determine our future.

Rodrik posits that "we have to live in the world we have, with all its political divisions, and not the world we wish we had. The best way to serve global interests is to live up to our responsibilities within the political institutions that matter: those that exist, within national borders."[35] Again, although this sounds like a wonderful adage of pragmatic reason, it strikes me more like a powerful argument of normative vision. One needs to be reminded that many of the critiques of global governance in terms of "demo-cratic deficit, lack of legitimacy, and loss of voice and accountability"[36] are often true of democratic politics in the nation-state, too. For many excluded or disenfranchised groups within the nation-state, international governance mechanisms became important for voice and inclusion, whether in questions of civil and political rights or of the impact of grand development projects in their local communities.

Rodrik concludes by asking "Who needs the nation-state? We all do."[37] Well, there will be losers too, perhaps the globalist cosmopolitan class that has so far been the winner of hyperglobalization. Or the financial and corporate interests that have handsomely influenced and benefited from existing global rules and incentives. They may not need Rodrik's version of the nation-state. But the world Rodrik depicts would seem overall much saner. While I am very sympathetic to his vision, I profess a certain ambivalence about the nation-state. I can see both its beneficial and ruinous faces. At a time where the globalization backlash throws into question the assumptions and institutions of lib-eral globalization as we know it, there is also a unique opportunity to explore alternatives

---

[34] Ibid., 225; principle 7 reads, "Nondemocratic countries cannot count on the same rights and privileges in the international economic order as democracies."

[35] Ibid., 47.

[36] Ibid., 29.

[37] Ibid., 47.

between this ailing hyperglobalization and the retrenchment to economic nationalism. Perhaps we can explore, too, new forms of allegiance, of community and of governance that are not simply going back to the nation-state on offer.

Conclusion

Rodrik's book is refreshingly critical and honest. It reflects years of thinking hard and writing eloquently about the risks posed by globalization in its current form. Risks that, as he warned many years ago, have materialized. Rodrik has also taken on his discipline for not engaging honestly with the public about the potential negative effects of trade liberalization, thus preventing a wider and more robust discussion on how to address the social and distributive concerns with trade. He is dismayed by the tendency of many economists to peddle ever-increasing trade liberalization based on simplistic assumptions, even when they know better. This, he argues, tended to set aside valid concerns, raise unwarranted expectations, reduce the scope of debate and policy proposals, and help damage the credibility of the profession.

In our moment of crisis, when much of globalization and its institutions have been questioned, we see once again a knee-jerk reaction against this backlash. A reaction that seems to assume that things would be fine if we could only contain the backlash—be it the Trump administration trade wars or Brexit—by holding on to the institutions and arrangements that preceded it. Rodrik's work encourages us to resist that impulse by showing all that was wrong with the liberal globalization of the past three decades, whose effects and their dismissal are largely responsible for the current backlash. His work points in a different direction, one of reimagining and remaking the institutions of the global market, including slowing down its pace and refocusing on the greater welfare and prosperity that should animate its existence. As with any author, one may disagree with certain parts of his assumptions, analysis or conclusions. But Rodrik's highly original voice is essential to understanding our present conundrum and how we may chart a way out of it. He has certainly delivered what he promised: straight talk on trade.

Chapter Five

A RESPONSE TO THE COMMENTS BY THOMAS, GALLAGHER, SHAFFER AND SANTOS

Dani Rodrik

I am truly grateful for this wonderful and gracious set of comments on my book *Straight Talk on Trade: Ideas for a Sane World Economy*. An author cannot wish for more than this: to have his work taken seriously, and then elaborated or critiqued in light of further reflection. Kevin P. Gallagher, Alvaro Santos, Gregory Shaffer and Chantal Thomas do that and much more in a relatively small amount of space. What follows are some quick responses and rejoinders to their rich arguments.

I begin with Kevin P. Gallagher's point that perhaps I have been too hard on economists. I happily accept his corrective! Indeed, many other social scientists were complicit in misreading the consequences of the type of globalization we had embarked upon. This is especially true of mainstream international relations theorists in political science. Typically, these scholars took their cue from economists when they assumed the overall gains were large and the losers could be treated as merely rent seekers in the political system. Even though they should have known better, they treated trade agreements as efficiency-enhancing arrangements instead of the political documents that they were.

In a recent lecture, Robert Keohane, one of the most distinguished scholars of international relations, was quite honest about the shared responsibility and engaged in some self-criticism:

"Those of us who have not only analyzed globalization and the liberal order but also celebrated them share some responsibility for the rise of populism. We did not pay enough attention as capitalism hijacked globalization. Economic elites designed international institutions to serve their own interests and to create firmer links between themselves and governments. Ordinary people were left out."[1]

---

[1]   This is from the piece Keohane wrote jointly with Jeff D. Colgan in *Foreign Affairs* (see https://www.foreignaffairs.com/articles/world/2017-04-17/liberal-order-rigged). The article is based on Keohane's Warren and Anita Manshel Lecture in American Foreign Policy, delivered at Harvard University in December 2016.

As Keohane indicates, and as I argue in the book, the policies pushed by the US elite undermined what another political scientist, John Ruggie, called "embedded liberalism." Too many international relations scholars overlooked the consequences.

Alvaro Santos provides a deep and nuanced reading of the book and raises three important questions. First, he is skeptical about the project of "model diagnostics" or "model selection" I advocate for applied economists. I propose this approach as a way of moving from a position of relative agnosticism ("there are many contending models") to reasonable policy prescriptions ("the evidence indicates we can rule out these models while these other ones may well apply"). Being able to move down this path, Santos writes,

> presupposes that there is a meta-level standpoint, free from the influence of method, from where we can choose [...] The view of the utility of one or another model will be colored by one's own assumptions, that is, by one's own implicit or explicit meta model. And at that level, too, there will be competition and uncertainty.

I do not necessarily disagree. I certainly do not want to underplay the difficulty of engaging in a model selection process that is truly objective. But in my defense, I would point out that empirical analysis does in fact discipline this process, and does so in a somewhat nonideological manner. We have seen, for example, how empirical work on the labor market consequences of trade (considerable) or the growth effects of financial globalization (not much) has moved the discipline's priors. Ideology plays a role in shaping the questions we ask and the priors we take on—but it is not everything. Objective facts do exist and they do matter. Perhaps we can be more optimistic with respect to economics than legal scholarship here because positive, empirical analysis—did X cause Y? —plays such a larger role in economics.

Second, Santos wonders about my nation-state-centric approach to the determination of standards. I draw here a distinction between a country setting its own standards (which I say is justified) and a country imposing its own standards on others (not justified). As Santos rightly observes, the distinction may not matter a whole lot in practice. If the United States imposes its own fishing standards on all imports, Malaysia has little choice but to adopt the US standard—if it wants to sell in the US market.

I am not sure this is any different from the United States applying, say, the same health and safety standards to imports as it does to domestic production. Chinese exporters are not allowed to sell toys in the United States that contain more lead than what domestic regulations allow. We take this as perfectly normal and do not challenge it, even though it certainly constrains China's trading options.

None of this is to say that international harmonization of standards is necessarily bad or should not be attempted. My worry about international harmonization is that it gives trade interests—exporters, multinationals, pharma companies—too much say. Ultimately, regulatory standards have to be politically legitimized, and the international sphere falls far short of what is required with respect to political accountability compared to the domestic sphere.

This leads to Santos's third note of skepticism. "I profess certain ambivalence about the nation-state," he writes,

At a time where the globalization backlash throws into question the assumptions and institutions of liberal globalization as we know it, there is also a unique opportunity to explore alternatives between this ailing hyperglobalization and the retrenchment to economic nationalism. Perhaps we can also explore new forms of allegiance, of community and of governance that are not simply going back to the nation-state on offer.

I am in fact very sympathetic to this line of thinking. Even though my book does call for a reinvigoration of the nation-state, I am not averse to experimentation with the goal of creating new forms of political allegiance. At the same time, we should not overlook that the main proponents of such a project in recent decades have been precisely the hyperglobalizers, for whom transnational allegiances have provided a convenient cover for failing to live up to their local responsibilities.

Gregory Shaffer relates my work to that of legal realists: "To develop a pragmatic international economic law," he writes, "Rodrik's insight should be combined with the parallel ideas of the legal realists concerning the dangers of simple economic models that have been embedded in legal doctrine." Shaffer discusses a number of aspects of legal realism that indeed closely parallel my own thinking on economic models and institutional design. I confess this is a new area for me, but look forward to learning more about it from Shaffer and others.

Chantal Thomas poses two questions: First, have global value chains (GVCs) and the internationalization of production they entail made national economic governance no longer "realistically possible or effective"? Second, am I too pessimistic about the prospects for industrialization in developing nations, in view of the existing flexibilities in trade agreements and the possibilities of South–South trade? I will take them together, as they are closely related.

My sense is that we greatly exaggerate both the role that GVCs have played so far in developing countries' trade and their potential contribution to these countries' development. In a paper I have just finished,[2] I have looked at these questions and come out with largely pessimistic conclusions. First, the expansion of GVCs seems to have ground to a halt in recent years.

Second, developing-country participation in GVCs, and indeed in world trade in general, has remained quite limited, with the notable exception of certain Asian countries. Third, and perhaps most worryingly, the domestic employment consequences of recent trade trends have been quite disappointing. The job intensity of exports has steadily declined since around 2001 in not just advanced but also developing nations. This trend is not very surprising for the advanced nations, where skill-based technological change has been ubiquitous and the leading cause of declining employment shares in manufacturing industries. It is more puzzling and disappointing in low-income countries, where one would have expected to see the beneficial employment consequences of diversification out of natural resource exports and transition into labor-intensive manufactures.

---

[2] See Dani Rodrik, "New Technologies, Global Value Chains, and Developing Economies," Pathways for Prosperity Commission, University of Oxford, September 2018, https://drodrik.scholar. harvard.edu/publications/new-technologies-global-value-chains-and-developing-economies.

GVCs have of course made inroads in developing countries in manufacturing, services and agriculture. Many of the exports of developing countries are channeled through GVCs, which also act as conduits for new technologies. But in most developing countries, and certainly the poorest ones, sectors and activities touched by GVCs remain a very small part of the domestic economy. New capabilities and productive employment remain limited to a tiny sliver of globally integrated firms.

These trends suggest that there remains a substantial role still for national economic governance. The key challenge is to disseminate throughout the rest of the economy the capabilities already in place in the most advanced parts of the productive sector. We can call this a process of domestic productive integration to accompany the usual process of international economic integration. In addition to improving fundamentals—human capital and governance—governments require more proactive policies of government–business collaboration targeted at strengthening the connections between highly productive global firms, potential local suppliers and the domestic labor force. The principles governing such proactive policies have been laid out in discussions of "new industrial policy," with the important proviso that the policies in question would not concentrate exclusively on manufacturing.

PART II

SETTING THE STAGE FOR A PROGRESSIVE VISION: EMERGING ISSUES IN WORLD TRADE AND INVESTMENT LAW

SECTION 1

MAPPING THE NEW CONTEXT FOR TRADE AND INVESTMENT LAW

Chapter Six

THE END OF TRADE AND INVESTMENT LAW AS WE KNOW IT: FROM SINGULARITY TO PLURALISM

Poul F. Kjaer

The global trade and investment law regime is disintegrating. It is becoming increasingly impossible to speak of a singular regime spanning the globe; instead, there are now several regional-based regimes with quite distinct characteristics.

A rethinking of trade and investment law (TIL) needs to take this insight as its point of departure and is possible only by understanding the structural composition and direction world society is taking and the deep-seated cultural and social (including political) structures and contexts within which it operates. Both orthodox and heterodox TIL relies on assumptions concerning the state of the world and the driving forces behind it, but those assumptions need to be subjected to scrutiny and substantial rethinking.

For heterodox TIL, critical globalization studies (CGS) has emerged as a central counternarrative to the neoliberal globalization discourse of the preceding decades. CGS rightly points out the deficiencies of the neoliberal paradigm and the problems created through increased inequality, the straightjacketing of policy choices and the volatility created in the world economy due to the boom-and-bust culture installed through liberalization of capital markets and the like. But by digging a bit beneath the surface of policy discourses and practical politics, a number of structural transformations can be observed that might also need to be considered when rethinking TIL.

The core paradox we are dealing with is that increased globalization has implied an increase rather than a decrease in global diversity. A future-oriented TIL therefore should be thought of in the plural, not in the singular, as it is likely to fragment into a number of regional TIL regimes based on very different philosophies and institutional setups.

The End of the Western-Centric World

Claiming that the world is at a tipping point easily becomes tiresome—all ages and eras believe they live through a "special moment." However, we may indeed be experiencing a tipping point. The breakdown of the Eurocentric world is now being followed by the breakdown of the Western-centric world. The Eurocentric world started to collapse in the late nineteenth century with the rise of the United States, and later Japan and the Soviet

Union, and became manifested in the mid-twentieth-century decolonization processes. Today the concept of the West is disintegrating, with Europe and the United States moving steadily apart in political, economic, social and cultural terms and becoming strangers. Furthermore, this development unfolds with the rise of non-Western powers, most notably China, greatly exacerbating the consequences.

The rise of non-Western powers means that the relative centrality and weight of the West in the world is rapidly declining. The image of the secretary of state for international trade in the United Kingdom begging for a post-Brexit trade deal in India, the former jewel of the empire only 70 years ago, illustrates how much and how fast the tables have turned. The United States, the successor state to the British global empire, might not experience as rapid and deep a downfall as the United Kingdom, but the rules of the game have changed for the United States and will most likely continue to change.

The Absence of an Anchor Nation

From the Dutch in the seventeenth century to the British and then to the Americans, the global economy has relied on an anchor nation, which has served as the center of the global economy, its currency acting as the global reserve currency, creating and propping up the global economy's institutional architecture, including the institutions of TIL.

In the emerging global constellation, however, no anchor nation is in sight. China, in spite of its seemingly impressive growth, will not be able to take over the role of anchor nation for a range of political, economic, social and cultural reasons. An anchor nation typically possesses economic, political and institutional power, as well as cultural and ideological dominance. Even if China's economic clout continues to increase, transforming such importance into political power embedded in global institutions tailor-made for its needs tends to be a long and protracted affair. Measured by gross domestic product, the United States became the largest economy in the world in the late nineteenth century, but it was not until more than 50 years later, after World War II, that a US-centered institutional architecture with global reach was established. At the time, the United States also embodied a way of life and advanced political ideology with global attraction, an ideology and culture that in principle was universal in nature and as such could be transposed to other parts of the world. Chinese authoritarian nationalism does not possess such a pull factor. Engaging with China is a necessity, and many countries, especially developing ones, are likely to continue to increase their engagement with China, but few people outside of China dream of living a Chinese way of life.

Limits to Chinese power are also likely to emerge and be reinforced. China has become a dominant player and can now exercise influence globally, but its capacity to exercise real power with few restraints and from a dominant position is likely to be limited to the East Asian and Pacific part of the world as neither the United States nor Europe will accept unrestrained Chinese power in their respective backyards.

The United States is fighting a rearguard action and is essentially left with the choice to reconfigure its role and self-understanding as a global actor in either a graceful or pathetic manner. The Obama administration took the first route, and the Trump administration is taking the second. The long-term structural implications will, however, remain the same. The United States will continue to be a crucial and essential actor for the foreseeable future but will not enjoy the *primus inter pares* position of the past.

The European Union might become a more coherent strategic actor with its shrinking post-Brexit providing a stronger sense of strategic purpose. But even if the speed of integration and the degree of internal coherency is increased, it is unlikely to take over the anchor role. No single state or community of states will, in other words, be able to fulfill the role of an anchor nation. It is, of course, not the first time in history that a world with competing powers exists, but even in the era of the great power rivalry prior to World War I and during the Cold War, a single nation—the United Kingdom and subsequently the United States—served as the anchor nation for the institutional infrastructure of the global economy. It is unlikely that any nation will fulfill this role in the future.[1]

The paradox of globalization is that it is producing global disintegration and increased diversity rather than increased integration and uniformity. The world is likely to be made up by a number of centers with overlapping political, economic, social and cultural regimes, with none of them acting as a singular global anchor. These centers will be within one another's horizons but without the fraternal spirit that early modern European competing monarchical states shared with one another.

From TIL in the Singular to TIL in the Plural

One of the many consequences of this development is that we need to speak of TILs, not TIL. The evolution of TIL from 1945 onward was largely based on a relatively homogenous set of rules propped up by the United States. The future will most likely be characterized by different TIL regimes with each regional center developing its own version on the basis of the cultural, political and economic universe their institutions operate within. Lawyers specializing in World Trade Organization (WTO) law may need to find new interests as a global singular rule-based system withers away.

This development started when the General Agreement on Tariffs and Trade (GATT) transformed into the WTO, changing the system from a US monopoly to a US/EU duopoly. As the breakdown of the Doha Development Round, launched in 2001, reveals, this duopoly was short-lived as countries like China, Brazil, India and South Africa refused to engage with terms dictated by the West. Although the WTO dispute settlement system has continued to work until recently, providing a basis for a gradual shift of power toward non-Western powers, the overall architecture of the system has not been reformed.

The major players are likely to develop TIL philosophies that correspond to their own societal structures and ways of life. The genetically modified organism (GMO) saga between the European Union and the United States, and China's prioritization of economic growth with little interest in the environmental, social and human rights

---

[1] Ole Wæver, "International Leadership after the Demise of the Last Superpower: System Structure and Stewardship," *Chinese Political Science Review* 2, no. 4 (2017): 452–76.

dimensions of TIL, are cases in point, because in different ways, they both reflect different understandings of TIL's purpose and limits.

Rethinking the Rethinking of TIL

The academic discourse on TIL does not seem to have fully acknowledged the implications of the decentering of the world. In fact, both the preceding implosion of the Eurocentric world and the ongoing end of the West has not yet been sufficiently understood.[2]

The rethinking of TIL needs a rethink. Scholars based in China, Europe, the United States and elsewhere should engage in meaningful exercises of rethinking, but that will not lead to the emergence of a new singular paradigm for the world. TIL in the singular was largely an American product, developed on the backdrop of American politics, economy and cultural affinities and subsequently exported through a mixture of persuasion and imposition to the rest of the world. Paradigms and models developed for Nebraska arrived in Sicily and Hunan.

In the wake of the progressive decentering of the world, the persuasiveness of the American academic worldview is diminishing, along with the status of the American societal model at large. From a non-American perspective, a rethinking of TIL should be an exercise of reconnection, developing models that match the cultural universes, economic structures and political worldviews of the world's different regions. TIL needs to become part of the cultural political economy and understood as a broader societally embedded exercise that takes the idiosyncratic structures of the societies where they are developed, deployed and exercised seriously.[3]

Breaking the Hegemony of Economics

For both institutional and social praxis reasons, academia tends to transform more slowly than the world that surrounds it. The economic rise of the United States in the late nineteenth century was not matched by a comparable status of US academia before 1945, and just like the Sorbonne is still the Sorbonne more than 100 years after its peak, Harvard will in all likelihood still be Harvard 100 years from now.

The discursive universe that TIL scholarship operates within will largely remain dominated by American-based scholarship for decades to come. The change will be very slow.

The core element needed for a rethinking of TIL and its transformation into TILs is, however, beyond the control of lawyers. When the current world order, which is now dying away, was created in the wake of World War II through the establishment of Bretton Woods, GATT, the International Monetary Fund and the like, the legal discipline was in

---

2 Hauke Brunkhorst, "Constitutionalism and Democracy in the World Society," in *The Twilight of Constitutionalism?* ed. Petra Dobner and Martin Loughlin (Oxford: Oxford University Press, 2010), 179–98 (185).

3 Ngai-Ling Sum and Bob Jessop, *Towards a Cultural Political Economy: Putting Culture in Its Place in Political Economy* (Cheltenham, UK: Edward Elgar, 2013).

charge as the diplomatic world at the time was overwhelmingly dominated by lawyers. Despite influential economists like John Maynard Keynes, lawyers and their worldview re-created the world while economists acted as the technicians tasked with implementing the plan. Also in this respect the tables have turned. Today the economists, on the basis of their worldview, develop the policies, and the lawyers are the technicians engaged in implementation. Unless this changes, any rethinking of TIL will be futile and a potentially pitiable exercise with little or no effects.

The lost world of the hegemony of the legal discipline is unlikely to come back. The biggest impetus of change will have to come from within the economic discipline itself. This change will occur only to the extent that the discipline is pluralized through a breakdown of the hegemonic status of a handful of economics departments, which currently control the definition of what is good and sound economics scholarship.

The discipline will have to be opened up to insights from disciplines such as anthropology, history, sociology and—of course—law. Rather than integrating economics into legal tools and insights, legal tools and insights might be integrated into economics instead. Achieving that would probably be the biggest possible contribution one could make to the rethinking of TIL and its transformation into TILs.

Chapter Seven

HETERODOX MARKET ORDERS IN THE GLOBAL TRADE SYSTEM

Andrew Lang

The root causes of the present instability of the international economic order are diffi-cult to diagnose. For some, the core problem is the radically unequal distribution of the gains and losses associated with the recent period of globalization: existing economic institutions and structures have been challenged as those who have lost (or gained little) from globalization withdraw their support from a system that appears not to work to their advantage. For others, the primary explanation is the relative erosion of US global economic hegemony, which has both left the United States less willing to act as the guar-antor of the system in its present form and given rise to increasingly urgent efforts to reshape the system in ways that may more reliably sustain existing distributions of eco-nomic power. And for yet others, the present system is under attack because it has failed to deliver on its promise of economic self-determination at the national level, as political communities feel their futures constrained and directed by global rules, institutions and logics that seem out of their immediate control.

This short essay starts with the claim that the current period of instability is also the result, in part, of far-reaching changes to the institutional underpinnings of the global economy that occurred during the last quarter century or so after the end of the Cold War. At the time, the years following the collapse of communism seemed to herald a radical reduction in the global economy's institutional diversity as states throughout the former Second and Third worlds converged toward a single model of market capitalism. But the reality has proved more complicated: the national marketization projects initiated during this period have each evolved according to different dynamics, resulting in the emergence of a variety of new and heterodox market forms in different countries and regions of the world. "Every transition to capitalism," it has been observed, "produced a new variety of capitalism."[1] These economies have become more deeply integrated with global markets, reopening one of the fundamental questions the postwar international economic order has always faced concerning the legitimate range of institutional diver-sity fairly permitted in global competition conditions: At what point do heterodox market

---

[1]   Neil Fligstein and Jianjung Zhang, "A New Agenda for Research on the Trajectory of Chinese Capitalism," *Management and Organization Review* 7 (2011): 39–62, 47.

forms cease to constitute legitimate experimentation and become a form of "cheating" on the terms of fair competition in international trade?

The question is an existential one for the contemporary rules-based international trading system. As any game theorist will attest, mutual cooperation based on agreed rules can rapidly—and perfectly rationally—devolve into tit-for-tat retaliation, where each party has a different understanding of what constitutes cheating on their bargain. This is one way of understanding what we are seeing now, as latent disagreements on the question of institutional diversity have been uncovered as a result of the emergence of new and unanticipated market forms during the last two or three decades. A key task for those interested in reestablishing or sustaining cooperation in the international economic order, then, is to address the question of institutional diversity afresh, with a view to establishing a new *modus vivendi* responsive to contemporary social, political and material conditions. Exactly what this accommodation should look like, and how it might be produced and maintained, will be—and indeed must be—a matter of sustained and detailed debate.

We can learn quite a lot about the different options available to us, and the possibilities and challenges associated with each, by looking at how this issue has been addressed in past periods in the history of the postwar international economic order. A distinction is commonly made between two ways of understanding the approach to the question of institutional diversity reflected in General Agreement on Tariffs and Trade (GATT)/World Trade Organization (WTO) law and practice. On the one hand, some see international trade law merely as an "interface mechanism" between different national economic systems, providing a pragmatic basis for trade among states that remain essentially and irreducibly plural in their economic structures.[2] With this view, the international trade regime does not aspire to establish a single consensus understanding of fair competition, nor does it seek to dictate the domestic economic structures of participants in the trading system. Instead, it reveals participants' different views of what constitutes fairness and provides for the pragmatic resolution of consequent frictions through ad hoc bargaining over specific institutional variations while permitting states to determine their own domestic economic systems. On the other hand, some believe the international trade regime establishes a set of common rules of the game, which—implicitly or explicitly, narrowly or broadly, clearly or ambiguously—define a range of normal market forms and discipline deviations from it.[3] With this view,

---

[2] John Jackson, *The World Trading System: Law and Policy of International Economic Relations*, 1st ed. (Cambridge, MA: MIT Press, 1989), 218; John H. Jackson, William J. Davey and Alan O. Sykes, *Legal Problems of International Economic Relations*, 3rd ed. (Eagan, MN: West Publishing, 1995), 668–72, 1140–42. For a discussion of this view, see David Kennedy, "The International Style in Postwar Law and Policy: John Jackson and the Field of International Economic Law," *American University International Law Review* 10, no. 2 (1995): 671–716, especially 707 and surrounding.

[3] For a recent articulation of this view, as a criticism, see Dani Rodrik, "The WTO Has Become Dysfunctional: Trade Rules Must Acknowledge the Benefits of Divergent Economic Models Such as China's," *Financial Times*, August 5, 2018, available at https://www.ft.com/content/c2beedfe-964d-11e8-95f8-8640db9060a7.

the international trade regime acts as a force for institutional convergence, addressing competitive concerns raised by institutional differences by seeking to establish a level playing field and disciplining deviation from a more or less well-defined range of legitimate institutional variations.

In fact, both of these tendencies have been present, and in tension, throughout the history of GATT/WTO, and the institution's practice is best understood as an evolving compromise between the two viewpoints. In the early years, the most important context in which this tension played out related to the participation of socialist and communist economies in the GATT. There was some divergence of views among the key architects of the postwar trading order on this issue: some saw the GATT primarily as a club of like-minded market economies and a champion of liberal market values; others had a more universalist vision for the organization.[4] Accordingly, while the original contracting parties were almost exclusively market economies of one form or another, after some discussion an invitation was extended to the USSR to join the initial GATT negotiations. Although the invitation was ultimately declined—and indeed the socialist bloc as a whole avoided the GATT and initially viewed it with some suspicion as an instrument of capitalist expansion—at the very least it represented an important signal that the key founders of the system saw it as potentially compatible with many kinds of domestic economic systems. Some years later, when a number of Eastern European countries changed course and expressed an interest in participating in the GATT, a way was ultimately found for them to do so, albeit gradually.[5] Yugoslavia, Poland, Romania and Hungary all attained first, observer status, then associate membership, then ultimately full accession as contracting parties between 1950 and 1973. Bulgaria was granted observer status in 1967, though never acceded as a GATT contracting party. It is relevant that, although some special arrangements were required, no major changes to the rules of the GATT 1947 were needed to accommodate these accessions. The rules, in other words, were designed to be largely facially neutral with respect to the structure of contracting parties' domestic economies, which was seen to be a matter of sovereign prerogative not amenable to international legal discipline.

In part as a result of these episodes, the GATT's flexibility and pluralism regarding its members' domestic economic systems is now commonly remembered as one of

---

[4]   Douglas A. Irwin, Petros C. Mavroidis and Alan O. Sykes, *The Genesis of the GATT* (Cambridge: Cambridge University Press, 2008), 63, 73–74. The Canadian delegation proposed that only market economies be invited to the initial GATT negotiations. On the other hand, the US vision of the postwar economic order from its inception envisioned a pluralist framework for economic cooperation between a variety of economic systems: see H. D. White, *Preliminary Draft—Proposal for United Nations Stabilization Fund and Bank for Reconstruction and Development of the United and Associated Nations*, World Bank Archives (April 1942), e.g., II-63.

[5]   For accounts of the GATT's relations with socialist economies, see M. M. Kostecki, *East-West Trade and the GATT System* (Basingstoke: Palgrave Macmillan, 1979); James R. Reuland, "GATT and State-Trading Countries," *Journal of World Trade Law* 9 (1975): 318; Kazimierz Grzybowski, "Socialist Countries in GATT," *American Journal of Comparative Law* 28 (1980): 539–54; Kazimierz Grzybowski, "East-West Trade Regulations in the United States, The 1974 Trade Act, Title IV," *Journal of World Trade Law* 11 (1977): 506.

its "central strength[s]."[6] But it is important also to note that, in practice, the GATT contracting parties' commitment to universal inclusion only ran so far. Despite the facial neutrality of its rules and the formal accessions just described, the participation of socialist economies in the trading order established by GATT remained extremely limited. The USSR, after all, never joined the negotiations. Those original GATT contracting parties that changed their domestic economic systems were effectively excluded from significant participation in the GATT trading order by one means or another: China withdrew from the GATT after its 1949 revolution, while both Cuba and Czechoslovakia were subject to, among other restrictions, US sanctions on trade with communist countries after their political transitions.[7] The Czechoslovakia experience also prompted the addition of a special interpretive note to the GATT Article VI, which facilitated the use of special procedures in the imposition of antidumping duties against nonmarket economies.[8] Furthermore, the accession of Eastern European countries is best understood in political terms as part of a larger strategy of economic rapprochement with the less doctrinaire members of the socialist bloc. It reflected, in other words, not so much a deep commitment to institutional pluralism but rather a pragmatic calculation that engagement represented the most effective way of encouraging marketization of socialist economies over the longer term.[9] That Hungary and Yugoslavia had undertaken steps to decentralize their economies over a number of years was an important factor in their accession negotiations, while Romania and Poland also restructured their foreign trade arrangements to facilitate greater direct involvement of producers.[10] In any case, trade flows between these countries and the GATT contracting parties remained insignificant as a share of global trade—and were, in any case, subject to special safeguard regimes. Indeed, the association of accession with domestic marketization and liberalization, as well as the ongoing exclusion of socialist economies in the absence of any serious indications of market-oriented reforms, became an enduring feature of the GATT. The facial neutrality of the GATT rules then, while important, needs to be understood alongside the GATT's practical character as a club of market-based economies[11] and a quiet champion of market values.

In addition to the participation of socialist economies in the GATT, there is the quite separate issue of the way in which institutional diversity *within* the capitalist world was handled within the GATT. In the discussion so far, I have followed much of the existing

---

[6] Petros C. Mavroidis and Merit Janow, "Free Markets, State Involvement, and the WTO: Chinese State-Owned Enterprises in the Ring," *World Trade Review* 16, no. 4 (2017): 571–81 (572).

[7] See Reuland, "GATT and State-Trading Countries"; Grzybowski, "East-West Trade Regulations in the United States"; Kent Jones, "Revolutionary Cuba and the GATT/WTO System," *Journal of World Trade* 51 (2017): 817–42.

[8] Kostecki, *East-West Trade and the GATT System*, 24.

[9] Ibid.

[10] Kennedy, "The International Style in Postwar Law and Policy"; Kostecki, *East-West Trade and the GATT System*; Grzybowski, "East-West Trade Regulations in the United States."

[11] For an insightful account of club dynamics in the history of the GATT, see Nicolas Lamp, "The Club Approach to Multilateral Trade Lawmaking," *Vanderbilt Journal of Transnational Law* 49 (2016): 107–90.

literature in referring generically to "market economies" and "socialist economies," but this terminology obscures the tremendous variety that exists within each category. Many different kinds of capitalist market economies have emerged at different times and in different places, and the fundamental character of capitalism and markets as a highly variegated social and economic form is well established.[12] Indeed, the core institutional innovations of many of the most well-known historical market forms—American liberal market capitalism, German social market economy, French dirigisme, Scandinavian social democracy, British postwar mixed economy and so on—were established in the years on either side of World War II. As Jackson has noted, the significant institutional differences between even these relatively similar economic systems inevitably gave rise to tensions and frictions as their respective systems of production were consolidated, new patterns of comparative advantage were established, and trade flows intensified.[13] How then did the GATT address these frictions?

It is fair to say that, at least for the first two or three decades of the GATT, this form of intracapitalist diversity was—with some exceptions—managed in a spirit of tolerant pluralism, without serious difficulty. As a formal matter, the drafters of the GATT designed a system of rules that clearly reflected, and accommodated, the diverse institutional choices made by contracting parties. As is well-known, few, if any, formal requirements were included to reduce state ownership of commercial enterprises; state trading enterprises and other state monopolies were permitted and subject to only the relatively relaxed disciplines of the GATT Article XVII; large-scale governmental stabilization programs in the agricultural sector were explicitly permitted; and the original GATT agreement contained no serious disciplines on either domestic or export subsidies. Furthermore, liberalization in much of the developing world was generally pursued in a manner consistent with highly diverse forms of direct state intervention and infant industry protection. The reasons for this are in part prosaic. There was never any serious prospect of contracting parties agreeing to rules that required changes to any of the core institutions of their market structure, such as their domestic corporate governance arrangements, the structure of their financial systems, their industrial and regional development strategies or their domestic industrial relations frameworks. Such matters are not readily amenable to international legal discipline.

In this sense, intracapitalist institutional diversity was treated by the GATT contracting parties simply as a fact that demanded accommodation. But it is also fair to say that

---

[12] See generally, e.g., Jamie Peck and Nik Theodore, "Variegated Capitalism," *Progress in Human Geography* 31 (2007): 731–72; Geoffrey Wood and Christel Lane, eds., *Capitalist Diversity and Diversity within Capitalism* (London: Routledge, 2012); Peter A. Hall and David Soskice, eds., *Varieties of Capitalism: The Institutional Foundations of Comparative Advantage* (Oxford: Oxford University Press, 2001); David Lane and Martin Myant, eds., *Varieties of Capitalism in Postcommunist Countries* (Basingstoke, UK: Palgrave Macmillan, 2007); Gregory Jackson and Richard Deeg, "Comparing Capitalisms: Understanding Institutional Diversity and Its Implications for International Business," *Journal of International Business Studies* 39 (2008): 540–61; Bruno Amable, *The Diversity of Modern Capitalism* (Oxford: Oxford University Press, 2003).

[13] Jackson, *The World Trading System*, 218.

tolerance of such diversity emerged as a genuine institutional value. There is a larger context here that needs to be recalled. The mid-twentieth-century market economies of Western Europe took shape in the specific context of US-led projects of postwar reconstruction and development, under the auspices of the Marshall Plan and other aid programs.[14] The structure of the Marshall Plan gave the United States a significant say in the development of European market institutions during this period, and it undoubtedly represented, in significant part, a transatlantic transplantation of American market institutions.[15] The need to establish and support core capitalist institutions of whatever form quickly became an imperative in the emerging context of the Cold War. This required, in Cox's words, a "conscious shaping of the balance among social forces within states" to support new political and economic institutions.[16] Since in each state the constellation of the social forces required was different, significant national institutional variation emerged and was tolerated. The GATT's commitment to (intracapitalist) institutional diversity should be partly understood in this context. The construction of a liberal international economic order, and the postwar reconstruction of Europe, were of course two elements of a single project, and part of the immediate purpose of the GATT regime was precisely to create an international environment conducive to the flourishing of Western European market institutions. During this time, pluralist tolerance of the variety of institutional forms across the advanced economies flowed naturally, and this larger context structurally limited the incentives and abilities of particular GATT contracting parties to harness the institutions toward a more doctrinaire and less flexible vision of market capitalism, at least for some time.[17]

There was, however, another crucial element of the compromise. The GATT liberally permitted contracting parties to continue to use, on a unilateral basis, trade defenses to counteract the effects of what they perceived to be unfair trade—namely, "dumped" and subsidized imports. Jackson first perceptively noted that these trade defense mechanisms can act in practice as "an 'interface' or buffer mechanism to ameliorate difficulties [...] caused by interdependence among different economic systems."[18]

---

[14] See generally, e.g., Michael J. Hogan, *The Marshall Plan, America, Britain, and the Reconstruction of Western Europe, 1947–1952* (Cambridge: Cambridge University Press, 1987); Michael J. Hogan, "American Marshall Planners and the Search for a European Neocapitalism," *American Historical Review* 90, no. 1 (1985): 44–72; Robert W. Cox, *Production, Power, and World Order: Social Forces in the Making of History* (New York: Columbia University Press, 1987); Gabriel Kolko and Joyce Kolko, *The Limits of Power: The World and the United States Foreign Policy, 1945–1954* (New York: Harper & Row, 1972); Charles S. Maier, "The Politics of Productivity: Foundations of American International Economic Policy After World War II," *International Organization* 31, no. 4 (1977): 607–63.

[15] Maier, "The Politics of Productivity"; Maria N. Ivanova, "Why There Was No 'Marshall Plan' for Eastern Europe and Why This Still Matters," *Journal of Contemporary European Studies* 15, no. 3 (2007): 345–76.

[16] Cox, *Production, Power, and World Order*, 215.

[17] Of course, this did happen on occasion—challenges in the GATT to the agricultural programs of the European Economic Community and to certain key aspects of US and EC tax systems are probably the most significant examples during this period.

[18] Jackson, *The World Trading System*, 244.

His point was that even apparently minor institutional differences among similar market economies can significantly affect patterns of comparative advantage and global trade flows, and often give rise to claims of "unfair trade." Establishing a consensus view of what constitutes "fair" trade—in the sense of establishing a single baseline of universal market institutions—was not only impossible but also in tension with the pluralist institutional ethos of the GATT just described. The approach taken was to give each state relatively broad freedom to take unilateral defensive action on the basis of its own vision of what constituted fair and unfair trade—or, equivalently in this context, legitimate and illegitimate institutional variation. Such defensive measures, as long as they were kept within certain bounds, could act "as a crude or blunt instrument to cause different economic systems to more equitably share the burdens of adjusting to shifts of world trade flow."[19] As we shall see, this highly permissive approach to trade defenses proved in due course to be very important, notwithstanding the exceptional character of such measures initially.

Another period in the GATT's history, in which the question of institutional diversity was reopened, was the turbulent "new protectionism" period during the 1970s and early 1980s. During the 1960s and 1970s, a range of East Asian economies—Japan, South Korea, Singapore, Taiwan, Hong Kong—emerged and had become newly competitive across a range of globally traded industrial goods. Together, these economies represented the emergence of a new family of capitalist forms "fundamentally distinct" from all prior Western models. Notwithstanding their considerable variety, a number of features characterize the institutional structure of East Asian capitalisms.[20] One is the relative importance of interpersonal trust, as compared with institutionalized trust. This has deeply shaped the character of interfirm relationships, giving rise to a predominance of longer-term contracting, a substantial degree of informality and, importantly, the consolidation of large business conglomerates linked together through strong family and social ties or through complex cross-shareholding arrangements. Other features have to do with the particular role of the state characteristic of East Asian economies. Witt

---

[19] Ibid.

[20] See generally, e.g., Michael A. Witt and Gordon Redding, *The Oxford Handbook of Asian Business Systems* (Oxford: Oxford University Press, 2014); Michael A. Witt and Gordon Redding, "Asian Business Systems: Institutional Comparison, Clusters and Implications for Varieties of Capitalism and Business Systems Theory," *Socio-Economic Review* 11, no. 2 (2013): 265–300; Robert Boyer, Hiroyasu Uemura and Akinori Isogai, eds., *Diversity and Transformations of Asian Capitalisms* (Abingdon: Routledge, 2012); Frank B. Tipton, "Southeast Asian Capitalism: History, Institutions, States, and Firms," *Asia Pacific Journal of Management* 26 (2009): 401–34; Amable, *The Diversity of Modern Capitalism*; Suzanne Berger and Ronald P. Dore, eds., *National Diversity and Global Capitalism* (Ithaca, NY: Cornell University Press, 1996); Cornelia Storz, Bruno Amable, Steven Casper and Sebastien Lechavalier, "Bringing Asia into the Comparative Capitalism Perspective," *Socio-Economic Review* 11, no. 2 (2013): 217–32; Richard Whitley, *Business Systems in East Asia: Firms, Markets and Societies* (London: Sage, 1992); David Hundt and Jitendra Uttam, *Varieties of Capitalism in Asia: Beyond the Developmental State* (Basingstoke: Palgrave Macmillan, 2018); Andrew Walter and Xiaoke Zhang, eds., *East Asian Capitalism: Diversity, Continuity and Change* (Oxford: Oxford University Press, 2012).

and Reading, for example, refer to their typical "multiplexity," referring to the simultaneous presence of different business systems—state-owned, state-supported and private sectors—within a single economy.[21] This is also associated with the development of a variety of innovative modalities of cooperation, exchange, guidance and direction between the public and private sectors. Others have focused on the particularly active role of the state in shaping the dynamics of competition within important sectors of the economy.[22] Although the precise tools differed from country to country, a number of East Asian states (South Korea, Japan, Taiwan) all famously chose to conduct a relatively active industrial policy, including through direct participation in corporate governance, some bureaucratic control over the provision of credit, government enterprise purchasing decisions, active facilitation of the transfer of know-how and technology, the establishment of government-controlled cartels, relaxed enforcement of antitrust laws and direct subsidies for competitive exporters.

These institutional features are often counted among the key explanations for these countries' efficiency and comparative advantages, but they equally gave rise to claims of unfairness. This is best illustrated in the context of US–Japan relations between the 1970s and the 1990s, when these and other institutional differences became an important focus of trade disputes. Famously, the structure and operation of large Japanese business conglomerates—the *keiretsu*—was commonly identified as an important reason for the difficulties facing US exporters in penetrating Japanese markets.[23] The tendency of such conglomerates to make purchasing decisions that favored suppliers within the group tended to exclude foreign actors from domestic markets, while patterns of in-group cross-shareholding helped insulate these firms from takeover pressure and acted as a barrier to foreign investment. Where such conglomerates were organized around a financial institution as the central pillar (common in Japan), the conglomerate structure afforded them privileged access to capital, insulating them from some of the discipline associated with financial markets and stock market fluctuations and leading to problems of overborrowing and overlending. In addition, a number of US exporters objected to the conduct of large state-owned enterprises in the Japanese economy, which they argued

---

[21] Witt and Reading, "Asian Business Systems."

[22] See, e.g., Chalmers Johnson, *MITI and the Japanese Miracle: The Growth of Industrial Policy 1925–1975* (Stanford, CA: Stanford University Press, 1982); Robert Wade, *Governing the Market: The Role of Government in East Asian Industrialization* (Princeton, NJ: Princeton University Press, 1990); Alice H. Amsden, *Asia's Next Giant: South Korea and Late Industrialization* (Oxford: Oxford University Press, 1989); Richard W. Carney and Michael A. Witt, "The Role of the State in Asian Business Systems," in *Embedded Autonomy: States and Industrial Transformation*, ed. Peter B. Evans (Princeton, NJ: Princeton University Press, 1995); Witt and Redding, *The Oxford Handbook of Asian Business Systems*, 538–60.

[23] For some contemporary examples, see Dorothy Christelow, "Japan's Intangible Barriers to Trade in Manufactures," *Federal Reserve Bank of New York Quarterly Review* 10 (Winter 1985–86): 11–18; Bela Belassa, "Japan's Trade Policies," *Weltwirtschaftliches Archiv* Bd. 122, H. 4 (1986): 745–90; William V. Rapp, "Japan's Invisible Barriers to Trade," in *Fragile Interdependence: Economic Issues in U.S.-Japanese Trade and Investment*, ed. Thomas A. Pugel with Robert G. Hawkins (Lanham, MD: Lexington Books, 1986), 21–45.

tended to favor Japanese goods in their purchasing decisions.[24] And of course, Japan's mechanisms of public-private coordination in the field of industrial policy—not only its promotion of competitive exporters but also its "administrative guidance" to importers, programs for the defense of depressed industries as well as measures to facilitate rapid inward technology transfer—were cast as illegitimate and unfair interferences with fair market competition.[25]

The emergence of the East Asian family of capitalisms seriously tested the original commitment to intracapitalist institutional pluralism, such as it was, of the major GATT powers. Their response—again best illustrated by US action in relation to Japan—was multipronged. One prong was the maximal use of unilateral defensive measures against unfair trade practices, to the limits of what was formally permitted under the GATT, and indeed beyond. Safeguard and antidumping investigations were initiated during the 1970s and 1980s on steel products, footwear, certain consumer electronics, computer chips, photo paper, automotive parts and other products, leading to voluntary export restraints and orderly marketing agreements in these sectors.[26] Where such agreements were negotiated with the United States, the European Economic Community typically also demanded similar treatment.[27] Although countervailing duties were not used against Japanese imports in this period, antidumping duties were used heavily in many of the same industries to slow import penetration and minimize the associated market disruption. A large proportion of such duties levied during the 1970s and 1980s were directed against Japanese products.[28]

Other prongs of the response were targeted at opening Japanese markets to US imports. Importantly, for the purposes of the present argument, they included a number of efforts to address certain underlying institutional features of the Japanese economy. For example, the United States stepped up its use of GATT dispute settlement against Japan, including disputes that raised aspects of Japanese retail distribution mechanisms,

---

[24] E.g., in the context of markets for telecommunications equipment, satellites, supercomputers, see Belassa, "Japan's Trade Policies"; Ka Zeng, *Trade Threats, Trade Wars: Bargaining, Retaliation and American Coercive Diplomacy* (Ann Arbor, MI: Michigan University Press, 2004), chap. 5.

[25] There was, it should be said, an important contingent that did not see them this way but rather saw many of them as facilitating, replicating, speeding up or intensifying market forces, or overcoming impediments to them: see, e.g., Gary R. Saxonhouse, "What's All This about 'Industrial Targeting' in Japan?," *World Economy* 6 (September 1986): 253–74; Philip H. Trezise, "Industrial Policy Is Not the Major Reason for Japan's Success," *Brookings Review* 1 (Spring 1983): 13–18; Charles L. Schultze, "Industrial Policy: A Dissent," *Brookings Review* 2 (Fall 1983): 3–12. The difference in characterization is important and of course precisely what is at stake in conflicts of this kind: support in accordance with market pressures and signals.

[26] Useful overviews of this practice can be found in Chad P. Bown and Rachel McCulloch, "US-Japan and US-PRC Trade Conflict: Export Growth, Reciprocity, and the International Trading System" (working paper no. 158, Asian Development Bank Institute, Tokyo, November 2009); Thomas O. Bayard and Kimberly A. Elliott, *Reciprocity and Retaliation in U.S. Trade Policy* (Washington, DC: Institute for International Economics, 1994).

[27] E.g., Zeng, *Trade Threats, Trade Wars*: chap. 5.

[28] Bown and McCulloch, "US-Japan and US-PRC Trade Conflict."

government procurement practices as well as other matters.[29] More important, a number of Section 301 actions were taken in response to Japanese industrial policies and industry structures—including most prominently in the semiconductor and satellite sectors in the mid- to late-1980s.[30] Such measures were designed in large part to pressure Japan to modify its practices and were accompanied by a series of bilateral working groups and negotiations seeking to achieve that effect.[31] In the present context, one of the most interesting of these was the US–Japan Structural Impediments Initiative, a set of trade negotiations concluded in 1990, which were designed to address the underlying institutional determinants of the persistent US trade deficit with Japan. These discussions covered a wide range of matters, from the restrictive business practices of Japanese conglomerates to Japanese land-use policy, the enforcement of Japanese antitrust law, the structure of the Japanese retail distribution sector and other sources of apparent domestic market rigidities—a list that still appears extraordinary today, even if the results of the negotiation were nonbinding.[32]

In addition, and importantly, a number of these efforts were also pursued (albeit in a very different form) through new *general* rulemaking at the multilateral level in the GATT and subsequently the WTO. Many of the additions and modifications to international trade rules that were negotiated during the Tokyo Round, and especially the Uruguay Round, grew out of this period and sought to establish new concepts and techniques for distinguishing between legitimate and illegitimate institutional experimentation across market economies. These included most prominently new rules that sought more clearly to discipline industrial subsidies (the Tokyo Round Subsidies Code and the WTO's Agreement on Subsidies and Countervailing Measures) and open up procurement markets (the Government Procurement Code and Agreement on Government Procurement) as well as universal standards of minimum intellectual property (IP) protection applicable across the entire GATT/WTO membership (the Trade-Related Aspects of Intellectual Property Rights agreement), but a range of other clarifications and modifications seek to also limit the effects of restrictive business practices as well as measures to facilitate technology transfer. The Subsidies and Countervailing Measures agreement was particularly important in the present context, as it added enforceable disciplines that entirely prohibited the use of export subsidies and domestic subsidies in certain circumstances, rather than merely permitting importing states to use countervailing duties to counteract their effect in particular cases.

It is a matter of legitimate disagreement whether, and precisely how far, the new WTO agreements have in fact limited the freedom of WTO members to innovate new institutional forms of market capitalism—they likely did less than is commonly perceived,

---

[29] Ibid.

[30] See Zeng, *Trade Threats, Trade Wars*: chap. 5.

[31] Including the so-called Market-Oriented Sector-Selective (MOSS) talks, the US–Japan Working Group on High Technology and the US–Japan Strategic Impediments Initiative.

[32] Joint Report of the US–Japan Working Group on the Structural Impediments Initiative (June 28, 1990), available at https://tcc.export.gov/Trade_Agreements/All_Trade_Agreements/exp_005583.asp.

even as a formal matter. Nevertheless, they clearly represent a new compromise between the alternative approaches to institutional diversity—the "interface" model and the "convergence" model—which have been in tension in GATT law and practice since its inception. One of the legacies of the new varieties of capitalism that emerged across East Asia has been to elevate the latter and to dilute (or at least to expose the latent weakness of) the regime's earlier commitment to the qualified tolerance of intracapitalist institutional diversity. Experience during that period, furthermore, teaches us a great deal about both the strengths and the risks of the GATT's original compromise on institutional diversity, lessons that are highly relevant for thinking about the present challenges.

Turning then to the present, the boundaries of legitimate institutional diversity in the international trading system are again in a process of renegotiation. While in the earlier period Japan became the cipher for the general question of institutional diversity and its limits, now China occupies that position. Since the creation of the WTO, when a number of transition countries sought to become members of the multilateral trading system, WTO accession negotiations have been used to exert pressure on transition economies to move more quickly and more completely toward marketization. Particular attention has been paid, for example, to the progress of ongoing privatization programs, the administration of government pricing policies (for example, in the energy sector) and the extent of administrative discretion in the regulation of economic life, and certain obligations on these and other matters frequently found their way into these states' accession protocols.[33] Accordingly, when WTO members agreed to China's accession in 2001, it was on the basis of an understanding that the Chinese economy was moving relatively swiftly toward a free market economy. As the hybrid quality of contemporary Chinese capitalism coalesced, and the expectation of its convergence toward something resembling liberal market capitalism was exposed as unrealistic, the perception is that China has reneged on its implicit promise. China's model of capitalism, it is said, is both novel and unanticipated, and some strongly believe that it gives Chinese enterprises an unfair advantage in global trade, just as Japan's institutional innovations were said to have done decades earlier.

The responses of major trading powers, most prominently the United States, also resemble those responses to East Asian experimentation decades earlier. Trade remedies actions, including this time both antidumping and antisubsidy proceedings, have been aggressively pursued against exports from China, not only by the United States and the EU but also by a range of developing and middle-income countries.[34] In addition, the United States has initiated Section 301 proceedings against Chinese imports, just as it

---

[33] See, e.g., UNCTAD, "The Non-Market Economy Issue in International Trade in the Context of WTO Accessions," UNCTAD/DITC/TNCD/MISC.20 (October 9, 2002), available at http://unctad.org/en/docs/ditctncdmisc20_en.pdf; Constantine Michalopoulos, "World Trade Organization Accession for Transition Economies: Problems and Prospects," *Russian and East European Finance and Trade* 36, no. 2 (2000): 63–86; Dylan Geraets, *Accession to the World Trade Organization: A Legal Analysis* (Cheltenham, UK: Edward Elgar, 2018).

[34] See Bown and McCulloch, "US-Japan and US-PRC Trade Conflict"; Mark Wu, "Antidumping in Asia's Emerging Giants," *Harvard International Law Journal* 53 (2012): 101.

did against Japanese imports, and on this occasion has infamously imposed further trade restrictions on grounds of national security. At the same time, at the multilateral level, there have been efforts to interpret WTO law to permit challenges to a range of Chinese practices and measures relating to currency manipulation, forced technology transfer, IP enforcement and others. Such measures may have led to on-again, off-again bilateral talks between the United States and China akin to those between the United States and Japan earlier, though it is too early to say what, if anything, might come of them. Efforts have also been underway for more than a decade to develop new rules in recent trade agreements explicitly addressing some of the challenges associated with the emergence of heterodox market capitalism in China, most notably the conduct and activities of state-owned enterprises.

In light of the brief history told above, the present system has at least two apparent serious flaws. The first has to do with the way in which, and the extent to which, trade defenses are being used against imports from heterodox market economies. I noted earlier Jackson's conceptualization of antidumping and antisubsidy law as a blunt but at least potentially effective instrument for pragmatically addressing the frictions inevitably caused by trade among different economic systems, including different varieties of market capitalism. His point is an important one, and it has been underappreciated for some time. If this role of trade defenses had been recognized more fully, the Appellate Body's jurisprudence under the Antidumping Agreement might have gone in a different direction, and one of the main sources of pressure on the current dispute settlement system may have been avoided. That said, it is also true that existing trade defense regimes are a particularly blunt method of fulfilling that function and are constantly in danger of going beyond it. Even in the 1980s, the United States' use of such measures against imports from heterodox economies was strongly criticized for being inefficient, politically captured and ideologically driven.[35] This criticism now appears inescapable. It is not only that their use has become much more common and more geographically dispersed, but also that they are so disproportionately targeted against products from heterodox market economies. Indeed, this has been made worse by new interpretive techniques that have emerged, having the effect of inflating dumping margins and subsidy levels, where foreign markets are characterized as "distorted."[36] The result is a system of trade defenses

---

[35] Daniel Tarullo, "Beyond Normalcy in the Regulation of International Trade," *Harvard Law Review* 100, no. 3 (1987): 546–628.

[36] See, e.g., Bernhard Kluttig, Christian Tietje and Martina Franke, "Cost of Production Adjustments in Anti-dumping Proceedings: Challenging the Raw Material Inputs Dual Pricing Systems in EU Anti-dumping Law and Practice," *Journal of World Trade* 45, no. 5 (2011): 1071–102; Edwin Vermulst, Juhi D. Sud and Simon J. Evenett, "Normal Value in Anti-dumping Proceedings against China Post-2016: Are Some Animals Less Equal Than Others?," *Global Trade and Customs Journal* 11, no. 5 (2016): 212–28; Ming Du, "China's State Capitalism and World Trade Law," *International and Comparative Law Quarterly* 63 (2014): 409–48; Sherzod Shadikhodjaev, "Input Cost Adjustments and WTO Anti-dumping Law: A Closer Look at the EU Practice," *World Trade Review* (January 2018); Weihuan Zhou, "Australia's Anti-dumping and Countervailing Law and Practice: An Analysis of Current Issues Incompatible with Free Trade with China," *Journal of World Trade* 49 (2015): 980–91.

that, to a significant enough degree, is targeted in a discriminatory and even punitive manner against heterodox institutional forms, in ways that can only disincentivize institutional experimentation. Instead of being a blunt but legitimate instrument to pursue goals of stability, cost-sharing or distributional equity, as Jackson described, it is too often a more questionable instrument of commercial policy or ideological projection.

The second concern is the continuing erosion of the value of institutional pluralism in the international trading regime. I have argued above that, while it is true that a commitment to intracapitalist institutional pluralism has been present in the system from the beginning, this value has always been in tension with a desire to promote institutional convergence, or at least to set boundaries on members' institutional choices. I also argued that the compromise between these two shifted considerably toward the latter during the last decades of the twentieth century, in part as a result of the disruptions to existing patterns of comparative advantage caused by the rise of new capitalist forms in East Asia. One possible outcome of the present period of trade tension, and indeed a likely one, may be to prompt a shift even further in that direction. It is now perfectly apparent that a large part of the new agenda of rulemaking in international trade agreements is designed specifically to place additional constraints on new institutional forms emerging in China and elsewhere. The development of new rules on state-owned and state-controlled enterprises, alongside the concerted use of existing subsidies rules to challenge the practices of Chinese state-owned enterprises, is the best example.

If this is true, it is a cause of some concern. Many of the specific concerns that have been raised about China's trade policy have merit and must be addressed. However, one of the lessons of the history and development of the postwar trading system is that global institutional innovation contributes to the long-term strength, resilience and dynamism of the global economy. Some of the major periods of structural transformation in the global economy, including periods of major gains in productive efficiency and the integration of marginalized populations, have been associated with periods of profound institutional experimentation. While it is common to focus attention on the transaction costs associated with institutional differences—and to treat their persistence as a necessary concession to the value of political and economic self-determination—the better view seems to be that the presence of multiple market forms is efficiency-enhancing at the systemic level, even if it imposes specific costs on individual firms conducting business across borders.

To be clear, this has much more to do with the nature and distribution of opportunities for institutional experimentation and innovation globally than with the extent of institutional diversity as such. Those who study capitalism comparatively more or less unanimously believe that international economic integration on its own is unlikely to lead to reduced institutional diversity—indeed, it may perhaps lead to the opposite, as countries intensify their efforts to gain comparative institutional advantage.[37] The risk, then, is not that international trade law will impose institutional convergence in any simple sense. But what is apparent even from the brief historical survey presented here is

---

[37] See, for one among many examples, Hall and Soskice, *Varieties of Capitalism*.

that domestic institutional configurations always arise in the context of particular international structures, even as they express local values, preferences and histories. This is as true of Chinese "state capitalism"—which could not have emerged without the broader structures of neoliberal globalization characteristic of the late twentieth century[38]—as it is of the varieties of capitalism established in Western Europe in the decades spanning the period after World War II. To approach the question of institutional pluralism sensibly, then, it would be helpful to move beyond thinking of the international trade regime primarily as a constraint on states' institutional choices and a limitation on the degree of institutional diversity globally. Just as domestic institutional configurations enable firms to define their interests and strategies, the international institutional order could act in the same way in respect of states: enabling certain kinds of institutional strategies, discouraging others and distributing the capacity for institutional innovation and experimentation differentially across different states.

What, finally, of the distinction between the "interface" and "convergence" approaches to the question of institutional pluralism? One conclusion we might draw from the history above is that the governance techniques associated with each are more ambiguous in their institutional effects than might be expected. On the one hand, the "interface" model is more explicitly pluralist in its orientation—but its emphasis on pragmatic ad hoc bargaining for the resolution of consequent trade frictions can, in practice, problematically treat institutional choices as bargaining chips in reciprocal negotiations and lose sight of their systemic effects. On the other hand, the "convergence" model's preference for general limits on institutional diversity appears antipluralist in orientation but can be the opposite in practice. Depending of course on their content and nature, general rules can facilitate institutional experimentation by establishing common understandings of what is (and is not) acceptable, thereby reducing the risks of retaliation by affected trading partners. This is another of the clear risks of the contemporary erosion of support for the multilateral system. We may need to think beyond both models, imagining the present system not just as a mechanism for managing the interface among different economic systems or as a force for reducing institutional frictions, encouraging institutional convergence and leveling the international competitive playing field, but also as a system for encouraging genuinely democratically driven institutional experimentation.

---

[38] See, e.g., Jamie Peck and Jun Zhang, "A Variety of Capitalism [...] with Chinese Characteristics?," *Journal of Economic Geography* 13 (2013): 357–96.

Chapter Eight

EMBEDDED NEOLIBERALISM AND ITS DISCONTENTS: THE UNCERTAIN FUTURE OF TRADE AND INVESTMENT LAW

Sonia E. Rolland and David Trubek[1]

An era marked by an uneasy truce between developed countries and the developing world is coming to an end. This era, which reached its apogee in the 1990s, could be characterized as "embedded" neoliberalism, where developing countries signed on to an international economic law (IEL) system premised on neoliberal tenets but softened by de jure and de facto exceptions and derogations ostensibly to accommodate developmental needs and policies. Initially, developing countries resisted rules that imposed unwanted restrictions and that limited growth options. But it was the best they could secure at the time, so they accepted much of the regime thus creating a temporary truce. With this truce between market-oriented globalization and state-based developmentalism unraveling, we look at how things might evolve and ask if there is another set of relations that would address changing conditions, manage conflicting interests and restore some stability.

The world economy is rife with clashes of values and interests. States in the North, encouraged by multinational corporations (MNCs), push to further open global markets, reduce the role of the state in the economy and provide special protection for foreign investors. States in the South resist some of these pressures in the name of development, maintain a commitment to state-led growth and demand more control over their domestic markets and opportunities abroad for their exporters. These tensions translate into stalemates over the scope of existing rules, struggles to create new ones and even the possibility that the multilateral rule-based system itself will collapse.

Over all this looms China. In recent years, China has become more assertive on the world stage, doubled down on its commitment to state-led growth and announced policies that conflict with existing and proposed rules. As its economy grows in both absolute terms and relative to that of the United States and the European Union (EU) and it strengthens relations with other developing countries, China's capacity to influence trade and investment policy may grow apace. Could we be witnessing the end of the postwar

[1] This essay draws on Rolland and Trubek, *Emerging Powers in International Economic Law: Cooperation, Competition, and Transformation* (Cambridge: Cambridge University Press, 2019).

liberal order and the emergence of a China-led order more supportive of Global South values?

It is clear that China will have more and more to say about the multilateral ordering, but it is neither ready nor willing to remake the current system from which it has benefited significantly. If one looks closely at the struggles of China and the rest of the Global South with the liberal trade and investment regime, one finds a much more complex picture. Far from trying to overturn the liberal trade order, China and other emerging economies have sought to use it to promote their interests while resisting efforts to extend the regime in ways that challenge their core values and interests. Similarly, while emerging economies have also resisted aspects of the global investment protection system, most have accepted many of its tenets and some continue to sign bilateral investment treaties (BITs) albeit in modified form.

At this juncture, it is worth noting that although developing countries are a highly diverse group and the analysis we provide below applies differently to specific countries, some trends remain true for developing countries generally.

The first part of this essay argues that despite tensions between the current IEL system and the policy preferences of many emerging economies, countries of the Global South have managed to achieve some kind of balance between the neoliberal thrust of the system and their desire to pursue strategies that—from a neoliberal viewpoint—are heterodox. The result is a system they can use to further their own ends and one that only intrudes on their policy space to a tolerable degree.

Think of it as a truce between a radical liberalization campaign and strong resistance in the name of state-led growth and sovereignty. The truce is acceptable to developing countries because the system benefits them to some extent, they lack a clear alternative ordering and even if they had identified a substitute model, they lack the political structure and discipline to mount concerted action to implement it. Likewise, the truce is acceptable to developed countries because it has given those economies sufficient access to lucrative markets in the developing world and cheap imports while ostensibly allowing social protection at home for those dislocated by trade liberalization.

We might think of this truce as embedded neoliberalism, echoing John Ruggie's famous description of an "embedded liberalism" regime that emerged from World War II. Ruggie coined the term to describe the compromise between allowing goods and capital to flow freely around the world as they had in the heyday of the Gold Standard and allowing national governments to control such flows and develop social protection systems to protect against destabilizing shocks. Updating the idea of a compromise between discordant policies, we might call today's regime "embedded neoliberalism" where free market globalization is governed by a multilateral rule system designed for capitalist market economies but tempered by a series of policies and strategies that allow some protectionism along with social protection to cushion import shocks.

While we believe that a form of embedded neoliberalism has emerged, we argue, in the second part of this essay, that it may not endure. It was understood that China and other countries committed to state-led growth deviated from the free market capitalist model the rule system presupposed, but it was assumed they would eventually join the mainstream. What happens when that faith fades? Will the North no longer tolerate the favorable rules, exceptions, avoidance and evasion upon which the truce rested?

There is evidence that the truce is unraveling. Some of the premises underlying the settlement have come unstuck. China has made it clear that it has no intention of abandoning its state-led model. Systems of social protection in the North are proving inadequate to protect the losers from the shocks of market opening, thus undermining the legitimacy of adherence to the multilateral system as it is currently designed and creating domestic backlash against the system. The United States now questions many of the trade rules and processes of the post–World War II regime, as does the EU in the field of investment. The World Trade Organization (WTO) (and the General Agreement on Tariffs and Trade (GATT) before that), long the linchpin of the regime, has largely stalled as a negotiation forum, and its preeminence is being challenged by unilateral moves by the United States, as well as the Comprehensive and Progressive Agreement for Trans-Pacific Partnership (CPTPP), Regional Comprehensive Economic Partnership (RCEP) and other megaregional agreements. If the truce flounders, can a new equilibrium be found? We turn to that in the final section.

Making the System Work for the South: Embedded Neoliberalism

Behind the theory of embedded neoliberalism lies the claim that developing economies have been able to make use of the liberal trade and investment regime to support their development strategies without having to adopt the full gamut of neoliberal prescriptions. The evidence supports that thesis. A growing number of emerging countries are successfully utilizing the existing trade law system in support of development policies. Particularly noteworthy are victories in dispute settlement, the use of flexibilities such as trade remedies and successful resistance against the expansion of free trade disciplines. Similar changes impend in the investment regime where countries like South Africa and India have pushed back and Brazil has pursued a different approach altogether, all without significantly affecting the flow of foreign direct investment (FDI) to their economies.

Developing countries use the WTO to gain access to markets in the North and South

At the WTO, emerging countries have prevailed in a number of disputes against developed members whose policies restricted their access to markets. The EU lost challenges brought by China, Brazil, Thailand, India, Argentina, Indonesia and Peru. The United States lost against China, Brazil, Thailand, India, Argentina, Indonesia, Venezuela, Chile, Antigua and Barbuda, Ecuador, Mexico and Pakistan. Brazil prevailed over Canada. Indonesia won against South Korea.

However, implementation problems have dampened apparent victories. Developing members make up a disproportionate number of complainants in retaliation proceedings and other findings of noncompliance. A number of additional cases were withdrawn or settled without a decision by a panel or arbitrator.

Developing members also successfully challenge one another's trade restrictions. China, Brazil, India, Indonesia, Argentina, Costa Rica, Honduras, Guatemala, El Salvador, the Dominican Republic, Mexico, Panama, Colombia, Turkey, Egypt, the Philippines and Thailand have all been involved in disputes against one another where one party was found in breach of its obligations.

Developing countries use trade remedies and other flexibilities to protect domestic industries

One way developing countries can try to maintain industrial policies in the face of neo-liberal restrictions is the widespread use of trade remedies such as safeguards, antidumping duties and countervailing duties. For instance, in the period March 2013–March 2018, Brazil initiated 55 antidumping investigations and two countervailing duty investigations against various WTO members, resulting in duties imposed against products from India, South Korea, South Africa, China, Russia, Thailand, Egypt, Mexico, Saudi Arabia, Japan, the United States, the United Arab Emirates, Sweden, Germany, the United Kingdom, Canada, Mexico, the Ukraine, the EU, Germany, Israel, Italy, Malaysia, Taiwan, France and the Netherlands. Another 17 trade remedy actions, involving the products from several of the same countries and a few others, were terminated during this period. China and India were the most frequent targets of trade remedies imposed by Brazil. Meanwhile, China imposed countervailing duties and antidumping duties on products from the EU, Japan, the United States, Korea and India, as well as Singapore, Thailand, Malaysia, Thailand and Taiwan, among others. China also terminated duties that had been imposed against other products from Russia, Indonesia and some of these members.

In some cases, these measures have been challenged at the WTO, and countries have been required to end them. But not all efforts to curb the use of trade remedies have been successful, and the cases that have reached the WTO are merely the tip of the iceberg when it comes to trade remedies implemented by emerging countries to protect their domestic policies and markets. In the face of massive use of these measures, the system lacks the capacity to effectively deter potential abuse of the measures.

Trade remedies are not the only escape from restrictions: developing countries avail themselves of additional flexibilities within the WTO trade regime, including exceptions to most-favored-nation obligations for the Generalized System of Preferences (GSP), preference programs among developing countries and ad hoc waivers to other provisions in particular circumstances.

Although most flexibilities and derogations are equally available to developing countries, their usage varies greatly. Middle-income countries tend to make little use of flexibilities specifically available to developing countries, such as special and differential treatment (SDT) at the WTO, but make heavy use of economic policy instruments available generally, such as trade remedies. At the other end of the spectrum, least developed countries (LDCs) are exempt from some provisions (for instance, with respect to certain intellectual property obligations at the WTO) and benefit more heavily from certain forms of SDT (such as the Everything But Arms initiative and other preferences).

In many cases, LDCs use de facto flexibilities resulting from breaches that go unchallenged because their markets are marginal to trade dynamics. However, their ability to use de facto and de jure flexibilities is tempered by their greater susceptibility to coercion by developed or developing trade partners (including threats to lose public aid to development, withdrawal of GSP preferences, etc.).

In practice, the dispute process allows developing countries to temporarily adopt policies that contravene the rules

Even when an exception or waiver is not available, the design of the dispute settlement system, in practice, results in members breaching their obligations while suffering relatively little economic cost because of the long time it takes an injured party to secure the right to retaliate. Disputes should reach a final panel or Appellate Body decision in a maximum of 18 to 19 months, but currently they average more than two years, from a consultations request to adoption of a report. Implementation procedures can take another couple of years before the member in continued breach would be required to begin compensating the complaining member. Overall, a member could readily implement a subsidy or other industrial policy in violation of WTO law for a duration of four or five years before it would have to withdraw its measure or face economic consequences other than paying the legal fees for defending its measure.

Developed and developing members make use of this de facto flexibility mechanism. Infamously, the dispute regarding bananas pitting various African, Caribbean and Pacific Group of States (ACP) members and the United States against the EU has been ongoing since 1995. More recently, India's solar energy development program, which includes subsidies, mandates for the purchase of domestic goods over imported products and other requirements that tend to be problematic under WTO rules, was launched in 2010. A request for consultation by the United States followed in 2013. Compliance proceedings are ongoing, and although the United States requested retaliation rights in 2018, the matter is still unresolved. Meanwhile, the original target for completion of the Indian program is 2022.

China appears to pursue a slightly different strategy. Rather than exploiting procedural delays, China atomizes potential challenges by imposing sectoral trade restrictions, targeted subsidies and other constantly varying industrial support measures. Business entities are left to navigate the regulatory maze, identify potential WTO violations, lobby their governments to consider bringing a dispute, possibly organize the financing of such a dispute and eventually perhaps persuade their government to launch a formal request for consultations or impose a trade remedy. By that point, the Chinese measure might have changed or shifted to another sector. Although it defends challenges to its policies vigorously, China typically does not end up facing postdispute compliance proceedings.

Developing countries have successfully blocked extension of the rules

Lastly, and perhaps most importantly, developing countries have been able to mount effective resistance to the expansion of the trade liberalization agenda at the WTO. From the roll back on the so-called Singapore issues, to the reckoning at the Seattle Ministerial Meeting, to the Doha Work Programme, emerging countries have asserted their voice to exclude from the negotiations or circumscribe items they disfavor and include topics of interest to them. By coordinating coalitions in negotiations and targeted litigation, they improved their outcomes on access to medicine, extracted subsidies reduction commitments from the United States on cotton and were key architects of the Trade Facilitation Agreement, which inaugurated a new type of progressive, capacity-based commitment.

Most emerging economies initially embraced the global investment protection system and signed restrictive BITs. However, many became disillusioned as the implications of these relatively novel instruments became clearer. As cases were brought or decided against them, countries found that BITs imposed unexpected limits on their regulatory powers. At the same time, experts began to doubt whether BITs actually increased capital flow. Resistance to BITs grew. India, South Africa, Indonesia and Ecuador withdrew to one degree or another. These moves did not seem to stem the flow of foreign investment: like Brazil, which has never ratified BITs yet has been a premier location for foreign investment, India, South Africa, Indonesia and Ecuador apparently have been able to limit their participation in BITs without suffering major investment loss.

While we argue that these compromises and strategies resulted in something of an equilibrium, we do not suggest that the international trade and investment law system serves the interests of developing countries adequately or equitably. It has worked more or less well in the area of trade, but not in finance. Moreover, hard-won concessions in favor of emerging countries often revealed themselves to be pyrrhic victories. The status quo was, in many ways, an agreement to disagree made up of a combination of effective resistance to new rules, de jure and de facto derogations and strategic noncompliance. The post-2008 period, however, called this truce into question.

Is the Truce Broken?

From every quarter of the globe, unpredictable political economy choices and normative heterogeneity suggest that we are in a period of legal and institutional instability. We view changes in Chinese and US trade policies and development strategies as particularly salient.

Trade policy changes in the face of resurgent Chinese state capitalism

Far from promising to further move toward market-oriented policies and liberalization, China has made clear that it is committed to maintaining its unique form of state-dominated economic strategy. In an effort to catch up with and surpass the more established economies, China has announced the Made in China 2025 action plan, which outlines a 10-year strategy to build intelligent manufacturing capabilities, enhance innovation and upgrade 10 key sectors. Many believe this vast new industrial policy contains numerous violations of WTO law. China is expanding its influence all over the world, creating new alliances and institutions and making massive investments. Its rapid upgrading of industrial and technological skills has allowed it to emerge as a major competitor to the older industrial powers. Chinese producers and investors' dramatic expansion into Asian, African and Latin American markets is settling into an enduring trend that offers destination countries alternatives to their traditional partners.

Strategies in response to this new reality are eroding the embedded neoliberalism truce. Across the political spectrum in old industrial powers, progressive and conservative voices, liberal and protectionist interests concur to cast China as a political, economic and military threat, a manipulator of the rules. The March 2018 consolidation of power by China's Xi Jinping further heightened concerns. Taking the lead is the United States. The first US effort to roll back China's influence was the Trans-Pacific Partnership (TPP), which sought to create a more market-oriented space in the Asia-Pacific region: some saw this as an indirect way to pressure China to liberalize. After withdrawing from the TPP, the Trump administration announced a zero-tolerance reaction to China's heterodox strategies in a decisive break from the embedded neoliberal compromise. It has since launched an all-out trade war designed to pressure China to liberalize.

Elsewhere, critics differ sharply as to the appropriate response to China. Some opt to push back on the perceived threats with protectionist policies, trade litigation, investment restrictions, rapprochement with like-minded countries and a general hardening of the political discourse. Others prefer to join China as a new locus of power and influence, as demonstrated by the support of the Asian Infrastructure Investment Bank (AIIB), RCEP and Belt and Road Initiative. The collapse of Transatlantic Trade and Investment Partnership (TTIP) negotiations and rise of the AIIB are even causing some European countries to shift their negotiation efforts from West to East while Latin America seeks to maneuver between China, the United States and the CPTPP.

Investment law is unsettled

Investor-state dispute settlement is becoming a highly sensitive pressure point for states. The legitimacy of the International Centre for Settlement of Investment Disputes (ICSID) and other investor-state investment dispute resolution entities is called into question by developed and developing countries alike. A broad range of legal experimentations is afoot to reframe legal disciplines, the balance of rights of investors and host countries, and the nature and reach of dispute settlement. Countries as diverse as Brazil, South Africa, Ecuador and Bolivarian-oriented countries wish to reassert the preeminence of the state as an arbiter of investment policy and protection. China, which is also a proponent of such policies when it comes to inbound investment flows, finds itself more in line with the proinvestor protections enshrined in traditional BITs when it comes to its outward investment.

Restricted by IEL and other factors, social safety nets fail to offset shocks

International economic regulation implemented in the 1990s, including the proliferation of BITs and trade agreements generally aligned with the WTO, was fundamentally designed to achieve convergence in economic and social policies toward a capitalist, liberal democracy model. SDT at the WTO assumes temporary deviations pending full commitment to a mainstream free trade agenda; Washington Consensus policies require privatization and a general curtailing of state intervention in the economy.

The theory was that states would manage and offset the costs of liberalization domestically, as dictated by their particular social contracts. But a number of states are unable or unwilling to uphold these social contracts. While theories abound as to the reason for such failings, IEL arguably plays a role because it increasingly constrains domestic policy instruments in the name of market opening. In other words, the notion that IEL would manage external liberalization for the greater good and that states would mitigate individual costs domestically was doomed as soon as IEL limited states' ability to accomplish the domestic part of the equation.

The WTO agreements ostensibly leave it up to states to determine the level of regulatory protection they wish to maintain in these areas, but in practice, interpretative standards such as the requirement for the least trade-restrictive alternative, the expiration of exceptions for certain subsidies and the tightening of government procurement disciplines all constrain states' policy options. Rules on patents have also constrained developing countries with major public health challenges to provide the necessary access to medicines. Efforts to curb agricultural subsidies in emerging countries clash with the provision of basic food rations by the government (in India, for instance), food security and the support of poor agrarian populations. Washington Consensus mandates to privatize vast sectors of the economy in developing countries in the 1980s and 1990s to rein in public expenditures also restricted these countries' ability to control the delivery of services and to provide employment.

At the same time that IEL has restricted social protection in the South, austerity programs and other factors have limited the capacity of social safety nets in much of the North to fully cushion trade shocks. This is one cause of the populist backlash against the trade regime and provides support for those who want to forego the embedded neoliberal bargain by cracking down on deviations from market principles. At the same time, it poignantly reveals to China and other emerging countries the flaws in liberal capitalism, thus reducing their incentive to join the system.

A New Equilibrium?

If the truce we have described is indeed faltering, what could come in its place? There is, of course, the worst-case scenario of an out-and-out trade war, complete breakdown in the regime, a retreat to autarky and a serious decline in global GNP. Tariffs imposed on many countries by the United States in 2018, and the retaliatory responses from China, the EU and others, make this a very real possibility. The escalation of tariffs on Chinese goods announced by the Trump administration amount to outright economic warfare, and China is retaliating. Unless the respective parties step back from the brink, there is no guarantee that such a doomsday scenario can be averted.

The most important issue moving forward is how to work with China *as it is*. We have to recognize that visions of China evolving into a nice Asian version of France or Germany were never very realistic and now are completely dashed. Despite apparent efforts by the United States to slow its growth, China will soon be the largest economy in the world. How is it at all reasonable to think that a combination of IEL restrictions and US tariffs can force China into a neoliberal straightjacket?

So how might things develop? Some may have thought that China and the other BRICS economies (Brazil, Russia, India and South Africa) would band together to demand a systematic revision of global trade and investment rules. But this hasn't happened. Such a transformation would have required shared agreement on a heterodox vision for the world economy in a move similar to the design of the New International Economic Order (NIEO) in the 1970s. No such vision is yet on offer. While countries like Brazil, India and China all want more space for policy experimentation, they have not coalesced around the kind of systematic alternative to global capitalism that might support a unified effort to radically revise the regime.

A more feasible goal would be a new version of the embedded neoliberal truce in which China and other emerging countries trade increased access to their markets for some relaxation in rules that hamper their developmental-state, state-capitalist strategies. Both sides have a lot to lose from the collapse of the system, and both have a lot to gain from a new version of the compromise. The issue facing the world today is how a new bargain could be struck in the face of the decline of the WTO as a venue for multilateral negotiation, the proliferation of regional free trade agreements (FTAs), the poisonous effect of populist policies in the North, the aggressive and ill-informed unilateralism of the United States and the strident nationalism in China.

Finding a new equilibrium that satisfies developed and developing countries will take a long time and will not happen through one grand bargain. It will have to emerge out of a series of parallel developments in various parts of the world. There are promising initiatives that point toward a new equilibrium. The African Union is devising templates for trade and investments that deserve attention, although the hesitation of Nigeria and South Africa to adhere reflects the difficulty of regional integration in today's fragmented world. The EU is exploring a new architecture for the investment regime that might serve as a model for a new approach worldwide. In Asia, the CPTPP members have modified the original agreement, making some changes that fit developing-country priorities. The Association of Southeast Asian Nations, China and India are moving ahead on the RCEP, an alternative form of FTA that embraces some of the norms developing countries have pushed for and lacks some they object to. There are some tensions between the rules in the RCEP and CPTPP. Could these be reconciled and serve as a basis for a new regime that both China and even the United States might eventually embrace? Or will they develop as opposed spaces, adding to the already troubling fragmentation?

As the world faces the possibility of a protracted trade war generated by the United States, it is not easy to be optimistic. Will the United States settle for minor changes in Chinese state capitalism and its restrictions on market access, declaring victory but leaving the current Chinese system largely intact? The minimal revisions of the North American Free Trade Agreement (NAFTA) in the wake of the Trump administration's boisterous decrying of the agreement illustrate such a "much ado about nothing" approach. Will the Chinese use their growing power to build alliances that challenge US efforts? Or will Trump's onslaught—which combines mercantilist and neoliberal approaches—force real changes in the Chinese system with repercussions for other emerging economies pursuing heterodox strategies?

Only time will tell. The odds are that we will endure a long period of conflict, tension and uncertainty before the dust settles and the major protagonists are ready to sit down and hammer out something new. But promising developments in many parts of the world offer hope that with time we will struggle toward a new equilibrium.

Chapter Nine

RETHINKING THE RCEP IN THE THIRD REGIONALISM: PARADIGM SHIFTS IN WORLD TRADE LAW?

Pasha L. Hsieh

The Regional Comprehensive Economic Partnership (RCEP) represents a new era of regionalism and offers a distinct paradigm for world trade law. When it is launched, the RCEP will be the world's largest free trade agreement (FTA) and a clear alternative to the extant neoliberal trade regime. Built upon the Association of Southeast Asian Nations (ASEAN) free trade areas, the 16-party RCEP covers half of the global population and 30 percent of global gross domestic product (GDP).[1] It also encompasses the world's most vigorous economies, such as China, India and Indonesia. These countries significantly contribute to the bloc's GDP growth rate of 4.6 percent, which is more than double that of the United States and the European Union (EU).[2]

The RCEP, which is double the economic scale of the now 11-member Comprehensive and Progressive Agreement for Trans-Pacific Partnership (CPTPP), will be a key milestone in trade agreements.[3] Yet the RCEP is not simply the latest stage of evolving Asia-Pacific regionalism. It also exhibits the Global South's contemporary normative vision, which challenges the dominant neoliberal approach and the Indo-Pacific strategy of the Trump administration. Since the RCEP combines regional integration with a new perception of economic ordering, it is the harbinger of what I call a New Regional Economic Order (NREO).

In this essay, "The RCEP in the Third Regionalism" analyzes the geopolitical backdrop of the RCEP by detailing the current wave of regionalism and the Global South's

---

[1] Regional Comprehensive Economic Partnership, http://asean.org/?static_post=rcep-regional-comprehensive-economic-partnership.

[2] Baker McKenzie, "ASEAN Connections: What Is Shaping Business Strategy in the Region?" (April 2016): 13, https://www.bakermckenzie.com/en/insight/publications/2016/04/asean-connections; PwC, "The Long View: How Will the Global Economic Order Change by 2050?" (2017): 8, https://www.pwc.com/gx/en/world-2050/assets/pwc-world-in-2050-summary-report-feb-2017.pdf.

[3] "Minister Champagne Welcomes Progress on the Comprehensive and Progressive Trans-Pacific Partnership," November 10, 2017, https://www.canada.ca/en/global-affairs/news/2017/11/minister_champagnewelcomesprogressonthecomprehensiveandprogressi.html.

backlash against trade agreements based on the North-mandated neoliberalism. "Trade Policies of Emerging Powers" explains the economic priorities and FTA strategies of China, India and ASEAN to illustrate the converging policies of Asia's emerging powers on the RCEP. "Distinct Features of the RCEP" examines the selected arenas where the RCEP departs from Western-style regionalism and discusses the aspects of the RCEP's institutional design that may serve as the trade-development model for developing nations. "New Dynamics of Asia-Pacific Regionalism" sheds light on the role of the RCEP in expanding and accelerating regionalism in the Doha Round of the World Trade Organization (WTO). Finally, the conclusion offers legal and policy advice for policymakers and trade negotiators.

The RCEP in the Third Regionalism

The RCEP can be seen as part of the third wave of regionalism, which denotes the creation of FTAs within the broader WTO ambit. Such trading blocs are mostly confined to a defined geographic region. The first wave took place in the 1960s but encountered political resistance and did not progress far.[4] In comparison, the second wave, represented by the EU and the North American Free Trade Agreement (NAFTA) in the 1980s and 1990s, was much more successful.[5] Since the 2000s, the third wave, which I call the "Third Regionalism," grew out of the deadlock of the Doha Round and has resulted in a proliferation of bilateral FTAs and megaregionals, such as the RCEP and the CPTPP.[6]

Multilateral and regional trade initiatives have been developed in tandem with the Global South's resistance to the Western notion of neoliberalism. This sentiment can be traced back to the 1955 Bandung Conference in Indonesia, where anticolonial nationalism of Asian African states escalated to the Non-Aligned Movement. In the 1970s, these states joined the Group of 77 in pushing for a New International Economic Order (NIEO) in the United Nations.[7] To argue for a more developmentally friendly global regime, the South demanded trade sovereignty and justified exceptions to principal trade norms largely developed by the North.[8] However, the NIEO movement faded when the Thatcher–Reagan alliance rejected their demands. The rising Washington Consensus, which imposed laissez-faire liberalization on the South, became the dominant trade model.

---

[4]   Jagdish Bhagwati, "Regionalism versus Multilateralism," *World Economy* 15 (1992): 535, 538–39.

[5]   Ibid., 540–42; Jagdish Bhagwati, *Termites in the Trading System: How Preferential Agreements Undermine Free Trade* (Oxford: Oxford University Press, 2008), 31–35.

[6]   Pasha L. Hsieh, "Reassessing the Trade–Development Nexus in International Economic Law: The Paradigm Shift in Asia-Pacific Regionalism," *Northwestern Journal of International Law and Business* 37, no. 3 (2017): 321, 335–36.

[7]   Programme of Action on the Establishment of a New International Economic Order (NIEO), A/RES/S-6/3201, May 1, 1974.

[8]   Antony Anghie, "Legal Aspects of the New International Economic Order," *Humanity* 6, no. 1 (2015): 145, 147–49.

Such neoliberalism prompted the WTO to adopt the single-undertaking modality, a take-it-or-leave-it approach that left the developing nations with marginal regulatory space. Absent bargaining power, the South was compelled under multiple WTO agreements to assume additional commitments that posed serious threats to domestic industries. Classic examples include the farming sector facing the inflow of agricultural imports due to slashed tariffs and the entry of professional firms undermining the business of local counterparts. While remedial measures, such as special and differential treatment provisions, were introduced to help developing countries, those measures have been criticized as insufficient to realize the WTO's development goals. This unequal North–South structure also overshadowed regionalism where developing countries acceded to US and EU demands, including the trade plus obligations on labor and environmental protection in FTAs.

As part of the Third Regionalism, the RCEP (and the NREO it represents) harks back to the development call for a NIEO and can be seen as the current manifestation of that desire now taking concrete shape. Distinct from the NIEO's ideological North–South clashes, the NREO reinforces the Global South's normative vision to rejuvenate South–South FTAs (i.e., agreements concluded between developing countries) that suit their development needs. The challenge to the North's neoliberal proposition became feasible because of the relative decline of Western hegemony, particularly given the rising Asian powers. Thus, with support from China, India and Japan, ASEAN introduced the RCEP framework as the ASEAN-led process in 2011 and issued the Guiding Principles for the pact in 2012.[9] In March 2018, RCEP countries announced the finalization of two chapters on Economic and Technical Cooperation and on Small and Medium Enterprises.[10] They also reiterated their intensifying efforts to conclude this 16-party pact within the year.

Trade Policies of Emerging Powers

The converging policies of Asia's emerging powers buttress the RCEP's standing in the Third Regionalism. China, India and ASEAN collectively contribute to a new paradigm in world trade law by shaping the RCEP's characteristics, which are distinguishable from prevailing Western-style FTAs. By representing the NREO, the RCEP signals the Global South's backlash against rising populist nationalism and poses a geopolitical challenge to the US Indo-Pacific strategy. Contrary to common belief, China has never monopolized RCEP negotiations. In fact, Beijing has been a major beneficiary of the trading system in the post-Mao era and seldom challenged the normality of the "Western" rules that sustain the system. To avoid direct conflicts with Japan in vying for regional leadership, China's stance is to enable ASEAN, Asia's third largest economy, to lead the RCEP.

---

[9] "Guiding Principles and Objectives for Negotiating the RCEP" (2012), https://asean.org/storage/2012/05/RCEP-Guiding-Principles-public-copy.pdf.

[10] Joint Media Statement, The Fourth RCEP Intersessional Ministerial Meeting (2018): 1.

Nevertheless, as the largest party that accounts for one-third of the RCEP's GDP, this mega-agreement will enhance China's right of discourse in global rulemaking. The Obama-backed Trans-Pacific Partnership (TPP) once deterred China's strategic goal. Ironically, Trump's withdrawal from the TPP in 2017 has enabled the Xi Jinping government to fill the power vacuum in the Asia-Pacific region. The RCEP complements Beijing's One Belt, One Road initiative, which facilitates the export of Chinese capital, labor and production.

The RCEP similarly supports India's efforts to be recognized as a rising power in the international economic order. To further integrate the country into Asia's supply chain, Prime Minister Narendra Modi's Act East policy adopted a more action-based approach than its preceding Look East policy. On the development ground, New Delhi adopted a two-pronged approach to the RCEP. The government aims to facilitate the provision of outbound professional services while resisting the import of agricultural products and TPP-level intellectual property standards.

For the 10-country ASEAN, its ASEAN Economic Community Blueprint 2025 places the RCEP as the top priority. Under the concept of ASEAN centrality, the RCEP strengthens the bloc's hub status and integrates its bilateral FTAs with six RCEP members. In addition, ASEAN agreements have consistently provided preferential treatment to its least developed country (LDC) members. By including the ASEAN mechanism that balances trade and development, the RCEP will serve as a model for the Global South.

Distinct Features of the RCEP

Seven Asia-Pacific countries are parties to both the RCEP and the CPTPP, whereas China, Korea and India have acceded only to the former. The CPTPP was primarily based on the 30 chapters of the TPP that 12 countries, including the United States, concluded in 2016. Agreed upon by the remaining parties in March 2018, the CPTPP amended and suspended 22 provisions of the TPP, which was heavily influenced by US FTAs.[11] The differences between the RCEP and the CPTPP illustrate the RCEP's departure from the dominant neoliberal approach.

First, unlike the CPTPP and the US and EU FTAs, the RCEP does not include a chapter on state-owned enterprises (SOEs), and labor and environmental protection.[12] The omission of SOE provisions, which contrasts with the CPTPP, which seeks to make SOEs behave like commercial market actors, signals that the RCEP will not impose a narrow market-economy approach to development policy. This exclusion particularly favors China, which has relied on SOEs to drive its economic growth. SOEs also serve the policy goal of developing nations to maintain employment and social stability. In the case of India, potential layoffs following SOE reforms will directly contravene the

---

[11] Comprehensive and Progressive Agreement for Trans-Pacific Partnership (2018), Article 2 and Annex.

[12] Outline of the RCEP Agreement (as of November 2017), Joint Leaders' Statement on the Negotiations for the RCEP (2017): 2–3.

government's goal of job creation. Thailand and Myanmar present different types of considerations. The military exerts a dominant influence in these countries. Placing ex-military officials as executives in SOEs ironically prevents them from causing political obstacles to economic reforms. Tellingly, the exclusion of labor and environment chapters also indicates the Global South's normative vision that avoids the trade-plus provisions the North often mandated. Moreover, the agreement's simpler structure avoids delaying negotiations and minimizes Western influences in domestic policy.[13]

Second, the RCEP's goods and services commitments will demonstrate its evolutionary approach, which recognizes different levels of development among members that range from Australia to Myanmar. Different from a single undertaking deal like the CPTPP and most FTAs, the RCEP will provide a framework under which the agreed agenda stipulates various stages of liberalization for different countries. For instance, consistent with ASEAN agreements but rare in Western-style FTAs, the RCEP will accord lengthier transition periods for tariff eliminations to Cambodia, Laos, Myanmar and Vietnam.[14] To alleviate the impact on the infant services industry in developing nations, the RCEP will also adopt successive packages of services commitments that accomplish intended liberalization incrementally.[15] The extensive special and differential treatment provisions highlight the RCEP's role in development.

Third, labor mobility is critical to the Global South because of remittances and skill transfer. Yet, due to the perception that it creates a back door for immigration, the WTO and the United States, subsequent to its FTAs with Singapore and Chile, made little progress in facilitating such mobility. Similar immigration concerns arguably prompted Brexit. To allow countries to retain regulatory space, the RCEP will follow ASEAN's model that confines labor mobility to skilled labor, which is narrower than the EU notion of free movement of labor.

Both the CPTPP and the RCEP have provisions on the movement of natural persons. However, adopting ASEAN's mutual-recognition arrangements will energize the RCEP more than CPTPP in facilitating professional services. The CPTPP's soft-law scheme only encourages relevant bodies to enter into recognition arrangements. In comparison, the ASEAN mutual-recognition arrangements cover eight professional services, such as architectural, engineering and medical services. ASEAN's most recent mutual-recognition arrangement on tourism professionals is particularly distinctive, as it is a rare scheme that facilitates unregulated services absent international standards for the industry. This scheme can have a great development impact because tourism services empirically enable up to 25 percent of tourism expenditures to reach the poor in LDCs.[16]

---

[13] Mari Pangestu and David Nellor, "RCEP Is More Than TPP-Lite," *Nikkei Asian Review*, February 10, 2017, https://asia.nikkei.com/Politics/RCEP-is-more-than-TPP-lite.

[14] Shujiro Urata, "Constructing and Multilateralizing the Regional Comprehensive Economic Partnership: An Asian Perspective" (working paper, no. 449; Mandaluyoung City, Philippines: Asian Development Bank Institute, 2013): 14–15.

[15] Hsieh, "Reassessing the Trade–Development Nexus in International Economic Law," 349–50.

[16] Jonathan Mitchell, "An Unconventional but Essential Marriage: Pro-Poor Tourism and the Mainstream Industry," *Private Sector and Development*, no. 7 (2010): 5.

Lastly, the investor-state dispute settlement (ISDS) mechanism has been an acutely contested topic in trade politics. ISDS entitles foreign investors to bring complaints against host governments before international panels. ISDS is criticized for transferring sovereignty to multilateral corporations and creating a regulatory chill that deters authorities from implementing public policy. Considering India's and Indonesia's resistance to ISDS, the RCEP is unlikely to exceed the level of ASEAN FTAs, which are based on the US Model Bilateral Investment Treaty, which incorporates more arbitration procedures than previous investment agreements.[17] Importantly, the *Philip Morris v. Australia* case, in which the tobacco company challenged Canberra's plain cigarette packaging legislation, created public concern and resulted in the tobacco carve-out clause of the TPP's ISDS provisions.

The CPTPP scales back the scope of ISDS by disallowing investors to sue the host government on the basis of the investment agreement and by suspending the minimum standard of treatment pertinent to financial services. Moreover, individual countries, such as New Zealand, signed side letters with counterparts to either exclude ISDS entirely or condition arbitration on governmental approvals.[18] As for EU FTAs, Brussels has adopted a new policy to replace ISDS with an investment court system, which has been incorporated in bilateral agreements with Canada, Vietnam and Singapore. The EU system creates a permanent tribunal and provides an appellate mechanism for investor-state disputes. Nonetheless, neither ASEAN nor the RCEP will adopt the EU model. These developments will shape the RCEP design, which may deviate from Western-style FTAs.

New Dynamics of Asia-Pacific Regionalism

Similar to the CPTPP, the emerging RCEP offers a new paradigm in the Third Regionalism and world trade law. Parallel to the WTO, multiple trade and investment agreements exist between the same countries. For instance, Singapore's trade relations with China will be governed by their bilateral FTA, the ASEAN–China FTA and the RCEP. Both the CPTPP and the RCEP will coexist with internal agreements rather than replace them. Exporters' choice among FTAs with different rules of origin that entitle preferential treatment will increase business costs and undermine trade liberalization.

On the positive side, the RCEP will consolidate ASEAN's six FTAs and construct the Free Trade Agreement of the Asia-Pacific (FTAAP). This process of expanding regionalism reinforces the normative vision of the Global South and the NREO that the RCEP represents. Presently, the Asia-Pacific Economic Cooperation (APEC) includes 12 parties to the RCEP. APEC's Bogor Goals aim to accomplish regional trade and investment

---

[17] See generally Amokura Kawharu and Luck Nottage, "Models for Investment Treaties in the Asian Region: An Underview," *Legal Studies Research Paper*, no. 16/87 (2016): 33–34.

[18] "CPTPP: The Five Countries That Won't Sue NZ, According to the Government," March 9, 2018, https://www.newshub.co.nz/home/politics/2018/03/cptpp-the-five-countries-that-won-t-sue-nz-according-to-the-government.html.

liberalization by 2020. In 2004, the APEC Business Advisory Council introduced the FTAAP, which includes 21 APEC economies. The 2010 APEC Leaders' Declaration identified ASEAN+3, ASEAN+6 and the TPP as pathways to the FTAAP. Given the existing literature's primary focus on the TPP, I offer an analysis on the RCEP as a feasible pathway to the FTAAP.

Amid the US–China rivalry, the RCEP first appeared in the Beijing Roadmap, in which APEC declared that the possible pathways to the FTAAP encompass the TPP and the RCEP.[19] Beijing argued vigorously for the FTAAP when it hosted the APEC meetings in 2014. The Obama administration opposed the Chinese proposal because it could have detracted from the TPP, thereby damaging the pivot-to-Asia strategy.[20] A compromise was reached to enable Beijing to conduct APEC's Collective Strategic Study on revitalizing the FTAAP. In 2016, APEC leaders' endorsement of China's study, which emphasizes the RCEP's impact on the global economy, buttressed the status of the RCEP.

Trump's withdrawal from the TPP substantially reduced its share of global GDP from 38.2 percent to 13.5 percent.[21] The TPP's original provision makes it difficult for the remaining parties to continue the deal. The absence of the United States is detrimental, as the TPP's entry into force depends on the approval of members that account for 85 percent of the combined GDP of the original signatories. Under the leadership of Japan and Australia, the CPTPP remedied this obstacle by altering the requirement to six, or 50 percent, of the number of participating countries.

In terms of Asia-Pacific regionalism, the open accession clauses of the CPTPP and the RCEP are also noteworthy. The CPTPP is open to "any State or separate customs territory" after it becomes effective. In comparison, the RCEP allows "any ASEAN FTA partner" or "any other external economic partners" to accede to the pact. Neither agreement provides detailed conditions and procedures for accession. Markedly, the new ASEAN–Hong Kong FTA made China's subsovereign region a potential RCEP member. Chile and Peru, both CPTPP and APEC members, are considering joining the RCEP. Their accession will enable the RCEP to be a TPP alternative and accelerate APEC's FTAAP goal.

Conclusion and Suggestions

As the world's largest FTA, the RCEP ushers regionalism into a new era and contributes to the shaping of world trade law. It not only challenges the existing neoliberal FTA approach but also represents the Global South's normative desire to request development

---

[19] The 2014 Leaders Declaration: The Beijing Roadmap for APEC's Contribution to the Realization of the FTAAP, Annex A.

[20] Patrick Low, "Beijing Must Take a Different Route with the US to Realise FTAAP Goals," *South China Morning Post*, November 13, 2014, http://www.scmp.com/business/economy/article/1637967/beijing-must-take-different-route-us-realise-ftaap-goals.

[21] Yasu Ota, "TPP 11: How Asia Took the Lead in Free Trade," *Nikkei Asian Review*, March 7, 2018, https://asia.nikkei.com/Spotlight/Cover-Story/TPP-11-How-Asia-took-the-lead-in-free-trade.

needs. The converging policies of China, India and ASEAN on the RCEP have reinvigorated the structure and negotiations of the 16-party agreement. The comparison between the RCEP and the CPTPP illustrates how the former departs from Western-style regionalism and may proffer a model for developing nations. Furthermore, the RCEP will help accelerate the APEC goal of establishing the FTAAP, which will in turn energize Doha Round negotiations.

To ensure the RCEP's legal and geopolitical significance, I provide the following suggestions for fortifying the trade-development nexus. First, the RCEP provides a new momentum for Asia-Pacific economic integration. Currently, China lacks FTAs with Japan and India. The RCEP will fill the FTA gap between these nations and solidify the regional supply chain. Nonetheless, multilayered agreements may hinder the effectiveness of FTAs because of the trade fragmentation problem commonly known as the "noodle bowl syndrome." I recommend that the governments remedy the low utilization of agreements by traders. The usage rate of NAFTA exceeds 60 percent, but the utilization rate of Asian FTAs is only 28 percent.[22] The usage of ASEAN agreements, such as 2.3 percent of the ASEAN–Japan FTA for importers, is strikingly low.[23] The RCEP provides a timely opportunity to align the diverse rules of origin to increase the business sense of FTAs. The efforts of the authorities to enable small and medium enterprises to utilize FTA preferential treatment in a cost-effective manner could strengthen the RCEP's development impact.

Second, the RCEP's incorporation of appropriate forms of flexibility reinforces ASEAN's implementation of the Doha Development Agenda and the UN Sustainable Development Goals. RCEP negotiators are advised to consider the ASEAN Minus X formula, which crystallized special and differential treatment provisions by permitting flexible participation. As ASEAN's services liberalization illustrates, two or more members could liberalize selected sectors and allow other members to participate at a later stage. To eliminate the free rider problem, the concessions are conferred only on a reciprocal basis. However, this formula could result in fragmented commitments at divergent speeds. A legal loophole may emerge when a country initially agrees to its commitments but later decides to opt out of such commitments because they are too difficult to implement. The RCEP's clarification of ASEAN's flexibility rules will offer a model for the Global South.

Finally, a sound administrative structure is critical for monitoring and enforcing FTAs. The CPTPP provisions that create the Committee on Development and the Commission comprising government representatives failed to consider the practical significance of an impartial, permanent secretariat. Hence, I propose that the ASEAN Secretariat provide

---

[22] Jaime de Melo, *Developing Countries in the World Economy* (Singapore: World Scientific Publishing Company, 2015), 280; Masahiro Kawai and Ganeshan Wignaraja, "Main Findings and Policy Implications," in *Asia's Free Trade Agreements: How Is Business Responding?*, ed. Masahiro Kawai and Ganeshan Wignaraja (Cheltenham, UK: Edward Elgar, 2011), 33, 34.

[23] Lili Yan Ing, Shujiro Urata and Yoshifumi Fukunaga, "How Do Exports and Imports Affect the Use of Free Trade Agreements? Firm-Level Survey Evidence from Southeast Asia," in *The Use of FTAs in ASEAN: Survey-Based Analysis* (South Jakarta: Economic Research Institute for ASEAN and East Asia, 2015), 1, 7.

institutional support for the RCEP and function as the contact point for the global partnership with the WTO and UN agencies. For development purposes, the institutional
memory of the ASEAN Secretariat in enforcing the Initiative for ASEAN Integration
that assists LDCs is indispensable. The RCEP could streamline intra-ASEAN initiatives
with external technical assistance projects. The consolidation of the funding basis and
the capacity building for the Secretariat will further augment the trade-development
linkage. In sum, these suggestions are important to the RCEP's indispensable position in
regional integration and world trade law.

Chapter Ten

BEYOND NORMAL TRADE LAW?

Robert Wai

What is normal trade law? The completion of the Uruguay Round in 1994 and the establishment of the World Trade Organization (WTO) seemed to mark the achievement of normal trade law, both in the sense of normalizing regulation of international trade relations by legal norms and institutions and in the sense of a normal content of trade law involving significant international convergence rather than sovereign diversity. Both of these senses of normal trade law now seem to be under pressure. The stalemate at the WTO, the turn to preferential agreements and the more recent return of belligerent sovereign unilateralism all suggest the need to interrogate again the legal context in which global trade and investment is embedded. Going forward, trade law may need to emphasize less convergent substantive concepts such as exceptions, differential treatment, interface and variable geometry. But this may also be the moment to rethink whether normal trade law involves a return to a more open role for international politics (including negotiation, threats and conflict), as well as a normal role for law better understood through the frames of transnational law and legal pluralism.

The Concept of Normal Trade

Defining normal trade in international economic relations was clearly a contested and negotiated task during the era of the General Agreement on Tariffs and Trade (GATT), with relatively thin international-level trade regulation combined with plural varieties of domestic market regulation, including in socialist states. The contested nature of normal trade was strikingly exemplified by US–China trade relations before 2000, which were significantly framed around the annual political maneuvering to grant the presidential waiver that would allow for the formal status of normal trade relations with China under US trade law. Normal trade relations involved the continuation of the most-favored-nation (MFN) treatment already extended by the United States to most of its trading partners, including all of the WTO–GATT membership. A major change in the character of the trade relationship between two distinct national economies therefore was marked when Congress passed legislation to grant China permanent normal trade relations (PNTR) in anticipation of the accession of China to the WTO in 2001. Similarly, Russia gained PNTR in 2012. With these changes in the United States and in the extension of WTO membership to include almost the entire world of major trading states, trade relations were now governed by a similar set of substantive provisions, centered especially around the content of the Uruguay Round agreements. Most favored became normal; less than most favored, exceptional.

What became permanently normal with respect to China–US trade also reflected a more general turn associated with the completion of the Uruguay Round and the establishment of the WTO to a normal role for law in international trade relations. Normal international trade relations seemed to include an augmented role for law, in particular, for the public international law and institutions associated with trade treaties. The scale of the commitments in the Uruguay Round agreements, the strengthened institutional features associated with the establishment of the WTO and the expanded scope of the WTO membership to include the most significant international trading states (particularly the accession of China and Russia) could be argued to have inaugurated a truly legalized set of world trade relations.

Viewed from 2018, the new normal trade law seems to be much less permanent in content and form. The content is now open to a critical contest in a variety of ways. And consequently, the attendant role and form of law in trade relations may vary. As in the relations between the United States and China, significant differences on substantive content may mean that legal agreements coexist with continuous negotiations and renegotiations through international politics.

Law's Role in Substantive Construction of the Normal Economy

Before turning to the issues related to the normal form and role of law in trade relations, it is important to see how the substantive content of normal trade relations has significantly moved away from any policy consensus on normal market regulation that emerged during the time of the Uruguay Round.

The turn toward legalized international trade relations came with more substantive constraints on sovereign autonomy with respect to the permitted range of institutional configurations (including sovereign laws and regulations from border measures, such as tariffs and quotas, to domestic measures, such as tax statutes, product regulations and intellectual property [IP] protections), and hence a new normal range for possible alternatives in national institutional forms for economic production, regulation and distribution. This was generally consonant with, and maybe dependent on, the contemporary Washington Consensus about the best forms of economic governance.

Defining market normalcy through international trade law

In groundbreaking articles from the 1980s, Daniel Tarullo traced back the fundamental relation of trade laws to the definition of the normal economy.[1] For Tarullo, US and

---

[1] Daniel Tarullo, "Beyond Normalcy in the Regulation of International Trade," *Harvard Law Review* 100 (1987): 546; Daniel Tarullo, "Logic, Myth and the International Economic Order," *Harvard International Law Journal* 26 (1985): 533.

GATT trade remedy law illustrated the necessity of defining the subsidy against which countervailing duties would be imposed. Since then, 30 years of experience, including during the WTO era, have seemingly not changed scholarly assessment that "there is no natural, self-evident, objectively determinable baseline against which to identify and evaluate subsidies."[2] Efforts to define subsidies—for example, through porous or arbitrary concepts like specificity or the use of market comparators—quite transparently involve fundamentally contentious line drawing with respect to what is a normal market and, in particular, the acceptable and unacceptable roles of government in the economy.

With this critical insight about the constructed rather than naturally defined nature of the normal market, the content of the Uruguay Round agreements and preferential trade agreements (PTAs) of the 1990s—with increasing regulation of subsidies but also provisions to protect intellectual property rights (IPRs) and foreign investors, such as NAFTA Chapter 11—seemed to amount to global-level discipline on states to normalize the neoliberal foundations of domestic markets in line with the Washington Consensus.[3]

The resulting impact of international trade law in constraining the policy space for experimentation with a more diverse range of institutional configurations for national economic development and market construction has been critiqued powerfully by many states and also scholars in economics, law and other fields since the WTO moment.[4] Such critique has clearly affected beliefs about the normal content of trade law. The current understanding of normal trade may be changing with the revived emphasis on trade theories other than liberal free trade theory based on comparative advantage, including forms that were ascendant in the pre-WTO era of the GATT, such as theories of dependency, strategic trade[5] or competitive advantage.[6]

Normal trade law and the rise of the normal exception

Part of why the WTO seemed to mark the arrival of a new centrality of law in trade relations was that it seemed to deliver a central feature of legalization: the comprehensive legal regulation of a social field under general rules of general application with limited exceptions. The Uruguay Round agreements deepened general rules such as quota prohibition, tariff bindings and nondiscrimination with respect to domestic regulation, and reduced the scope of subjects of trade (such as textiles and clothing, agriculture, subsidies, services and IP) that were largely excluded from the GATT-era trade regime.

In contrast to that aspiration, the WTO experience since 1995, including in dispute settlement, has arguably demonstrated that the content of normal trade relations is defined as much by the exceptions as by the general rules. The meditations on the

---

[2] Andrew Lang, "Governing 'As If': Global Subsidies Regulation and the Benchmark Problem," *Current Legal Problems* 67 (2014): 135–68 (147).

[3] E.g., most recently, Quinn Slobodian, *Globalists: The End of Empire and the Birth of Neoliberalism* (Cambridge, MA: Harvard University Press, 2018).

[4] E.g., Dani Rodrik, *Straight Talk on Trade* (Princeton, NJ: Princeton University Press, 2018).

[5] E.g., Paul Krugman, *Rethinking Trade Policy* (Cambridge, MA: MIT Press, 1990).

[6] E.g., Michael Porter, *The Competitive Advantage of Nations* (New York: Free Press, 1990).

centrality of the state of exception as articulated by Carl Schmitt and Giorgio Agamben have been pronounced in international law, especially since 9/11.[7] The WTO ambition for general rules and limited exceptions now appears to be exceptional rather than normal.

That the WTO moment involved a thin legalization over an unresolved substantive dissensus was evident almost immediately in WTO dispute settlement in cases involving the scope of the exceptions for various forms of social regulation, such as Article XX of the GATT 1994, Article XIV of the GATS (General Agreement on Trade in Services) and Articles 7, 8, 30 and 31 of the TRIPS (Trade-Related Aspects of Intellectual Property Rights). The WTO's increasing willingness to allow member states to justify trade-restricting regulation as having legitimate social policy purposes is an important part of the move to posit a "trade law after neoliberalism," even within the trade institutions.[8] The *US–Shrimp* cases, the *EC–Asbestos* sequence and the access-to-essential-medicines struggles all demonstrate that much of the terrain of normal law would be fought in the realm (and, in turn, the scope) of the exceptions. In this jurisprudence, Andrew Lang traces some of the technical forms through which policy dissensus about proper levels of regulation can be recognized through a more chastened approach at the WTO Dispute Settlement Body (DSB) involving techniques such as balancing analysis, greater and more prominent use of deference to national regulators and proceduralization in the sense of more oversight on procedural aspects of national regulations rather than on their substantive content.

The role of exceptions has perhaps been most evident in the continued and increased significance of realms of trade relations that overlap with national security. That recent US steel and aluminum tariffs were framed within domestic legislation oriented toward national security rather than safeguards is a sharp reminder of a wide domain of sovereign governmental policy with trade implications that remains almost exclusively outside of international trade law. Expansive treaty exceptions such as GATT Article XXI align with a more generally political and diplomatic consensus not to bring such disputes within the legalized domain of, for example, DSB dispute settlement. The significant trade restrictions that resulted from the post-9/11 security situation also were largely left to the domain of diplomacy, not to the world of the trade treaties. When such a large exception applies in a legal regime, the regime must see that the de facto trade disciplines (or regulatory pressures) sit largely without that law.

With the expanded prominence of exceptions, the Uruguay Round consensus appears in retrospect to be rife with gaps, contradictions and ambiguities. For example, the negotiations over new topics of the Uruguay Round clearly evidenced policy dissensus about key areas of increasing international economic significance, such as IP, investment and services. The Uruguay Round agreements used various strategies to balance the underlying dissensus, such as an agreement to leave the topic of investment

---

[7]   E.g., Fleur Johns, "Guantanamo Bay and the Annihilation of the Exception," *European Journal of International Law* 16, no. 4 (2005): 613.

[8]   Andrew Lang, *World Trade Law After Neoliberalism* (Oxford: Oxford University Press, 2011), chap. 10, 313–53, especially 320–30.

measures to other contexts, including bilateral investment treaties (BITs). With respect to services, the GATS established a normal general framework, but largely a prospective one for the application of key provisions because of the reliance on specific commitments. The simultaneous need to achieve significant domestic reforms to permit full international competition in services, and to recognize that many services sectors involve areas of significant sovereign domestic regulatory concern, left the GATS not only with important exceptions like Article XIV but also with the to-be-negotiated extension of the specific commitments strategy. The significant and controversial provisions of TRIPS, including positive harmonization commitments on important subjects of domestic protection of IP holders' rights, also included important exceptions (such as the compulsory licensing provisions for patents of Article 31) and left many areas of significant concern to technology producers outside of the agreement. This sense that the international trade law contained in existing international trade agreements was incomplete with respect to core areas of trade relations seems to be evidenced by the United States' emphasis on taxation, data exclusivity, privacy restrictions, antipiracy and protection against technology transfer, including in current bilateral disputes with China but also as priorities in earlier PTA negotiations (such as for the Trans-Pacific Partnership (TPP)). Similarly, the competitive successes of China's development model have disclosed for the United States, but also for other WTO members, a significant lack of consensus with respect to the normal permitted range for subsidies and state-owned enterprises.

Trade remedy law as normal trade law

Parallel to and related to the rise of the normal exception, the more central form of normal trade law may be turning out to be trade remedy law. Trade remedy law has always seemed an uncomfortable and troubling "other" to tariff reduction and quota prohibitions, an alternative realm of international trade relations based on managed protectionism.

A significant number of recent high-profile trade disputes are being addressed mainly through trade remedy law. Trade remedy actions have become an important part of the current US administration's international trade policy with competitors and allies, whether China or Canada. They cover a wide array of sectors, from the traditional commodity and industrial sectors (such as softwood lumber and steel) to the leading innovation sectors (such as semiconductors, solar panels and civil aircraft).

While the GATT, the Uruguay Round agreements and various chapters of PTAs clearly address countervail and antidumping, it would be hard to argue that these were intended to be the center of normal trade law. But these regimes may be emerging as the most representative form of contemporary trade law.

The basic approach of permissive but managed protectionism as a response to the diverse sovereign views about the policy problems of subsidies and dumping could be seen as a complex form of transnational law. Permission for sovereign discretion to apply protective duties is tempered by multilateral requirements of both substantive elements (e.g., determination of subsidy or dumping, and determination of injury to domestic industry caused by the subsidy or dumping) and procedural elements. The delicate task of adjudicating complaints at the multilateral level in turn raises the appropriate level of review of domestic determinations in trade remedy that recall the difficult issues of standards of review in administrative law. For all the resulting complexity and uncertainty, this mix of self-help domestic remedies, paired with case-by-case oversight for some substantive and procedural requirements, may in fact become the more typical form of normal trade law at the international level. In some ways, the DSB's approach in some of its later jurisprudence on national regulations under GATT Article III and Article XX, and under the WTO's SPS (Sanitary and Phytosanitary) and TBT (Technical Barriers to Trade) agreements, now resembles the approach to antidumping and countervail with respect to issues of proper standards of deference and procedural oversight.

Normal Trade Law as Interface

A turn to the trade remedy regime and the realm of exceptions as being normal trade law suggests that perhaps normal trade law is returning to what John Jackson, among others, considered as an interface. During the GATT era, Jackson used interface to conceptualize a trade law that sought to manage interactions between domestic orders even where the underlying policies implemented in each order were significantly diverse. Jackson turned to interface in dealing with a set of trade issues that seem to again be far more central to conflicts in current trade relations. For example, his book *The World Trading System* first references interface in a discussion of safeguards and adjustment policies.[9] He turns to the concept again in the chapter on unfair trade, in particular when discussing the approach adopted with respect to dumping. Finally, it plays a prominent role in the chapter about nonmarket economies, although he also generalizes the underlying analysis to disagreements among market societies as to the proper role of state-owned enterprises. Elsewhere, Jackson observes that the concept of international trade law as an interface system in relation to differences of national systems, with respect to differences in national markets and institutions, could also operate with respect to issues such as distribution and human rights, where there clearly remains significant substantive pluralism among sovereign societies.[10]

Viewing the normal role of international trade law as interface seems especially relevant now for trade law. The interface function might make better sense of the stalled WTO negotiations, the many continuing exceptions and the resistance to deeper harmonization. It also provides an approach that international trade law can take with existing or new topics that impinge closely on regulation or distribution concerns, such as in services and internet regulation. The interface concept also expressly accommodates diverse development strategies at the national level. For example, Dani Rodrik has

---

[9] John Jackson, *The World Trading System: Law and Policy of International Economic Relations*, 2nd edition (Cambridge, MA: MIT Press, 1997), 178–79.

[10] John Jackson, *Sovereignty, the WTO, and Changing Fundamentals of International Law* (Cambridge: Cambridge University Press, 2006), 226, 230–33.

recently adopted this frame in advocating that the "purposes of international economic arrangements must be to lay down the traffic rules for managing the interface among national institutions."[11] For Rodrik, interface would provide sufficient international coordination but otherwise promote significant room for autonomy and diversity in the national venues that he considers the best locations for institutional experimentation in a policy environment that should be moving beyond the Washington Consensus.

What specifically would a normal trade law based on interface involve? The passages from Jackson are relatively undeveloped, but the techniques related to interface include practices of subsidiarity and the requirement of national treatment in relation to state-owned enterprises. In the most elaborated discussion, that of trade remedy law, interface involves a recognition of disagreement between trading partners about a policy problem (such as dumping) and both permission for a state to act to protect itself against some aspects of the problem as well as some international-level oversight of the substance and procedure for protection. Some other basic techniques found in the GATT and other trade agreements may fit well with the interface goal, including regulation based on negotiated commitments rather than minimum requirements (e.g., tariff bindings or specific commitments in services) and regulation premised on nondiscrimination rather than harmonization or prohibition. Within the Uruguay Round agreements, therefore, the core would be techniques such as negotiated tariff bindings, nondiscrimination principles or procedural commitments (as found in the GATT) with priority over tighter harmonization instruments, such as the TRIPS agreement or the SPS or TBT agreements.

More generally, the articulation of trade law as interface could foster a broader consideration of the techniques of interaction among normative orders. The legal pluralist observation that plural normative orders coexist in the same temporal and spatial frame invites further consideration of the nature of their interaction. The pluralist notion of interlegality recognizes the possibility that these normative orders can interact in relations of conflict or coordination, and in forms of both hierarchy and heterarchy. Heterarchy is much less emphasized in the legal literature, so much framed by statist legal centralism. But this ignores the many forms of intersystemic relation that need not be hierarchical. I have argued, for example, that private international law significantly relies on the conscious realization of the coexistence of parallel normative systems, in which there is no hierarchical relation but where parallel systems may nonetheless share concerns, including in their particular disputes with ties (whether of persons, subject matter, effects) to more than one normative system.[12] Conflict of law rules, then, are final decisions of institutions supreme within their own normative order, but that often take into account not just the existence but the content of these other normative orders. The application of a foreign law as governing law, a decision to decline jurisdiction or the recognition and

---

[11] Rodrik, *Straight Talk on Trade*, 225.

[12] Robert Wai, "Conflicts and Comity in Transnational Governance: Private International Law as Mechanism and Metaphor for the Relationship among the Plural Orders of Transnational Social Regulation," in *Constitutionalism, Multilevel Trade Governance and Social Regulation*, ed. Christian Joerges and Ernst-Ulrich Petersmann (Oxford: Hart Publishing, 2006), 229–62.

enforcement of a foreign judgment are decisions based not on hierarchical supremacy, but rather on varied transnational policy considerations, including efficiency, fairness and comity.

Normal Trade Law as Less Law or as Transnational Law

What is the role of law if substantive dissensus has increased about the normal form of the underlying domestic economies, notably with respect to the role of the state? As the discussion of interface above suggests, legal form might track substance, and in the trade law context, this might involve a reorientation of the role and form of law in normal trade relations.

Normal trade order without/with less law

One view on normal trade law is that the emphasis on international law and legalism overstates the degree to which trade relations were fully legalized and the extent to which they really need to be.

Scholarship on enforcement in international law that criticizes legal centralism and instead looks to the wider forms of institutions and of cooperation and coordination is of this vein. Joel Trachtman, for example, emphasizes the range of alternative institutional forms for international economic law based on the insights of the new institutional economics, contract theory and game theory.[13] In work developed from the new institutional economics, the potential contribution of state institutions to trust and cooperation is identified, but alternative institutional arrangements are also emphasized, ranging from vertical integration to more horizontal solutions like moral suasion, deposits or hostages, sunk costs, incentives of future business or continued relations.[14]

In the context of international economic relations, the emphasis on institutional solutions, including nonstate solutions, together with awareness of game theory and strategic negotiations, clearly has a relationship to the work of the limits school of international law.[15] The renewed emphasis on hard bargaining, diplomacy and interstate politics associated with the current US administration may be seen as simply a more assertive and express adoption of this perspective that involves a more limited role for formal law in international trade relations. The emphasis on constant negotiations and dealing may not provide much certainty, but some claim that this kind of international trade policy can still achieve sufficiently orderly international trade relations. Whether

---

[13] Joel Trachtman, *The Economic Structure of International Law* (Cambridge, MA: Harvard University Press, 2008).

[14] For a discussion of this literature, see Robert Wai, "Enforcement in the Shadows of Transnational Economic Law," in *The Transformation of Enforcement: European Economic Law in a Global Perspective*, ed. Hans-Wolfgang Micklitz and Andrea Wechsler (Oxford: Hart Publishing, 2016), 15–46.

[15] Jack Goldsmith and Eric Posner, *The Limits of International Law* (New York: Oxford University Press, 2005).

formal legal instruments play more or less of a role is contingent on the distribution of power and interests at play. In this way, international trade relations would be like the ranchers in Shasta County: there can be tolerable order without law.[16]

Normal trade law still as law but as transnational economic law

If normal trade relations include such a variable and contingent role for law, it may be better to discard the notion that there is any normal trade law at all. However, this in turn seems to be a fantasy account of order not in accord with the existence of many legal instruments and significant deployment of various forms of law. Finding the normal role of law in trade may therefore require a broader sense of the legal orders that help structure not just particular legal claims but also the political and economic bargaining of trade relations.

Such an account of normal trade law would need to encompass a broader realm of relevant legal orders than simply public international law. In particular, normal trade law will involve a turn to transnational law and global legal pluralism.

Philip Jessup, of course, is most identified with this move against the centralism of public international law toward a frame of transnational law that includes "all law which regulates actions or events that transcend national frontiers."[17] The forms of transnational law include domestic and international law, public and private law, and different forms of nonstate law and practice. Many examples in Jessup's 1956 lectures relate to cross-border economic relations, and the transnational approach has been influential in the study of the laws of international business transactions.[18]

The move to transnational law is consistent with older traditions of international trade law, where the emphasis was very much away from public international law instruments and toward the plural forms of law relevant to international transactions, including domestic public and private law, but also nonstate forms such as the lex mercatoria. In the move to establish international trade regulation as a distinct area of international law, the origins of the field of international trade in this more plural and transnational setting were deemphasized. Normal trade law should now perhaps be reconceived again as transnational economic law, involving a plural set of state and nonstate orders including but not limited to public international trade law.[19]

Normal trade law would clearly include international trade treaties but only as part of a plural and transnational context that relied on a significant backdrop of transnationalism in economic law. The task would be to foreground all the legal regimes that are relevant to cross-border economic activity. This would include not

---

[16] Robert Ellickson, *Order without Law: How Neighbors Settle Disputes* (Cambridge, MA: Harvard University Press, 1994).

[17] Philip Jessup, *Transnational Law* (New Haven, CT: Yale University Press, 1956), 2.

[18] Detlev Vagts, *Transnational Business Problems* (Mineola, NY: Foundation Press, 1986).

[19] E.g., Wai, "Enforcement in the Shadows of Transnational Economic Law," 17–19; more generally, Terence Halliday and Gregory Shaffer, eds., *Transnational Legal Orders* (New York: Cambridge University Press, 2015).

just international trade and investment treaties but also other substantive areas of public international law (such as the regimes related to carriage of goods or arbitration, or the environment). As important, normal trade law would include private law and nonstate private ordering, such as the lex mercatoria. It would also examine more kinds of national public law, such as tax, privacy or competition law. Normal trade law analyses would consider the full range of relevant transnational law and ask about their significance in tempering the rise/fall of the multilateral or regional/bilateral trade treaties. Chris Brummer's recent work on minilateralism in international financial law demonstrates a similar view, seeing normal regulation in this area as much less dependent on formal international law treaties and multilateral institutions, instead deploying a mix of minilateral alliances, national laws and soft law, as well as political negotiations.[20] Such an account of financial law may be a more realistic account of contemporary trade law as well: the form of the law of international finance may in fact be the form of trade law's future, not vice versa, as might have seemed the case at the WTO moment.

Understanding normal trade law as transnational law would also make more sense of the current emphasis in international trade on the variable geometry of plurilateral and preferential agreements among subsets of trading states.[21] From a transnational law perspective, the existence of a variable blend of multilateral and preferential agreements is hardly a radical change. Periods of significant international trade have occurred when a variety of preferential arrangements existed, such as the mix of imperial preferences and bilateral commercial treaties during the nineteenth century. Obviously, the GATT period was seriously restricted in its coverage of states and subject matter and coexisted with a variety of other forms of trade preferences, including managed trade arrangements such as voluntary export restraint agreements. Most generally, many of the sovereign parties to international treaties themselves reflect variable forms of economic integration, such that the level and form of integration is varied and dynamic, for example, not just within the European Union (EU) but also within federal states such as the United States or Canada.

Finally, a transnational law sense of normal trade law would also recognize that a significant source of de facto legal regulation would be the extraterritorial effects (intended or not) of national laws. For example, competitive conditions in many domestic markets are effectively being constituted by policies and actions under the competition law of foreign jurisdictions. For many foreign consumers, the most relevant forms of market and consumer regulation of technology giants have been occurring through EU laws. Examples include the General Data Protection Regulation (GDPR), fines imposed on Qualcomm and Google related to anticompetitive practices and decisions like the European Court of Justice's *Costeja* ruling on the right to be forgotten. This transnational

---

[20] Chris Brummer, *Minilateralism: How Trade Alliances, Soft Law, and Financial Engineering Are Reforming Economic Statecraft* (New York: Cambridge University Press, 2014).

[21] Thomas Cottier, "The Common Law of International Trade and the Future of the World Trade Organization," *Journal of International Economic Law* 18 (2015): 3–20.

law perspective on normal trade law would not be simply the triumph of domestic uni-lateralism over international law. Instead, national law would operate in conjunction and interaction with international law instruments, as well as with both an awareness of and in combined effect with the domestic laws of other states.

Trade law is still present, just in more than the normal places.

SECTION 2

DEALING WITH MAJOR CHANGES
IN THE WORLD ECONOMY

Chapter Eleven

TRADE, DISTRIBUTION AND DEVELOPMENT UNDER SUPPLY CHAIN CAPITALISM

Dan Danielsen

Despite significant global growth in both trade and foreign investment volumes during the past 40 years, many developing nations and their domestic firms still struggle to realize the development benefits of this economic expansion. Although the Asian Tigers—China, India and a few others—have achieved significant increases in income per capita and reductions in poverty rates, most developing countries remain woefully short of their development goals notwithstanding a major shift in the composition of developing-country exports from resource-based products to manufactured goods and a significant increase in developing-country manufactures as a percentage of total global manufactures.[1] One factor contributing to these disappointing development results is the now dominant organization of global production through disaggregated, geographically disbursed, nonproprietary supply chains governed increasingly by concentrated buyer firms, which I term "supply chain capitalism."

In this essay, I will suggest how the organization of global production into supply chain capitalism limits the bargaining power and innovative capacity of many (if not most) developing states and their domestic firms, as well as their ability to capture an equitable share of the rents from participation in global trade. In addition, I will describe ways in which supply chain capitalism complicates national trade and development policymaking and makes it more difficult for many developing countries to achieve sustainable development benefits from global trade.

In the face of these challenges, standard progressive prescriptions for development through trade seem insufficient: for developing-country firms, focus on innovation and upgrade your position in global supply chains; for national development policymakers, secure sufficient domestic policy space to support your firms and their access to the chains.[2] If the goal is a more equitable global distribution of power and resources,

---

[1]   See Raphael Kaplinsky, *Globalization, Poverty and Inequality* (Cambridge: Polity Press, 2005), 164–70 (and supporting data).

[2]   For examples of the "upgrading" prescription, see, e.g., Gary Gereffi, "International Trade and Industrial Upgrading in the Apparel Commodity Chain," *Journal of International Economics* 48 (1999): 37; Peter Gibbon, "Upgrading Primary Production: A Global Commodity Approach,"

we will need a much richer understanding of the complex of norms and institutional formations that underpin the allocations of power and resources within supply chain capitalism. The traditional tools for national trade policy—tariffs, subsidies, strategic liberalization, industrial policy—and the global trade rules that govern them will be part of the story but not the most significant part. Explicating the key legal and institutional drivers that enable, facilitate, reinforce and sustain supply chain capitalism should bring into focus the significance of numerous legal regimes—national and transnational, public and private—beyond trade law and policy that constrain the bargaining power, policy choices and development outcomes of much of the developing world. Such a shift in focus should also illuminate new legal tools and policy strategies to enable developing countries and firms to gain greater advantage in the global economy.

At the same time, a more informed and clear-eyed analysis of the challenges and opportunities for achieving sustainable and equitable growth through supply chain capitalism may lead progressive trade theorists and development policymakers to question whether competitive participation in global markets remains a promising (or even viable) pathway to development for many countries. Perhaps more plausibly, it may prompt trade theorists and development policymakers to consider the possibility that the greatest challenge to equitable distribution and global prosperity is not the trade effects of protectionism by nation-states but the unacknowledged power of dominant firms governing global commerce through their supply chains.

Supply Chain Capitalism—An Introduction

Since the 1980s, a global shift has taken place from the transnational corporate model of vertically integrated networks of subsidiaries providing supply, production and distribution functions for geographically proximate markets to the disaggregated, geographically disbursed, nonproprietary and contractually coordinated relational chain structures that characterize supply chain capitalism.[3] One important effect of this shift has been an increasing concentration of power over the coordination and governance of supply

---

World Development 29, no. 2 (2001): 345; Kaplinsky, *Globalization, Poverty and Inequality*, 107–21. For examples of the "policy space" prescription, see, e.g., Dani Rodrik, "The Global Governance of Trade as if Development Really Mattered," in *One Economics, Many Recipes: Globalization, Institutions and Economic Growth* (Princeton, NJ: Princeton University Press, 2007), 213–36; Joseph E. Stiglitz and Andrew Charlton, *Fair Trade for All: How Trade Can Promote Development* (Oxford: Oxford University Press, 2005), 86–105; The Barcelona Development Agenda, September 24–25, 2004, http://www.bcn.cat/forum2004/english/desenvolupament.htm.

[3] See, e.g., Gary Gereffi, "Global Value Chains in a Post-Washington Consensus World," *Review of International Political Economy* 21, no. 1 (2014): 9; Robert C. Feenstra, "Integration of Trade and Disintegration of Production in the Global Economy," *Journal of Economic Perspectives* 12, no. 4 (1998): 31; Kaplinsky, *Globalization, Poverty and Inequality*, 120–59; *UN Conference on Trade and Development World Investment Report 2013: Global Value Chains: Investment for Trade and Development*, http://unctad.org/en/PublicationsLibrary/wir2013_en.pdf (global value chains account for 80 percent of global trade).

chains in large buyer firms. This can be observed in both traditional buyer-driven chains (such as the ready-made garment sector, furniture and toys) and producer-driven chains (such as electronics, autos and smartphones).[4] As a consequence, the power of buyer firms over commercial terms and the allocation of rents across their supply chains has also increased.

From a business perspective, the need for centralized coordination and governance of global supply chains seems to arise in large part from their disaggregated character. To ensure adequate efficiency gains and total returns to justify the costs and risks of these structures, supply chains need to be managed carefully, coordinated tightly and, to the maximum extent possible, structured to minimize potential disruption of chain operations by individual suppliers, groups of suppliers, geographically concentrated suppliers and the regulatory or policy interventions of national governments. The gains from disintegration, disaggregation and geographic dispersion of production need to exceed the very high transaction and agency costs these structures entail. In these circumstances, large buyer firms are best positioned to assume these chain coordination and governance functions, organizing their global corporate structures and the geography and structure of their supply chains to maximize chain efficiency, resilience and ultimately their own global returns.

Moreover, the distributed geographic scope of global supply chains, the interdependence of participants in chain structures and the dependence of suppliers and intermediaries on chain structures for access to markets give large buyer firms extraordinary bargaining advantages over firms and states competing for their favor. As a result, buyer firm directives have a significant impact on the business practices and behavior of entities across the chain.

Such directives can be conveyed through legal techniques or practices designed to direct the activities of chain suppliers and intermediaries such as supply contracts; corporate codes of conduct; policies regarding subcontracting by suppliers or intermediaries; punitive commercial measures that punish noncompliant firms; multisourcing practices that leverage competitive pressure to induce supplier compliance; limitations on supplier sourcing of production inputs; supplier monitoring, reporting, auditing and due diligence requirements; and many others. In addition to these more direct modes of chain management, buyer firms also shape chain governance through the design and structure of their own business operations. Some common examples include buyer firm strategies to maintain global proprietary control over innovation, intellectual property and brand assets through complex ownership and licensing structures, as well as inventory control and production management systems that minimize technology transfer to suppliers, or the use of complex corporate structuring to distribute buyer firm business

---

[4]   See, e.g., Kaplinsky, *Globalization, Poverty and Inequality*, 122–59, 170–78; Gereffi, "Global Value Chains," 12–17; Feenstra, "Integration of Trade and Disintegration of Production," 35–41; Mihir A. Desai, "Why Apple Is the Future of Capitalism," *New York Times*, August 6, 2018, https://www.nytimes.com/2018/08/06/opinion/apple-trillion-market-cap.html (describing the virtues of Apple's financial model leveraging its disaggregated and geographically dispersed global supply chain).

functions and the recognition of revenues and profits geographically to minimize global tax liability and maximize global returns.[5]

Whether implemented through downstream control mechanisms or strategic structuring of their own business operations, the governance activities of buyer firms impact not only the business practices, opportunities and performance of participants in their own supply chains but also the business practices and competitive environment for other buyer firms and their suppliers in the same business sector. As a result, both local firms and national development policymakers find their ability to increase the participation or performance of domestic firms in a business sector or the development effects of sector participation on the domestic economy shaped and constrained by the global effects of the commercial and governance practices of the leading buyer firms in that business sector. Once we move beyond a single chain or sector to consider the ubiquity of relational chain production structures across business sectors globally, the significance of buyer firm governance of supply chain structures and its potentially constraining effects on development policymaking and outcomes increases.

Supply Chain Capitalism and Key Challenges It Poses for Developing Countries and Firms

Supply chain capitalism constrains the policy autonomy of developing states, the innovative potential of developing-country firms and the bargaining power of each over rents from participation in chain structures in a variety of ways.

The power of buyer firms over chain operations and governance under supply chain capitalism shapes the strategic behavior of many developing countries and their domestic firms. This effect can be seen in an example from a business sector in which many developing countries are engaged: the ready-made garment sector. For domestic firms selling to global apparel brands concerned with reputational risk, national policy aimed at improving workplace safety and government oversight of labor conditions in garment factories may be important to retaining the business from those global brands. By contrast, for domestic firms selling to less reputation-oriented global brands or to buyer firms supplying low-price markets, a policy change imposing additional safety regulations or government oversight of labor conditions would likely increase production and compliance costs, resulting in tighter margins for domestic suppliers or the loss of business if supplier firms cannot absorb these additional costs and buyer firms seek alternative sources of supply rather than pay higher prices.

Whatever the national government opts to do with respect to safety and labor standards in the ready-made garment sector, each domestic supplier firm (especially firms selling to

---

5   For examples of the latter, see Jim Tankersley, "Tax Havens Blunt Impact of Corporate Tax Cuts, Economists Say," *New York Times*, June 10, 2018, https://www.nytimes.com/2018/06/10/business/corporate-tax-cut.html; Thomas R. Torslov, Ludwig S. Wier and Gabriel Zucman, "The Missing Profits of Nations" (working paper no. 2470, National Bureau of Economic Research, Cambridge, MA, 2018), http://www.nber.org/papers/w24701.

both types of buyer chains) will have to consider the needs and demands of the buyer chain(s) in which it believes it can most effectively compete and adapt its business practices accordingly (including its practices with respect to workplace safety and labor conditions). Similarly, national policymakers will need to anticipate the behavior of domestic suppliers in relation to the demands of the chains as well as the reactions of buyer firms, other developing countries and competing foreign supplier firms in order to assess what the development impact of one or another policy choice might be. Hence, both the national policy calculation and the safety and labor practices of supplier firms are determined with a view to their compatibility with the demands, requirements and sourcing alternatives of the global supply chains on which both the supplier firms and the domestic industry depend to reach global markets. In this way, global supply chains governed by foreign buyer firms may play a more significant role in establishing the business practices and competitive position of domestic supplier firms and the comparative advantage of the developing state in the global garment industry as a whole than the policy choices of domestic governments. The magnitude of this dynamic is compounded and the uncertainty increased for development policymakers and firms seeking to make strategic policy calculations in relation to multiple global supply chains in multiple export sectors.

This set of constraints implies an additional one: the power of developing states to shape the relative competitiveness and returns of domestic firms in global supply chains may be limited by a myriad of rules and business practices over which the developing state has no control. As we have seen in the ready-made garment industry, the behavior, competitiveness and business practices of supplier firms are shaped by numerous foreign legal and private ordering regimes, including supply contracts, corporate law in the buyer firms' home states, regulation or codes of conduct governing buyer firms, private industry standards, intellectual property rules, tax codes, loan agreements with foreign banks and many others. As a result, foreign rules and practices may be as or more significant than domestic rules and policies in determining the bargaining power and competitiveness of developing-country firms in global supply chains.

In addition, the focus of development policy has shifted under supply chain capitalism from establishing forward and backward linkages among domestic firms within a developing state to facilitating export-led growth through increasing linkages between domestic firms and global supply chains. This has caused developing-country suppliers to become increasingly dependent on global chains for access to markets, and developing countries to become increasingly dependent on participation by domestic firms in global chains for domestic revenue and development resources. Fierce and growing competition between suppliers of manufactures from developing countries has increased the power of buyer firms in global chains with respect to price and other commercial terms as evidenced in part by steady declines in both prices and barter terms of trade for developing-country manufactured exports.[6] To the extent developing states are reticent to pursue development policies aimed at improving wages or working conditions for

---

[6] See Kaplinsky, *Globalization, Poverty and Inequality*, 162–90.

workers or increasing domestic firm rents out of fear of reducing domestic firm competitiveness relative to supplier firms from other developing countries, buyer firm power would seem to be enhanced further.

In lieu of or in addition to top-down regulatory interventions that might put domestic firm competitiveness at risk, policymakers in developing countries could adopt incentive-based policy strategies such as tax forbearance or abatement, export zones or other infrastructure investment, or firm- or industry-specific subsidies aimed at increasing the attractiveness of domestic firms to global chains. For development policymakers, calculating the expected returns on these investments either for domestic firms or for national development will be both difficult and speculative because the dynamic and intense competitive conditions and bargaining power asymmetries that put downward pressure on supplier pricing will likely similarly limit the realization of returns on such incentive investments. Moreover, in order for this type of incentive investment to have the desired effect of making domestic firms or their geographic location more attractive to global buyer firms, the benefits of such investments would need to be shared beyond the domestic context with at least buyer firms and perhaps more broadly with other participants in their supply chains. As a consequence, economic returns on these types of incentive investments would also likely be dispersed across the chains and difficult to capture by developing countries and their domestic firms.[7]

An additional adverse effect of supply chain capitalism is its impact on the ability of developing countries or their domestic supplier firms to increase rent capture from participation in supply chains through innovation. The result may be a new global division of labor in innovation that seems related to but different from the concentration of manufacturing exports in the Global North and resource-based exports in the Global South that characterized global production and trade between 1945 and the 1980s. In this emerging division of labor, innovation generating high Schumpeterian rents (such as design, marketing, branding, governance, intellectual property, technology) is increasingly concentrated in buyer firms once located in the developed world and now strategically located globally for intellectual property management, tax avoidance and other purposes aimed at maximizing global returns from chain operations. By contrast, innovation by supplier firms located in poor and middle-income countries often seems to take the form of improvements in production processes, labor efficiency or worker skills. While such innovation could lead to increased supplier prices or higher wages, there are good reasons to think it might not. The fierce competition among developing-country suppliers in many business sectors will likely require supplier firms to make these innovations to gain access to or remain competitive in global supply chains with gains likely captured by buyer firms or shared across global chains.

---

[7] My image here is that these investments would have the character of a "public good" vis-à-vis the chain as a whole while contributing only incrementally to the competitive position of domestic supplier firms. If this is the case, one might expect the local development impact of such investment to be very limited as well.

As an example from the electronics sector, the sale of smartphones has recently begun to plateau, leading to slower sales growth for smartphone brands like Apple, Samsung and others. Significantly, the slowdown in smartphone sales has hit the financial performance of Foxconn, the world's largest contract electronics manufacturer, much more than its largest customer, Apple. In fact, while Apple's sales of iPhones increased by only 1 percent in the quarter ended June 30, 2018, its revenue from iPhones increased 20 percent during the same period due in large part to a 20 percent price increase in the average selling price for iPhones. Apple (with its control of the brand, marketing, intellectual property and design) was able to increase iPhone revenues despite slowing sales growth by increasing end product prices, while Foxconn's revenues declined during the same period.[8] If Foxconn, a very large, highly sophisticated and uniquely skilled contract manufacturer based in China that Apple relies on for almost all its iPhone production, is unable to obtain even a small portion of a substantial unit price increase for iPhones, we might expect the difficulty for smaller, more substitutable and less skilled suppliers from the developing world to capture the value of their innovations to be substantially greater.

Several implications follow from the divergence in the types of innovation in which buyer firms and their supplier firms from developing countries engage and their relative bargaining power to capture Schumpeterian rents from innovations under supply chain capitalism. First, for developing countries and their supplier firms, production and human resource innovation may be better understood as a cost of access to or continued participation in global supply chains rather than a source of new rents. Second, the extent to which innovation rents can be captured by domestic supplier firms in developing countries from their supply chains will be contingent on numerous factors, including the type of innovation at issue, the magnitude of the innovation's impact on chain returns, the degree to which the innovation positively distinguishes domestic supplier firms from competing suppliers, the ability of the domestic supplier firms to protect the innovation from use by competitors, the capacity of domestic supplier firms to capitalize on the innovation through increased output and sales, the extent to which the innovation may make domestic suppliers attractive to more lucrative supply chains, the bargaining power of buyer firms and competing suppliers in the chains with which the domestic suppliers deal and others. As a result, we should expect that the competitive position and returns of developing-country firms will decline as a result of a *failure* to innovate. Assuming that innovation by developing-country firms will result in increased returns seems a much riskier enterprise. In fact, given the trend of declining prices and terms of trade for developing-country exports,[9] it would seem that uncompensated innovation may be more the norm than the exception for many developing countries and their suppliers—a cost of not falling further behind rather than a source of growth and wealth.

---

[8] See Jamie Condliffe, "Foxconn Hit by Slow Smartphone Sales," *New York Times*, August 14, 2018; Yoko Kubata, "Foxconn Posts Unexpected Decline in Profit: Earning Decline Despite Strong Demand for Apple's iPhone," *Wall Street Journal*, August 13, 2018.

[9] See Kaplinsky, *Globalization, Poverty and Inequality*.

The Limits of Current Progressive Strategies for Development through Global Trade

Recognizing that trade liberalization across the developing world has not delivered promised returns for many countries, progressive trade theorists commonly promote one or some combination of three approaches to assist developing countries in capturing more domestic gains from global trade. These approaches in broad-brush are the following: (1) to assert and secure more national policy autonomy from constraints imposed by the trade rules to enable more effective strategic management of domestic industrial policy and participation in global markets (the policy space approach);[10] (2) to increase domestic capacity for using and exploiting existing trade rules to extract more national advantage from participation in global trade (the capacity-building approach)[11] and (3) to focus national development policy on the creation and management of innovations that enable domestic firms to participate in global production chains and strategically upgrade their role in the chains through innovation (the upgrading approach).[12]

These three strategies take aim at different perceived problems with the global trading system. The policy space approach contends that the trade rules are too restrictive and stifle legitimate national development policies used in the past by the Asian Tigers and other countries (including most high-income countries) to chart successful paths to development. The capacity-building approach suggests that the problem is not overly restrictive trade rules but rather insufficient domestic capacity in developing countries to exploit the rules strategically and effectively to their advantage. The upgrading approach does not focus on the trade rules per se but rather on enhancing the competitiveness of developing-country suppliers in global supply chains by increasing the capacity of suppliers to develop proprietary innovation.

Although each of these strategies may occasionally lead to increased growth for some firms or in some developing countries, none of these approaches engages with the complex and multiple legal regimes, competitive conditions and commercial practices that seem to be constraining policy autonomy, bargaining power, innovative capacity and ultimately the development of many developing countries and firms under supply chain capitalism. Both the policy space approach and the capacity-building approach seem to overemphasize the significance of the global trade rules in shaping the policy autonomy of developing countries and the competitiveness of developing-country firms. Yet under supply chain capitalism, numerous other legal and private ordering regimes and business practices (from supply contracts to labor law to tax law to intellectual property law to multisource supply structures to the business practices of competing suppliers to the policy choices of competing developing states) are shaping the room to maneuver

---

[10] See, e.g., Rodrik, "The Global Governance of Trade"; Stiglitz and Charlton, *Fair Trade for All.*

[11] See, e.g., Alvaro Santos, "Carving Out Policy Autonomy for Developing Countries at the World Trade Organization: The Experience of Brazil and Mexico," *Virginia Journal of International Law* 52 (2012): 553.

[12] See, e.g., Gereffi, "International Trade and Industrial Upgrading"; Feenstra, "Integration of Trade and Disintegration of Production"; Kaplinsky, *Globalization, Poverty and Inequality.*

for policymakers in developing countries and the competitive conditions for developing-country firms. Moreover, the complexity, power asymmetries and intense competitive conditions of multiple supply chain structures in diverse sectors make assessing the anticipated national costs and benefits of development policy choices more uncertain and difficult. Even if the World Trade Organization (WTO) regime were reformed to impose fewer constraints on trade and industrial policy choices by developing countries and developing-country officials were better capacitated to assert their interests in multilateral trade institutions, there is no reason to expect that significant changes or improvements in development policymaking or outcomes would follow. Rather, the strategic room for maneuver for both developing countries and their supplier firms would likely continue to be constrained by the numerous other legal regimes and business practices that shape the relative power of buyer firms and supplier firms and the competitive conditions in the supply chains on which they depend. In fact, one of the most troubling (and challenging) aspects of supply chain capitalism is that the combination of powerful geographically dispersed global buyer firms and geographically dispersed, often substitutable, supplier firms functions as both a hedge and a limit on the power of states to affect governance or the allocation of surplus in supply chains through national regulation or policy.

With these things in mind, the difficulty for developing countries and their firms in following the upgrading approach to anything like the prosperity achieved by the Asian Tigers seems less a product of national innovation policy or national or firm investments in innovation and more a function of the complex interaction of regimes that enable and support the current structure of global production and the distribution of innovative capacity, bargaining power and rents it seems to foster.

Trade and development theorists and policymakers, both at the global and the national levels, continue to focus on tariffs, subsidies, strategic national trade policy and the risks of state protectionism, while the extraordinary concentration of power over trade and development in global supply chains governed by large buyer firms seems to escape notice and remain unchecked. The reorganization of global production and trade into supply chain capitalism could not have happened without bringing the developing world into the liberal trading order under the WTO and other multilateral and bilateral trade agreements. Yet the legal and other mechanisms through which buyer firms and their supply chains shape the policymaking and bargaining power of states and supplier firms are not only, or even principally, trade rules.

While this essay has focused on the impact of supply chain capitalism on developing countries and their firms, the challenges posed by this organization of global production reach virtually every aspect of global commerce and impact the policymaking of every nation-state. Substantial challenges posed by supply chain capitalism—the global and national regulatory impact of buyer firm power over chain governance; the complexity and uncertainty of designing national policy to enhance the competitive advantage of individual firms and the comparative advantage of the nation as a whole across multiple chains and diverse business sectors; the effects of foreign rules, private ordering regimes and business practices on the strategic policy options of states and firms; the difficulty for supplier firms to capture rents from innovation in the face of brutal competition and little bargaining power; the limited ability of even the most developed states to capture tax revenues from disaggregated and often denationalized firms engaged in geographically dispersed economic activity—all merit careful study and regulatory attention from trade and development theorists and policymakers.

To begin, theorists and policymakers will need to look beyond the trade rules and the innovative capacity of individual states and firms to the vast array of rules, practices and regimes that shape the division of labor, bargaining power and distribution of surplus among all states and firms in the global economy.[13] More sophisticated maps of the legal drivers, operations and vulnerabilities of supply chain capitalism should provide a clearer understanding of the limits and possibilities of this configuration of global production for economic growth, including the possibility that under current conditions many nations may be unable to achieve a competitive foothold in the global economy or increased economic welfare even if they do. At the same time, better maps should illuminate new legal tools and policy strategies beyond the traditional tools of trade law and policy for disrupting the current configuration of power and distribution of resources under supply chain capitalism and enabling more equitable patterns of trade and distribution to emerge.

---

[13] For a description of this type of legal mapping of global value chain structures, see the IGLP Law and Global Production Working Group, "The Role of Law in Global Value Chains: A Research Manifesto," *London Review of International Law* 4, no. 1: (2016): 57, https://academic.oup.com/lril/article/4/1/57/2413108.

Chapter Twelve

THE GLOBAL RISE AND REGULATION OF PLATFORM FIRMS AND MARKETS

Jason Jackson

Over the past few years, platform firms such as Amazon, Google, Facebook and Uber (and their global counterparts and competitors such as Alibaba and Tencent in China) have emerged at the vanguard of international business. These firms represent revolutionary forms of oligopolistic capital and may hold major implications for industry organization, market structure and perhaps even the future of the corporate organizational form.[1] However, despite their ubiquity, understanding the rise of these firms is anything but straightforward. On the one hand, their rapid growth is predicated on new disruptive technologies that generate market value through machine learning algorithms and big data. Yet, on the other hand, the success of their business models is fundamentally predicated on the now-familiar structural and institutional transformations of the global economy that have occurred during the past few decades of neoliberal globalization. These include changes in trade, investment, and labor laws and policies that have facilitated global capital flows and rendered workers vulnerable in countries around the world.

Indeed, a core feature of platform firm strategy has been to leverage the material power of their large size to take advantage of high levels of global liquidity to capture surplus finance and rapidly capitalize much more quickly than conventional multinational corporations in manufacturing and extractive industries. Further, unlike conventional firms, multisided platforms deploy novel techniques of aggregating and deploying labor *on demand* while leveraging the power of network effects to rapidly grow their consumer base and build scale. This may have allowed these firms to generate technical efficiencies, but it also enabled them to amass significant political power through both large size and pervasive presence across markets. Platforms have also developed mechanisms for co-opting and directly deploying their consumers as resources in aggressive efforts to challenge conventional regulation at the urban, national and global scale. These dynamics challenge simple narratives of innovation-led growth in platform firms in favor of explanations that are informed by the political economy. In other words, the technological and political are

---

[1] Gerry Davis, *The Vanishing American Corporation* (Oakland, CA: Berrett-Koehler Publishers, 2016).

deeply intertwined. This essay seeks to critically assess the growth of platform firms and markets in this latest development in global capitalism.

Historicizing Platform Firms

The rise of platform firms reflects a fundamental development in modern capitalism. It signals a shift in the types of organizational actors and institutions that structure the global economy. Large firms have long occupied central roles in the co-construction of global markets and modern states. In the latter stages of mercantilism, state-chartered trading companies were key figures in the reordering of the global political economy through military and economic adventures that extended imperial state power to new geographic locations.

While the mercantilism of the past was institutionally distinct from the industrial capitalism that came later, an analytically important feature that cut across both systems is the often blurry boundary between public and private, whether between imperial states and their chartered companies or later between modern states and the large corporation. In seventeenth- and eighteenth-century South Asia, for example, it was notoriously difficult to identify the line between the East India Company, the Colonial Office and the British Crown, a reality that animated much of the ideas that became classical political economy. Similarly, in the nineteenth-century United States, the large corporation, which was initially created to carry out functions aimed at the public good, became the subject of intense debate as corporations increasingly became oriented toward private gain. This issue came to a head around monopoly control of markets, an issue that has returned to the forefront of contemporary analysis of platform firms as public utilities.[2] We now see the rise of platform firms and accompanying market transformations with new modes of coordination and governance of the production of goods, and particularly services, including many that historically have been the domain of the state but now are deemed ripe for "disruption," such as urban mobility. This new reality demands further development of the analytic approaches that have thus far guided our understanding of the evolving global political economy.

Platform firms provide a particularly rich case through which to interrogate the political, economic and moral dimensions of market transformation under early twenty-first-century capitalism. Uber is the exemplary case. For scholars of industrial organization, ride-hailing firms are multisided platforms that serve as market makers allowing buyers and sellers to meet. While they may be increasingly raising monopoly concerns familiar from historical analyses of both chartered trading and various forms of diversified conglomerates and business groups, from this perspective, commercial success is due to algorithmic matching and machine learning technologies coupled with big data upon which they are based. These techniques are deemed to be simply more efficient than

---

[2] An excellent example is Sabeel Rahman, "The New Utilities: Private Power, Social Infrastructure, and the Revival of the Public Utility Concept," *Cordozo Law Review* 39, no. 5 (2018): 101–71.

conventional market technologies, such as the system of human taxi dispatchers in the case of urban transportation.

The preceding characterization of Uber's market advantage focuses solely on its deployment of disruptive technology. However, research in political economy, economic sociology, critical legal studies, and science and technology studies (STS) suggests that such a narrow, technical conception of platform markets may obscure as much as it reveals by masking highly contested political decisions at the regulatory and organizational levels, particularly in the arcane realm of complex technical infrastructure.

For example, in 2014, Uber made a high-profile hire of lobbyist David Plouffe, a well-known member of the Obama administration, as it sought to reconfigure its infamously aggressive regulatory engagement strategy—enter markets first, build a politically and economically valuable consumer base (and workforce) and then deal with regulators later. This strategy is multidimensional and often directly enlists the power of technology-enabled consumer activism. For example, on the eve of a crucial regulatory decision in New York City on whether to cap the growth of the ride-hailing firm, Uber infamously added a "de Blasio's Uber" feature to its app, offering a view of life if the bill passed. It showed no cars available for 25 minutes and, instead of summoning a ride, prompted users to email the mayor and the city council opposing the bill. It was made available to 2 million users in the city. De Blasio's bill was defeated.[3]

As such, the development of urban transportation in this particular case lends insight into the sociopolitical foundations of markets.[4] This brief vignette of Uber's engagement with politics to structure its market opportunities demonstrates how platform firms raise fundamental questions about the analytical lens through which they should be understood. Disruptive technological innovations certainly play an important role in these market transformations. However, urban transportation markets are highly politicized spaces, and commercial success depends heavily on strategies of regulatory and policy engagement, a point that is evident in the explosion of the often aggressive lobbying efforts by leading platform economy firms.

Structural Disruptions in the Global Political Economy: Labor and Finance

The rise of platform firms not only has implications for the reorganization of industries and the survival of the firms that constitute these markets but also provides a valuable window into broader concerns about inequality and the future of work. For example, in the case of Uber, the taxis-versus-Uber debate and Uber's transformation of urban transportation markets is occurring against the backdrop of broader structural shifts in the global political economy: neoliberalism and globalization. These structural shifts

---

[3] Facebook has attempted similar strategies in its attempt to combat net neutrality in India, though those efforts failed.

[4] Neil Fligstein, *The Architecture of Markets* (Princeton, NJ: Princeton University Press, 2001).

have specific features, particularly in input markets such as labor and finance. These areas are further discussed below.

Labor outsourcing and offshoring

Much of the discussion of platform firms in the literature, particularly the distributional effects of this new organizational form, has centered on questions of labor market institutions. In the United States, the variation in industry-level strategies was facilitated by post–New Deal legislative changes in employment regulation and judicial decision making, interestingly with taxi workers and their right to strike being a central issue.[5] These had major implications for industry structure and market politics across at least two key dimensions spanning patterns and logics of ownership and work. First, they facilitated a shift in the strategies and business practices of taxi firms in many municipalities (such as Boston and San Francisco) from owning taxicabs and engaging drivers as employees to relinquishing direct employer control through driver leasing. Second, they generated a different type of labor politics emerging from a shift in the status and identity of drivers from wage-earning worker-employees with the legal right to unionize and collectively bargain to independent contractors and working-class entrepreneurs.[6]

This had a huge impact on the internal structure of urban transportation markets and the organizations that constitute them, with concomitant shifts in distributional outcomes between firms and workers. It also raises many important conceptual questions in the politics of markets. First, it points to the distinction between macroinstitutional transformations, typically analyzed through political economy approaches, and micro-organizational changes, which are generally the focus of industry- and firm-level approaches.[7] It also focuses analytic attention on whether this new cultural representation of workers as independent entrepreneurs, at least in the United States, helps legitimize a structural shift that may preclude traditional modes of industrial relations, once again highlighting the normative and moralized dimensions of these debates. Comparative cross-national analysis is thus critical for understanding how these global shifts in industry structure and accompanying distributive implications (both among firms in increasingly consolidating market arenas where platform firms are establishing dominant positions and between firms and workers in labor markets) may vary across developing and industrialized country contexts.

---

[5]　Veena Dubal, "Wage Slave or Entrepreneur? Contesting the Dualism of Legal Worker Identities," *California Law Review* 105 (2017). Interestingly, taxi workers and their right to strike was a central issue in the National Labor Relations Act debates that guaranteed employee status and key rights of association, though these came under pressure with the Labor Market Regulatory Authority, which in turn was based in part on Cold War angst about protecting the individual from the collective (Dubal, "Wage Slave or Entrepreneur").

[6]　Ibid.; Brishen Rogers, "Employment Rights in the Platform Economy: Getting Back to Basics," *Harvard Law and Policy Review* 10 (2016): 480–520.

[7]　Fligstein, *The Architecture of Markets*, 6–7.

While the process of vertical disintegration by large American corporations played a central role in the global economic transformations that accompanied the transition from statist planning and Fordist-Keynesianism to neoliberal globalization, the rise of platform firms like Lyft and Uber appears to represent a novel organizational form of a "Nikeficated" networked firm.[8] In principle, they serve as intermediaries that match buyers and sellers and thus claim to simply facilitate transactions between willing parties. In this conception, they hope to assume few of the costs of conventional Fordist-era firms nor even the more limited responsibilities of contemporary multinational firms in their governance of global value chains (GVCs). However, despite these differences, there are also important structural similarities in their emergence. Both were facilitated by entrenched patterns of labor market inequality between developing and industrialized countries in globalized value chains, across the formal and informal sectors and along lines of race, class, gender, ethnicity and immigration status in localized urban transportation markets in both developing and industrialized countries. Ironically, the latter remains evident in the labor force of both traditional taxis and modern ride-hailing firms in the United States: both rely heavily on working-class ethnic whites and immigrant men of color. Similarly, in many developing countries, urban mobility markets rely on migrants from rural areas or poorer neighboring countries.[9] This is not due to chance; it rather reflects a set of power-laden social relations between these emerging firms and the workforce they rely upon that is central to the distributive logic of the business models that platform firms and markets represent.

Finance and financialization

A second crucial dimension of the global rise of platform firms and markets centers on the structure of global finance and ongoing processes of financialization. This has been as important an element of macrostructural change in the global economy as the fragmentation of production and accompanying transformation of employment relations and work. Financialization refers to the growing importance of finance in the global economy, particularly following the structural disruptions of the 1970s.[10] It can be seen at the micro level in new strategies where nonfinancial firms earn growing proportions of their profits from focusing on financial investments and tax efficiency rather than from production and trade; at the meso level as an outcome of changing corporate logics of governance, authority and ultimately business practices between firms and their

---

8 Davis, *The Vanishing American Corporation*; Sabeel Rahman and Kathleen Thelen, "Broken Contract: The Rise of the Networked Firm and the Transformation of Twenty-First Century Capitalism" (unpublished manuscript, 2018).

9 The examples abound, for instance, internal migrants from rural areas in India (often drawn from lower-caste groups) or migrants from neighboring countries in Singapore (e.g., from Malaysia) or South Africa (e.g., from Zimbabwe or Malawi).

10 Greta Krippner, *Capitalizing on Crisis: The Political Origins of the Rise of Finance* (Cambridge, MA: Harvard University Press, 2011).

investors; or at the macro level as intensified interstate and intercapitalist competition in the context of hegemonic transitions in the global political economy.

The meso-level perspective is advanced by studies of the shareholder value revolution where shareholders who passively ceded authority and discretion over firm strategy to managers in the pre-1970s Fordist corporation—thus facilitating a focus on long-term goals and relatively convivial relations with the state, labor and other stakeholders—now exert direct pressure on managers to meet aggressive short-term profit growth object- ives.[11] These pressures emanate from institutional investors, new organizational actors that increasingly deploy their finance-rooted market power to reshape how markets work, notably through pushing firms to vertical and horizontal disintegration of the manner that was noted before. This dynamic generates particular structural effects: vertical dis- integration pushes finance upstream and labor downstream as firms seek to shed low- value-added activities in favor of higher-value-added segments of the production chain, while horizontal disintegration leads to the dissolution of conglomerates as managers are forced to focus on core competency.[12] The end result is an inverted model of corporate ownership and control: the old model saw dispersed ownership and concentrated asset control, while the new model sees dispersed asset control and concentrated ownership.[13] Crucially, in this perspective, the structural and organizational power of finance (and financial market actors) is a key driver of the fragmentation of global production, not just techno-economic drivers of innovation and efficiency as in conventional analyses of globalization.

This meso-level analytic perspective has much that renders it compelling, though the role of states and the policy and legal rules they create often seem to fade to the background.[14] From this perspective, it is worth noting that the latter macro-level view might find evidence in the weight of sovereign wealth funds as active global investors. This perspective decenters the analysis from US-based institutional investors to high- light developments such as the massive $45 billion Saudi investment in Japan-based SoftBank's Vision Fund. SoftBank positioned itself as a major player in the emerging tech and platform space with an early and highly lucrative investment in the Chinese firm Alibaba ($24 million in 2000, now worth more than $60 billion post-IPO). More recently, SoftBank has emerged as one of the most important players in the organiza- tion and governance of platform markets making aggressive investments in firms across the global ride-hailing space, including a 15 percent stake in Uber, making it the lar- gest investor, as well as positions in Didi (China), Ola (India), Grab (Southeast Asia), 99 (Brazil) and others. Perhaps the most important element of this investment activity is the power it appears to have conferred to SoftBank to shape firm-level strategy. (Uber pulled out of China and Southeast Asia, respectively, following SoftBank investments and public signals from founder and CEO Masayoshi Son of his preference that Uber abandon its

---

[11] E.g., Davis, *The Vanishing American Corporation*; Krippner, *Capitalizing on Crisis.*
[12] Rahman and Thelen, "Broken Contract."
[13] E.g., Davis, *The Vanishing American Corporation*; Rahman and Thelen, "Broken Contract."
[14] See Rahman and Thelen, "Broken Contract."

expensive efforts in Asia, where it burns hundreds of millions of dollars per year, in an attempt to capture markets and focus on core markets in Europe and the Americas.) This dynamic around global investment activity in ride hailing is not idiosyncratic; it is part of a broader development where urban tech is now the largest arena of venture financing, attracting $44 billion, or 22 percent of all global venture capital, in 2017, more than pharma, biotech and artificial intelligence combined.[15]

This brings us back to the central issues identified at the beginning of the essay on the boundary between firms and the state, as well as the corollary issue of monopoly control of markets. An important distinction in institutional analyses of the evolving global political economy rests on patient versus short-term capital. The Fordist period in the United States was characterized by dispersed share ownership that resulted in little pressure on managers for short-term profits. As noted, this has changed with the shareholder-value revolution and new dominant role of active institutional investors in demanding short-term gains. Similarly, the varieties of capitalism literature suggest a contrast between this short-term orientation in liberal market economies, such as the United States, and coordinated market economies, such as Germany, where bank-based finance continues to dominate and further ties this institutional variation to key outcomes such as a focus on radical innovation in liberal market economies and incremental innovation in coordinated market economies.[16] Thus this provides an explanation of the concentration of radical technological innovation in the United States, perhaps most notably in Silicon Valley.

However, analysts focusing on platform firms have identified new structures that invert the varieties of capitalism literature's incremental-radical innovation logic. For example, a new model of patient capital (i.e., long-term finance) has emerged that underpins a new relationship between platform firms and powerful investors.[17] This approach is not directed toward supporting steady profit growth and relatively egalitarian distribution between capital and labor, as in the Fordist era (or the European welfare state model), nor does it seek short-term profits, as in the shareholder value model. Instead, the strategic objective is monopoly control of horizontally related markets through "winner-take-all" market strategies.[18] Ride-hailing platforms do not simply seek to control urban mobility markets but to imagine a future as multifaceted urban service platforms. Indeed, following Uber's recent capitulation to rival Grab in Southeast Asia, Grab CEO Anthony Tan outlined a vision of the average day of an ideal Grab consumer: "The minute they

---

[15] Richard Florida, "The Rise of Urban Tech," CityLab, July 10, 2018, https://www.citylab.com/life/2018/07/the-rise-of-urban-tech/564653/.

[16] Peter Hall and David Soskice, *Varieties of Capitalism: The Institutional Foundations of Comparative Advantage* (Oxford: Oxford University Press, 2001). Literatures on similar diversified business groups suggest the important role of long-term finance, albeit arising from different institutional arrangements, for example, families and kinship-based networks in Asia, transnational European financial networks in Latin America as well as, in all cases, the state.

[17] Rahman and Thelen, "Broken Contract."

[18] Martin Kenney and John Zysman, "The Rise of the Platform Economy," *Issues in Science and Technology* 32, no. 3 (Spring 2016).

wake up, they book a car. The car comes, and the guy has his car financed by Grab financial. He or she then pays for her lunch (at a) local noodle stall with Grab Pay, zips between meetings using a Grab bike, then orders Grab food on the way home."[19]

This offers a useful way to think about other firms such as Google (consider Alphabet's Sidewalk Labs experiment in Toronto) or Tencent in China (where potential rivals such as Google and Facebook are banned), as well as new public–private initiatives such as *aadhar* and the India Stack. Data is the key resource that lies at the heart of the extensive activities and enormous valuations of these platform firms, including their aggressive acquisitions that render them horizontally integrated conglomerates of the digital era (for example, Google and Facebook are aggressive players in the market for start-up acquisitions). It also suggests paying close attention to financial market actors such as SoftBank, which is playing a major role in facilitating new forms of cross-border relationships among these firms through its Vision Fund investment vehicle. Indeed, the ambition of SoftBank CEO Masayoshi Son has long been to create an internet *zaibatsu* or "*netbatsu*," a model that explicitly invokes the *zaibatsu* diversified business group structure that underpinned Japan's rise as a global economic power.

The implications of these developments extend well beyond (urban) service markets, not least given the emerging links between ride hailing and radical transformation of conventional industries such as automobiles through autonomous vehicles. Leading ride-hailing platforms like Didi, Grab, Lyft, Ola and Uber have extensive technical and financial partnerships with a host of conventional automakers, and Didi and Uber have their own autonomy programs. The GVC analytic would suggest that market power may no longer rest in the control of production of key physical subcomponents of the vehicle—given the existence of networked production structures and the modularization and commodification of auto production—nor even capabilities in system architecture and design, but rather of the data and computational tools that will guide them. These capabilities are disproportionately held by technology firms rather than traditional automakers, many of which not only are lagging in these new areas of technological expertise but carry balance sheets that render them financially vulnerable to being subsumed in new structures of global value and production. We thus may be at the cusp of a new era of monopoly forms of capital, as a growing number of observers have argued.

Summary

This essay has sought to outline an analytic approach to conceptualizing the rise of platform firms in global markets, highlighting two broad issues—the state–firm relationship and the question of monopoly—through discussion of the way platform firms shape and are shaped by labor and financial market institutions. This is a first step. In particular, most analyses of platform firms focus on national-level systems with less focus

---

[19] Cited in Nancy Hungerford, "It Won Out against Uber. Now Grab Is Setting Its Sights on Another Target," https://www.cnbc.com/2018/04/02/grab-co-founder-and-ceo-anthony-tan-on-uber-deal-fintech-indonesia.html.

on transnational actors and institutions. As such, in future work it will be important to incorporate the role of global rules in shaping the strategies and organizational forms that platform firms and markets are adopting. Relatedly, while some work, such as that done by Sabeel Rahman and Kathleen Thelen,[20] has begun to integrate political economic and legal analysis, this can be deepened, particularly by bringing critical legal insights on the mechanisms through which background rules shape bargaining power and distributive outcomes to the forefront.

---

[20] Rahman and Thelen, "Broken Contract."

Chapter Thirteen

HOW SHOULD WE THINK ABOUT A GLOBAL MARKET IN LEGAL CANNABIS?

Antonia Eliason and Rob Howse

Although the trade and distribution of cannabis is (largely) prohibited under international law, as well as in most domestic legal systems, there is now a noticeable trend to decriminalize and regulate its use for medicinal, and in some cases recreational, purposes. A number of US states have moved in this direction, although federal US law continues to criminalize the use of cannabis. Uruguay has legalized recreational use, and Canada recently enacted similar legislation. Should international law be modified or interpreted so as to facilitate trade and investment in cannabis (and related products and services) between domestic jurisdictions where legalization has occurred? How do the principles and rules of international trade and investment law relate to the United Nations (UN) regime and its possible evolution toward permissiveness of global market activity in cannabis?

Debates about the legalization of cannabis use have been intense in many jurisdictions. To understand the implications of the internationalization of an emerging legal cannabis market, we must start with the diverse policy objectives often asserted for legalization. In the case of medical cannabis, improved health outcomes is the obvious objective; for recreational use, the objective is to counter the negative consequences of criminal activity. As social values change, impetus for legalization may also come from the belief that it is unfair that a widely socially accepted activity should put individuals at risk of a criminal record; in many cases, the criminal law is applied in a manner grossly inconsistent with social equality, with primarily disadvantaged minorities targeted for criminal sanction and possible incarceration. Another motivation for legalization is fiscal: governments can capture tax revenue that is not available from the criminal market. Finally, many believe that cannabis is a social drug that, when not abused, is relatively benign and generates a market for many spin-off goods and services, therefore generating revenue and contributing to economic growth and development.

Shaping Global Markets to Support the Domestic Objectives of Legalization

Domestic governments may need to shape or control how international actors participate in the emerging legal market for cannabis. Two particular areas of concern are the roles that Big Pharma and Big Tobacco, and perhaps Big Alcohol, may play in markets where cannabis is legalized.

With medical cannabis there has been an intense effort to assert intellectual property rights in various medical applications, whether through biotechnologically modifying the plan to better adapt it to particular therapeutic purposes or through creating distinct devices or methods for delivering therapeutic doses. The intent is to enforce such rights globally. Aggressive patenting and other claims to intellectual property rights run the risk that ultimately medical cannabis will become a subdivision of Big Pharma. Several multinational pharmaceutical companies, including Novartis, GW Pharmaceuticals and Pfizer, have taken stakes in the medical cannabis industry or positioned themselves to enter the market in various ways. The large Canadian medical cannabis provider, Tilray, has made deals with the largest pharmacy chains in Canada for distribution, and as of August 2018, seven of Canada's top 10 cannabis patent holders were multinational pharmaceutical companies. The Open Cannabis Project notes that the United States Patent and Trademark Office has issued overly broad cannabis utility patents, which are not specific to single varieties and could consequently significantly limit innovation. Applying the prior art rule, filing patents in various jurisdictions may result in certain large patentees capturing broader markets, subsequently limiting acquisition of patents by other cannabis tech innovators. This is, of course, further reinforced by the World Trade Organization's (WTO's) Trade-Related Aspects of Intellectual Property Rights (TRIPS) agreement, which requires enforcement of intellectual property rights by all WTO members.

In addition to possibly killing innovation, prices to consumers may be driven up, with intellectual property rights holders earning monopoly rents. This in turn could result in consumers returning to illegal markets, thus undermining one of the most widely agreed rationales for cannabis legalization—the reduction of the social costs associated with criminal activity and criminal organizations. In early 2018 there were signs that while investment in the cannabis industry continued to increase sharply, spending on innovation and R&D had leveled off or decreased. This may be due to intensive patenting, which produces a "tragedy of the anticommons" effect, as described by Michael Heller.[1] Despite the concern about utility patents noted above, there is also a real limitation from the novelty requirement in patent law; merely *discovering* a new medical application for cannabis is not enough, arguably, for patenting. Some kind of alteration is required; thus, as noted, early patenting efforts in the medical field have focused on biotechnology and/or delivery devices such as dosing instruments.

With respect to recreational cannabis, Big Tobacco has an interest in locking up legalized cannabis markets but has been cautious and discrete in taking stakes in existing ventures, remaining largely under the radar through minority holdings, sometimes owned by intermediary companies (such as leaf companies). As social norms about cannabis continue to evolve and legalization spreads to more jurisdictions, Big Tobacco is

---

[1]   Michael Heller, "The Tragedy of the Anticommons: Property in the Transition from Marx to Markets," *Harvard Law Review* 111 (1998): 621–88.

likely to be more open and aggressive in attempting to obtain a strong, if not dominant, position in a global legal cannabis market. The risks here are multiple: public health may be endangered through comarketing of cannabis with carcinogenic tobacco products. Moreover, the exercise of market power and superior financing and political lobbying power by tobacco multinationals can easily threaten domestic local sustainable artisanal producers and undermine domestic economic development goals of cannabis liberalization. Even a minority equity share or similar participation by a foreign company in a legal cannabis market may allow that investor to bring an investor-state claim under a bilateral investment treaty if the regulatory environment develops in such a way that the particular company in question does not realize its expectations in terms of market access or share.

In contrast, the state-by-state legalization of recreational cannabis in the United States has resulted in the flourishing of near-anarcho-libertarian models of cannabis development, with a wide array of strains, luxury edibles and even cannabis-infused alcohol hitting the commercial market in fairly deregulated statewide environments. In comparison, efforts to legalize cannabis at a national level, as exemplified by Canada's legalization, impose a more heavy-handed regulatory regime, shaped in part by the initial focus on decriminalization but also on the continued stigmatization of cannabis as a harmful product, and brought to life through conventional market-based government-imposed regulatory limitations. Furthermore, the social justice aspects of cannabis decriminalization have never been a focus at the state or national levels, omitting an important component to developing an environment in which cannabis can be a vehicle for economic growth for traditionally marginalized or excluded communities (although some progressives are raising such concerns in the United States).

As cannabis industry participants and their legal counsel often stress, branding through trademarks is vital to successful large-scale commercial competition. Canada's legislation imposes considerable restrictions on marks and related forms of branding through packaging and labeling to discourage the marketing of cannabis as a desirable product, especially through symbols and content that appeal to young people. Such restrictions may eventually be challenged as violations of freedom of expression under domestic constitutional law but would have a reasonable chance of being sustained as justified limitations on rights. At the same time the WTO intellectual property regime disciplines how members can control the content and manner of presentation of trademarks. This issue was raised in the WTO *Havana Club* case, where the United States prohibited the use of a mark to enforce domestic laws concerning property taken by the Castro regime in the Cuban Revolution. The WTO recently published a panel report on its ruling in the Australian tobacco plain-packaging case, which is also relevant to restrictions on marks in the context of legal cannabis. Australia successfully defended its plain-packaging laws at the WTO, although this has been appealed to the Appellate Body. The public health implications of Big Tobacco or Big Alcohol establishing themselves as leading brands for cannabis may be considerable; for example, they could include drawing cannabis consumers to higher levels of tobacco or alcohol consumption as related lifestyle products. (These kinds of considerations appear to have influenced decisions to sell cannabis in parallel retail outlets and not liquor stores in some Canadian provinces, although the same liquor monopoly will control cannabis distribution and retailing.)

International Drug Conventions

The international drug conventions loom over the technical legal questions of compatibility with trade and investment law. Almost immediately after the Canadian legalization bill passed, the Russian government issued an official statement criticizing Canada for passing a bill that will breach the UN drug conventions. As more countries look to legalizing recreational cannabis, they must reconcile legalization with the strict prohibitions contained in the drug conventions, and possibly denounce these conventions (as has been discussed in Canada) or seek a reservation from the obligations of the conventions for cannabis. In grappling with how to justify legalization, scholars and policymakers have explored various possible avenues.

The drug convention regime consists of three treaties: (1) the 1961 Single Convention on Narcotic Drugs, as amended by the 1972 Protocol; (2) the 1971 Convention on Psychotropic Substances and (3) the 1988 United Nations Convention against Illicit Traffic in Narcotic Drugs and Psychotropic Substances. Cannabis is a prohibited substance under those conventions. The 1961 Single Convention provides limited opportunities to export cannabis; states are prohibited from knowingly permitting the export of drugs to any country except as authorized by the country and within the limits specified to the International Narcotics Control Board for scientific or medical research purposes or as required for the manufacture of other drugs.

Advocates of cannabis legalization point to the inaccurate and out-of-date scientific research that forms the basis for the restrictive treatment of cannabis, opium poppies, coca bushes and their derivatives in the drug conventions. The equivalency in treatment between cannabis on the one hand and opium and coca derivatives on the other is particularly troubling given the mounting scientific evidence pointing to the relatively innocuous nature of cannabis.

There are two main approaches to discussing the applicability of the drug conventions: the drug control and antitrafficking framework, which includes a medical and scientific purposes exemption, and the international human rights framework.

With respect to drug control and antitrafficking, the International Narcotics Control Board (INCB) is not sympathetic to cannabis legalization efforts, having stated unequivocally its view that Canada's scheme for legalizing recreational cannabis is a violation of Article 4(c) of the 1961 Convention, which requires parties to "take such legislative and administrative measures as may be necessary [...] subject to the provisions of this Convention, to limit exclusively to medical and scientific purposes the production, manufacture, export, import, distribution of, trade in, use and possession of drugs," and that further, Canada's measures are inconsistent with their obligations under Article 3(2) of the 1988 Convention, which requires criminalization of intentional possession, purchase or cultivation of cannabis.

Despite the INCB's assertion that the obligation in the 1961 Convention to prohibit nonmedical and nonscientific use of cannabis is unequivocal, it ignores the language in

Article 4(c) of the 1961 Convention that prefaces the obligation "subject to the provisions of this Convention." The words "subject to the other provisions of this Convention" mean that in fact the prohibition is not unequivocal; to the contrary, it may be circumscribed by "other provisions." The French version of the 1961 Convention underlines the limiting nature of "subject to the other provisions of this Convention" through its rendering of this clause as "*Sous réserve* des dispositions de la présente Convention" (emphasis added).

In both the 1961 Convention and the 1988 Convention, there is a clear contrast between the unequivocal obligations that relate directly and indirectly to the aim of preventing trafficking and the obligations that concern a state's control of the use and abuse of drugs by its own nationals, which are qualified by respect for domestic constitutional principles and basic legal concepts and contain significant discretion to determine the precise nature of criminal offenses and any defenses (which could be read to include justifications and excuses) to those offenses. In this respect, there is increasing recognition based on substantive evidence in many states party to the drug conventions that traditional criminalization approaches have not been effective in this regard and have, perversely, sustained demand for illicitly traded drugs—if anything, increasing human suffering from the collateral criminal activities and organizations sustained through a criminalization approach.

In addition to the interpretive flexibilities inherent in the drug conventions, there is a codified medical and scientific purposes exemption in the 1961 Single Convention. Article 2(5)(b) of the Convention states, in relation to Schedule IV drugs, which include cannabis and cannabis resin, that "[a] Party shall […] prohibit the production, manufacture, export and import of, trade in, possession or use of any such drug except for amounts which may be necessary for medical and scientific research only."

Elaborating on Article 2(5)(b), Article 4(1)(c) of the Single 1961 Convention provides that the parties shall take legislative and administrative measures necessary "to limit exclusively to medical and scientific purposes the production, manufacture, export, import, distribution of, trade in, use and possession of drugs." It has been noted that there is a lack of clarity in the Convention, as well as international law generally, on what "medical and scientific purpose" means.[2] In interpreting the scientific research exception in the International Convention for the Regulation of Whaling, the International Court of Justice accepted in the *Whaling in the Antarctic* case that in principle a scientific research purpose might be invoked even if the conduct in question had additional purposes beyond scientific research.

The truth is that without real-life experiments such as Canada's legalization scheme, it will be impossible to understand whether, in fact, an alternative of government-controlled legal use (combined with regulatory and other policy measures to address health and social issues) would be more effective than the criminalization model that still prevails in most countries. As one international tribunal, the WTO Appellate Body, observed in

---

[2] Megan Fultz, Lisa Page, Alysha Pannu and Matthew Quick, "Reconciling Canada's Legalization of Non-Medical Cannabis with the UN Drug Control Treaties" (Toronto: Global Strategy Lab, April 2017), 12.

the *EC-Hormones* case, there are instances where the science required to inform policy can be taken only in "the real world, where people live and die." Many countries are currently rethinking their approach to cannabis, and drug abuse more generally. In these circumstances, Canada's experiment has the possibility of providing indispensable information about the kinds of real-world effects that might emerge from regulated legal access. In this sense, the goal of progress in understanding the means of effectively dealing with drug abuse and collateral human harms is *served* by Canada's experiment.

Besides the UN drug control and antitrafficking framework, there is a growing body of scholarly literature that insists that the UN drug framework and the UN human rights framework are both part of the UN legal system as a whole and should be applied together in a consistent manner, avoiding tensions.

Article 2(2) of the UN Covenant on Civil and Political Rights requires each party "to take the necessary steps, in accordance with its constitutional processes and with the provisions of the present Covenant, to adopt such laws or other measures as may be necessary to give effect to the rights recognized in the present Covenant." What is most relevant in assessing the international legality of a country's scheme for legal recreational cannabis is that, where the country is a party to the Civil and Political Covenant, by virtue of its obligations under the Covenant, the human rights in the Covenant are to be considered basic concepts of their legal system within the meaning of the 1988 Convention. A similar situation exists with respect to the Covenant on Economic, Cultural and Social Rights, which contains the right to health, though the obligation to implement in domestic law is qualified by the capacities of the particular state at the time in question.

An additional human rights dimension is that in many parts of the world, vulnerable minority groups have disproportionately been victims of the criminal justice system in relation to cannabis-possession offenses. This inequity in law enforcement arguably engages the right of nondiscrimination under the UN Covenant on Civil and Political Rights. While reform of the criminal justice system may be an alternative solution to discrimination in law enforcement, which may be a matter of disparate impact or intentional discrimination in some cases, removing possession and use of cannabis from the criminal justice system, as Canada has done, is arguably a more effective remedy in the short term than attempting to alter the culture of law enforcement across the country, a much larger and more difficult task, if an imperative one from a human rights point of view.

The Canadian Approach to International Trade and Investment in Cannabis

In addition to the legal challenges under the drug conventions, there are questions of how legalized cannabis would operate within the framework of international trade and investment law.

In the *EC-Generalized System of Preferences* case, India challenged the practice of the European Union in giving preferred market access to a subset of developing countries that were deemed to be addressing problems with trafficking in or production of narcotic drugs. The WTO panel, while accepting the EU's argument that encouraging other means of economic activity as alternatives to drug production is an important dimension of drug-control policy acknowledged in the UN drug regime, found that the departure from nondiscrimination obligations was not justified, which the Appellate Body upheld on the basis that the EU scheme lacked objective criteria to determine which countries were eligible for special treatment based on their efforts against drugs. This was the first explicit encounter between the international economic regime and the drug regime. A WTO member state cannot deviate at will from its WTO obligations on the basis that it is pursuing objectives and policies approved by the UN drug regime.

This logic has been reinforced much more recently in a WTO dispute concerning anti-money-laundering measures in Colombia. Colombia implemented a special approach to the imposition of tariffs that deviated from the normal practice as provided in WTO rules on grounds that it needed to address artificially low-priced imports, which were a means by which money laundering occurred. The Appellate Body held that the fact that Colombia's government was addressing what Colombia considered to be illicit trade did not suspend the operation of WTO rules; instead Colombia would have to justify its anti-money-laundering measures under a specific exceptions provision in the relevant WTO Agreement. This suggests that any cannabis regime will need to adhere to WTO rules in its efforts to also adhere to the antitrafficking goals of the UN drug conventions.

Canada's legislation continues to allow import and export of medical cannabis through a system of licenses and permits, but import and export of recreational cannabis are absolutely prohibited, in an effort to not exacerbate drug trafficking. In the case of medical cannabis, restrictive import or export licensing would have to be justified under WTO law (for example, for public health reasons or management of critical supply). The outright prohibition of trade in recreational cannabis, a product that is legal albeit regulated domestically, however, is not consistent with General Agreement on Tariffs and Trade (GATT) rules (see Article XI and the GATT *Thailand-Cigarettes* case). Canada might justify this prohibition as necessary, in the context of a transition from a criminal to a legal market, to ensure that exports do not find themselves destined for illegal commerce or that imports are also not tainted by participation in criminal streams of commerce. This would most likely entail the invocation of either the public morals exception in Article XX(a) of the GATT or the Article XX(d) exception, which can be used to justify measures needed for the enforcement of domestic law and regulation.

While Canada has actively engaged in trade activity in medical cannabis, becoming the world's leading supplier to global markets, and the risk of the product being diverted to illegal markets has been dealt with through licensing arrangements, the potential scale of trade in recreational cannabis is such that controlling this risk would be difficult without extensive tracking arrangements. In addition, medical cannabis products increasingly focus on removing or reducing cannabidiol (CBD) with tetrahydrocannabinol (THC)—the active ingredient recreational users are interested in. This intrinsically limits the interest of the illegal market in diverting flows of such forms of medical cannabis in global markets. Between the licensing arrangements and the removal of THC from certain products, the risk of diversion to illegal markets is greatly diminished with respect to medical cannabis as compared to recreational cannabis.

It is clear from the drug conventions that "international trade" is conceived as the movement of a scheduled drug across international borders. However, if one is to analyze cannabis in contemporary supply chain or value chain terms, a significant contribution to the final product comes from services inputs such as research, testing and agricultural consulting. In the case of medical cannabis, firms have already circumvented export restrictions by selling know-how through licenses to jurisdictions where the production of medical cannabis products is legal.

In addressing potential negative impacts of Big Pharma's and Big Tobacco's involvement in the cannabis industry, as long as no discrimination based on national origin is involved, Canada can arguably use licenses and permits to prevent market dominance by large multinationals through limiting the market share that any one grower or distributor can have. This can obviate the impact of aggressive patenting or other claims to intellectual property. The Canadian legislation also permits individuals to grow their own cannabis at home (up to four plants per household at a given time), which is inherently procompetitive.

With respect to investment, the Canadian legislation would allow regulators to deny licenses and permits on a discretionary basis on the sole grounds of a business organization's or individual's non-Canadian nationality. Actually, doing so could violate Canada's obligations under any number of free trade agreements and bilateral investment treaties that contain a right to establishment. There is also a possible claim from foreign investors who have entered the Canadian cannabis market on expectations that they will be able to benefit from further liberalization. At the same time, the discretion to deny licenses and permits to foreign operators could be used as a tool to ensure that these operators enter the Canadian market on terms that support Canada's policy goals for cannabis liberalization.

How the General Agreement on Trade in Services (GATS) will apply is also instructive.

The Appellate Body has interpreted commitments scheduled by WTO members very broadly: in the *US-Gambling* dispute, for example, the Appellate Body held that gambling came under the US commitments with respect to entertainment services even though gambling was largely illegal or highly controlled at both the federal and state levels when these commitments were made. Canada's commitments on wholesaling, distribution and retailing include delivery of these services through establishment of a commercial presence. Under the Canadian legislation, a permit or license may be denied on the sole grounds that the applicant is "an organization that was incorporated, formed or otherwise organized outside of Canada." This seems a clear violation of Canada's obligation of national treatment in the GATS. Moreover, the mere fact of a service provider being the national of another WTO member would not lead to a viable basis for a public morals justification, or indeed a health justification, under the Article XIV exception. This is clear from the manner in which the Appellate Body applied the nondiscrimination requirement in the chapeau of Article XIV in the *US-Gambling* case.

Article VIII of the GATS applies in situations where members establish government monopolies on wholesale, distribution and/or retailing, permitting new monopolies to be established, provided that the monopoly respects GATS provisions in its operations. As such, where the monopoly obtains services such as testing, or research and development, for example, it must conform to the obligations of the GATS with respect to quantitative restrictions and national treatment. The ability of Canadian regulators to deny licenses on the grounds of the non-Canadian nationality of the business organization or individual would be inconsistent with obligations of any provincial monopoly under Article VIII of the GATS.

The GATS further provides in Article V(4) that licensing and qualification requirements must not be more burdensome than necessary to ensure the quality of the service. Licensing and qualification requirements under Canada's cannabis scheme may be in some tension with these provisions in GATS Article V(4). Canada's supporting regulations, for instance, with respect to a testing license, require that the head of laboratory have a Canadian science degree or one from a foreign university recognized by a Canadian university or professional association. This clearly would create an additional burden for some testing service suppliers from other WTO members.

Finally, the WTO's Trade-Related Aspects of Intellectual Property Rights (TRIPS) agreement contains a range of flexibilities or exceptions that can be used to address the anticompetitive impact through aggressive and broad assertion of intellectual property rights. The TRIPS agreement gives members the choice of protecting intellectual property in plants through either patents or plant breeders' rights. The latter, as defined in the International Union for the Protection of New Varieties of Plants (UPOV Convention), has been argued to restrict international trade even more than patent protection, to the extent of being in tension with free trade norms in the GATT.[3]

The Challenge of Understanding a Global Market Fragmented between Legal and Criminal Activity

Economists and trade lawyers have not generally paid sustained attention to the structure of global markets that are fragmented between legal and criminal activity (though there is important literature on the trafficking of sex workers).[4] The case of cannabis raises a range of interesting questions, for both lawyers and economists. Canada's first-mover role in the legalization of medical cannabis has made the country's industry into a global winner. It seems counterintuitive to expect to capture global markets by legalizing a product that is illegal or severely restricted elsewhere. Yet Canadian producers and services suppliers were able to do just that. Many countries have faced pressure to make medical cannabis available to their citizens but have not been ready to permit a domestic industry in an otherwise criminalized product. For such countries, Canadian imports have been an attractive solution. In other cases, where countries have wanted to take additional steps, Canada's reputation in medical cannabis has led to an openness

---

[3] Matthew Kennedy, "Export Restrictions in Plant Breeder's Rights," *Journal of International Economic Law* 20, no. 4 (December 1, 2017): 883–903, https://doi.org/10.1093/jiel/jgx035.

[4] For an early treatment, see Chantal Thomas, "Disciplining Globalization: Law, Illegal Trade, and the Case of Narcotics," *Michigan Journal of International Law* 24, no. 2 (2003): 549–75, http://repository.law.umich.edu/mjil/vol24/iss2/2.

to Canadian investment and know-how (for example, Greece recently legalized medical cannabis and turned to a Canadian concern to set up growing facilities locally).

This leads to a related point about comparative advantage. Climatic and soil conditions have limited impact on comparative advantage in cannabis; the plants can be grown under many different conditions, including indoors. Agricultural science and bioengineering are being intensively used in the cannabis industry and substantially affect the costs of producing cannabis. This may have important implications for countries in the Global South, which have been large producers of cannabis for the illegal market, as more and more countries in the North legalize. The fact that cannabis has become a knowledge-intensive industry (especially in the medical sector) can make classic trade restrictions largely ineffective. For instance, in the face of the export ban on medical cannabis in Israel, Israeli companies have already made deals whereby they will supply know-how and technology, instead of Israeli-grown cannabis, to the destination countries. The main losers are the Israelis, who might have had jobs growing the cannabis locally.

A similar logic drives cannabis tourism. Individuals who cannot legally use cannabis in their own country can travel to jurisdictions where use is legal. Both the Netherlands and Uruguay believe that cannabis tourism produces negative social externalities. In these countries, cannabis tourists are associated with antisocial behavior and increased costs of security, policing and so forth. In fact, in Uruguay the government has attempted to limit recreational use of cannabis to local residents, as have some Dutch municipalities in the case of coffee shops. As Canada moves toward legalization of recreational cannabis, the issue of cannabis tourism will most likely become significant, given the long border with the United States and the large number of populated communities situated in close proximity to the border.

Tourism is covered by the WTO's General Agreement on Trade in Services (GATS), and many countries have made substantial commitments in their schedules to free markets (meaning that they will not restrict their own nationals from going abroad specifically for tourism, including consuming recreational or entertainment services). Given the realities of sex tourism (exploitation, abuse of minors, sexual slavery), it is understandable and justifiable under the exceptions provisions in GATS that it is a criminal offense in a number of jurisdictions for a national to consume defined sexual services abroad. What if the United States were to make it illegal for its nationals to travel for purposes of cannabis consumption? One answer is that they would simply instead go to US states where cannabis is legal. This in turn would make such restrictions less likely to be justifiable under GATS (the *US–Gambling* logic).

The challenge of a global market fragmented between legal and illegal activity may lead to innovation in global finance or accelerate trends to innovation. The United States has become a de facto hegemonic regulator of global finance. Because global banks depend on correspondent relationships with US-regulated financial institutions, they may easily be forced to conform with restrictions imposed by US law on their activities, whether they are sanctions, US court orders (the Argentina vulture funds case) or, as in the case of cannabis, lack of financing for an activity that is illegal in the United States.[5]

---

[5]   Sections 319 and 320, USA PATRIOT Act.

In fact, today countertrade and barter (which may often avoid the intermediation of financial institutions) account for a nontrivial percentage of (legal) world trade.[6]

Several major Canadian banks have been willing to finance legal Canadian cannabis activity; on the other hand, Uruguayan banks moved out when US banks threatened that they would lose their correspondent relationships.[7] Clearly, because of the massive amount of transboundary financial activity the leading Canadian banks engage in, US institutions are reluctant to threaten to cease dealings with them, even at some risk of violating the PATRIOT Act. At least for now, one sees the competitive advantage of being located in a country with large international banks willing to finance the cannabis industry. Indeed this advantage may be leveraged by the Canadian industry to operate significant aspects of the market in US states where cannabis is legal but where, because of the federal legal regime noted above, large-scale business activity is hampered by the impossibility of financial intermediation by US-regulated institutions. In the longer term, new forms of international financing may emerge that are separated from US banking or indeed the use of cryptocurrencies in the cannabis market, as well as extensive use of barter or countertrade. Because of US sanctions, and the long arm of the US courts, many parties are interested in viable forms of financial intermediation that cannot be influenced by US law and regulation. At least one entrepreneur is proposing a form of cryptocurrency for transactions in cannabis: "potcoin."

Medical cannabis legalization is being used dynamically as a wedge by which firms are engaging in research for cannabis applications—for example, cannabis-based skin product—that are not medical but also not associated with the effects recreational users seek. A climate of legalization for nonrecreational uses also makes it possible to exploit the industrial hemp market, which—in the United States, for example—is significantly constrained by the highly restrictive environment for cannabis in general, even though a decision of the Ninth Circuit ruled that importing and exporting hemp is legal.[8] Environmental concerns are driving an increased interest in hemp, which can substitute for products with a much heavier environmental footprint. Big Tobacco is aggressively investing in hemp to the extent that it is legal in the United States, with a consequent lobbying push to remove hemp from the controlled substance list. Canada is the largest exporter of industrial hemp, and the Canadian industry has seized on the move toward legalization of recreational cannabis to argue for an even more favorable regulatory environment for industrial hemp. As global markets expand in an ever wider range of cannabis-related or cannabis-derived goods and services, the opportunity costs of a highly restrictive approach that is typified by the United States only increase. Sadly, it is not only the United States that suffers these opportunity costs, but also smaller developing countries that are susceptible to US pressure.

---

[6] See Robert Howse, "Beyond the Countertrade Taboo: Why the WTO Should Take Another Look at Barter and Countertrade," *University of Toronto Law Journal* 60, no. 2 (Spring 2010): 289–314.

[7] John Hudak, Geoff Ramsey and John Walsh, "Uruguay's Cannabis Law: Pioneering a New Paradigm," Brookings Institution, Center for Effective Public Management (March 2018).

[8] See "Hemp as an Agricultural Commodity," Congressional Research Service (2017).

Finally, as countries move away from criminalization toward legalization, it will be integral to work former victims of the war on cannabis into the legal system, creating a global industry that does not merely provide capital opportunities but also allows people once forced into illegal activities due to their economic insecurity and marginalization to flourish. As Big Tobacco and other large investors move into formerly independent spaces, women and people of color are increasingly at risk of being pushed out of the nascent economy. Measures addressing minority group participation will be crucial to creating an equitable cannabis economy. Massachusetts was the first state to mention including those "disproportionately harmed by marijuana law enforcement" in its ballot initiative. More recently, Oakland, California, implemented an equity permit program for cannabis businesses that is intended to benefit those who have suffered under the War on Drugs, particularly those with arrest records. Without social justice initiatives, cannabis legalization will simply result in a global market that echoes the global market of Big Pharma and Big Tobacco.

SECTION 3

FRAMING A MORE EQUITABLE INVESTMENT LAW REGIME

Chapter Fourteen

BILATERAL INVESTMENT TREATIES: HAS SOUTH AFRICA CHARTERED A NEW COURSE?

D. M. Davis

South Africa, in its attempt to encourage foreign investment by enthusiastically embracing bilateral investment treaties (BITs), encountered a conflict between two policy objectives: the establishment of a conducive legal framework for attracting direct foreign investment and the pursuit of economic justice for all South Africans.

After 1994, at the dawn of democracy in South Africa, the country eagerly endorsed the idea of entering into BITs, none of which had been concluded by the apartheid government. By 2012, South Africa had concluded 48 foreign investment protection and promotion treaties. This rush to treaty must be placed into context.

When the African National Congress (ANC) came to power, it was anxious to ensure that the international community regarded the country as a sound investment destination. Foreign investors were concerned about the legacy of the history of postcolonial African states, which had embarked on a course of economic nationalization together with a proclamation of redistribution of economic growth. With this history in mind, the British government, under the leadership of the then prime minister, John Major, who was concerned that the ANC might expropriate British assets in South Africa, was the first to approach the newly installed South African government with a BIT proposal.[1]

This initiative was launched during a BIT-signing frenzy in which more than 3,600 treaties were concluded worldwide during the following decade.[2] At the very moment that democracy dawned in South Africa, the Washington Consensus macroeconomic model propagated by the World Bank and the International Monetary Fund had achieved hegemonic status. This consensus encouraged developing countries to enter into BITs with capital-exporting countries as a means to incorporate key economic values into developing countries' economic development. This aimed to ensure that the

---

[1] "South Africa's Foreign Investment Regulatory Regime in a Global Context" (occasional paper, South African Institute of International Affairs, Johannesburg, South Africa, January 2015), 214.

[2] UNCTAD Investment Policy Hub, International Investment Agreements Navigator: South Africa.

national regulatory system of developing countries was congruent with a transnational legal and policy regime. At the same time, the Washington Consensus induced the belief that the conclusion of BITs would attract foreign direct investment, which was seen as an important component of government policy at the time. It was assumed that the attraction of foreign investment would significantly boost developing countries' manufacturing and export industries.

With the benefit of the ensuing 20 years, the hegemony enjoyed by the Washington Consensus has been replaced, at least to the extent that articulated differentiations regarding the appropriate development strategy for developing countries such as South Africa exist. During the 1990s, the World Bank's approach was aimed at creating a fully integrated global economic order in which investment would be unfettered by national regulation designed to promote indigenous objectives and would inevitably be located where significant returns could be obtained, hence the anxiety that without the conclusion of a network of BITs, foreign investment would not be forthcoming. Without suggesting that there are not a myriad of options outside of this framework, it is useful to document that at the other extreme a populist view has unquestionably gained traction in South Africa, namely to see foreign investment as part of "an imperialist project that will undermine inclusive development and should be limited to the extent possible."[3]

This essay seeks to track the responses of the South African government to its initial enthusiasm for BITs, in particular, the passing of the Protection of Investment Act (PIA) 22 of 2015 and the implications thereof. But we first need to sketch the reasons for the government's change of policy, which cannot be attributed alone to changing economic debates post the Washington Consensus.

The Beginning of Trouble

From the outset South Africa's BITs exhibited an incongruence between the country's domestic imperatives and the legal commitments made at an international level pursuant to the plethora of treaties into which it entered. At the most general level, as a United Nations Conference on Trade and Development (UNCTAD) document conceded in 2006, "it is in the very nature of international (investment) agreements to constrain policy options at the national level." Arguably, the most important national policy option for South Africa was contained in the constitutional provision dealing with property. In particular, Section 25(2) of the Constitution of the Republic of South Africa Act 108 of 1996 provides that property may be expropriated only in terms of a law of general application for a public purpose or in the public interest. Section 25(4) (a) of the Constitution describes the nature of public interest as including "the nation's

---

[3]	See Sonia Rolland and David Trubek, "Legal Innovation in Investment Law: Rhetoric and Practice in Emerging Countries," *University of Pennsylvania Journal of International Law* 39 (2017): 52; within the specific South African context, see Sam Ashman, Ben Fine and Susan Newman, "The Crisis in South Africa: Neoliberalism, Financialization and Uneven and Combined Development," in *Social Register 2011: The Crisis This Time*, ed. Leo Panitch, Greg Albo and Vivek Chibber (Pontypool, Wales: Merlin Press, 2010).

commitment to land reform and reforms to bring about an equitable access to all South Africa's natural resources." To avoid any doubt, this section provides that property is not limited to land.[4]

As indicated from the reference to the intervention of John Major shortly after the dawn of South African democracy, and flowing from the nature of BITs, one of the key reasons states enter into these investment treaties is to protect an investor's property or investments from being taken by a host country.[5] Equally important is the provision in the BITs for an investor–state dispute settlement mechanism whereby an investor can approach an arbitral tribunal, usually located outside the host country such as the International Centre for Settlement of Investment Disputes (ICSID) or the UN Commission for International Trade Law (UNCITRAL), if a dispute arises from a BIT provision. Given the documented research that arbitrators in these circumstances may well be biased in favor of corporate interests and take insufficient account of the needs of the domestic legal system and the unique circumstances in its states, controversy was, not surprisingly, likely once South Africa so enthusiastically embraced the conclusion of BITs within the context of its constitutional obligations to national redress flowing from decades of apartheid. For example, it has been shown that arbitrators have adopted expansionary interpretations to treaty provisions, such as the phrase "fair and equitable treatment," which has been interpreted to require compensation if regulatory changes upset investor expectations.

The Foresti Case

On November 8, 2006, the ICSID received a request by certain Italian and Luxembourg investors for the institution of arbitration proceedings under the Additional Facility Rules against the South African government. The proceedings were based on an alleged breach by South Africa of its BITs with Italy and the Belgo-Luxembourg Economic Union, respectively. The crux of the claim was the alleged expropriatory effect of the South African Mineral and Petroleum Resources Development Act (MPRDA) 28 of 2002, which, inter alia, required mining companies operating in South Africa to achieve a level of 26 percent ownership by historically disadvantaged South Africans. South Africa argued in the arbitration that, even if there had been an expropriation of the mining rights held by the claimants, which it hotly disputed, this policy had been adopted

---

[4]   See Section 25(4)(b) of the Constitution.

[5]   See the commentary to the Organisation for Economic Co-operation and Development's draft convention on the protection of foreign property (1960), 41, in which indirect expropriation is described as "to deprive ultimately the alien of the enjoyment or value of his property without any specific act being identifiable as outright depravation." This would appear to mean that what matters is not the express intention of the expropriating state but the effect of the conduct thereof. For a discussion on the expansionary approach to treaty interpretation, see Muthucumaraswamy Sornarajah, "A Coming Crisis: Expansionary Trends in Investment Treaty Arbitration," in *Appeals Mechanisms in International Investment Disputes*, ed. Karl Sauvant and Michael Chiswick-Patterson (Oxford: Oxford University Press, 2008), 39.

for important public purposes that were unique to South Africa and that, as already indicated, were enshrined in Section 25 of the Constitution.

By contrast, the claimants contended that there had been a series of breaches of the relevant BITs, including that the common-law mineral rights that were leased/owned by the claimants' operating companies in terms of the previous legal regime had been expropriated, whether directly or indirectly, through the introduction of a requirement to apply for a license to continue mining where the old order mining rights were held by them.[6] The introduction of a requirement that historically disadvantaged South Africans should hold at least 26 percent equity in mining companies amounted to an expropriation of the claimants' shares in the operating companies that were conducting mining activities on their behalf. These requirements were in violation of the BIT protections against possible expropriation. Further, the favorable treatment accorded to historically disadvantaged South Africans under the MPRDA was a breach of the national treatment obligations contained in both BITs.

Lastly, the claimants argued that the provisions relating to fair and equitable treatment and national treatment in the BITs had been further breached. They argued that the MPRDA and a mining charter that flowed therefrom were instruments that were not sufficiently tailored to the unique circumstances and peculiarities of the claimants' businesses, with the result that compliance by the claimants' businesses would be objectively impossible. They argued further that historically disadvantaged South Africans had been treated more favorably under the new mining legislation than was previously the case and that as a result foreign investors had been discriminated against.

On November 2, 2009, some three years after the initiation of these proceedings, the claimants sought South Africa's consent to discontinue the proceedings, given that a private agreement had been reached granting claimants mining rights without the 26 percent historically disadvantaged South African equity divestiture, which had been contemplated in the MPRDA in exchange for agreeing to a beneficiation offset together with a reduced 5 percent equity divestiture.

The Protection of Investment Act

Notwithstanding the eventual settlement on the merits, South Africa did obtain a costs order against the claimants through the Tribunal, although the actual order of costs was far less than the amounts incurred to defend the government against the claimants.

The outcome proved less important than the lessons learned from the long-running saga. It emphasized the manner in which foreign investors could use the provisions of a BIT to block legitimate legislative and regulatory change in South Africa, or at the very least to claim compensation for these actions. As a result, the government initiated a review of the BITs concluded at a time when the government's enthusiasm to prove that

---

[6] MPRDA introduced a system of state custodianship of natural resources that required a license from the state to undertake mining activities or "old order" mining rights were required to be updated and licenses applied for within a certain period to continue mining activities.

South Africa was an investment-friendly destination far exceeded its appreciation of the many risks inherent in the BITs for the government's ability to fulfill its constitutional mandate or the development of future policy.[7]

The passing of the PIA followed some years later. Although it guaranteed that existing investments under BITs would continue to be protected for the period in the terms stipulated by the treaties, it provided that any investments made after the termination of a BIT(s) but before the promulgations of the Act would be governed by the general body of South African law.[8]

The preamble to the PIA set out to challenge the normative framework for a new investment regime. It noted that "it was conscious of the obligation to protect and promote the rights recognized in the Constitution" but recognized "the importance that investment plays in job creation, economic growth, sustainable development and the wellbeing of the people of South Africa." It went on to say that it was important to secure "a balance of rights and obligations of investors to increase investment in the Republic" while "recognizing the obligation to take measures to protect or advance persons or categories of persons, historically disadvantaged in the Republic due to discrimination."

The PIA's purpose, set out clearly in Section 4, is to "(a) protect investment in accordance with and subject to the Constitution, in a manner which balances the public interest and the rights and obligations of investors; (b) affirm the Republic's sovereign right to regulate investment in the public interest; and (c) confirm the Bill of Rights in the Constitution and the laws that apply to all investors and their investments in the Republic."

The PIA treats national and foreign investors equally. In this, the PIA follows the Calvo Doctrine adopted by a number of South American countries like Brazil, which requires that a host state provide a foreign investor only the same treatment as enjoyed by a national investor.[9] The PIA provides that an investor is entitled to approach a domestic court or independent tribunal in South Africa for the resolution of a dispute. However, the South African government may consent to international arbitration, which is now to be coupled with a new International Arbitration Bill, which incorporates the Model Law of the UNCITRAL. This will aid legal certainty in respect of dispute resolution.

The 2012 report of UNCTAD[10] supports the idea of ensuring that investment is protected while simultaneously affirming the country's sovereign right to regulate investment in the public interest and to comply with the Constitution, in general, and Section 25, the constitutional protection of property, in particular. The report sets out a series of core principles for investment policy that are similar to those contained in the PIA. They

---

[7] South African Department of Trade and Industry, "Bilateral Investment Treaty Policy Framework Review," June 2009.

[8] Section 15.

[9] Wenhus Shan, "From 'North-South Divide' to 'Private-Public Debate': The Revival of the Calvo Doctrine and the Changing Landscape in International Investment Law," *North-Western Journal of International Law and Business* 27 (2007).

[10] World Investment Report 2012: Towards a New Generation of Investment Policies, UNCTAD (2012).

include requiring investors to comply with a host state's investment-related domestic laws including regulation regarding environmental cleanup, formulating a fair and equitable treatment clause as an exhaustive list of state obligations and limiting full protection and security provisions to physical security and protection only. The report also includes a carefully crafted set of exceptions to protect human rights, health, core labor standards and the environment.[11]

The introduction of the PIA and the consequent repeal of many of the BITs entered into by South Africa had no negative effects on the flow of foreign investment into South Africa. In 2017, foreign direct investment inflows increased by 43 percent over the previous year to $3.2 billion.[12] In 2018, Mercedes-Benz announced a R10 billion investment (approximately $800 million) in the expansion of its East London plant.[13]

When the government announced its legislative proposal to alter the investment regime, a possible alternative to the PIA was mooted, being the conclusion of new BITs by South Africa on the basis of the South African Development Community model BIT.[14] The preamble recognizes the important contribution investment can make to the sustainable development of state parties, including the reduction of poverty, the increase of productive capacity, economic growth, the transfer of technology, and the furtherance of human rights and human development. It further provided that the model treaty seek to promote and encourage increased investment opportunities while "reaffirming the right of the State Parties to regulate and introduce new measures relating to investment and their treaties in order to meet national policy objective" (p. 5). In the event of a dispute for which mediation failed, the model treaty provided for compulsory arbitration, in the case of a state–state dispute; for an investor–state dispute, the treaty also contained the further right of the investor to initiate an arbitration. In terms of Clause 29, the investor has to first submit a claim before the host state's domestic court for the purpose of pursuing local remedies.

In summary, a BIT drafted on the model treaty would have to contain similar provisions to those in the PIA. However, the model treaty had not been approved by the time the PIA was introduced into law. In addition, by introducing domestic legislation,

---

[11] See also World Investment Report: Investment and the Digital Economy, UNCTAD (2017), which reflects similar adherence to principle in a number of the 115 investment laws examined.

[12] *Business Report,* January 24, 2018.

[13] Eyewitness News, July 26, 2018. In one of the few comprehensive studies completed that sought to test this proposition, Neumayer and Spess found that there is a positive relationship between the signing of BITs and FDI flows. Yackee, on the other hand, found that the relationship of BITs to FDI flows is marginal and much smaller than they had suggested. The scant empirical evidence, then, is at best ambivalent, hence the anecdotal evidence cited with regard to South Africa may be more reliable. See Eric Neumayer and Laura Spess, "Do Bilateral Investment Treaties Increase Foreign Direct Investment to Developing Countries?" *World Development* 33 (2005): 1567–85 (1568, 1585); Jason W. Yackee, "Do BITs Really Work? Revisiting the Empirical Link between Investment Treaties and Foreign Direct Investment" (Legal Studies Research Paper no. 1054, University of Wisconsin, September 18, 2007).

[14] SADC model bilateral investment treaty template: South African Development Community, July 2012.

South Africa was able to exercise far more control over its own legislative framework. For this reason it was deemed to be a preferable route, given that international agreements of this kind unduly constrain national governments seeking to implement key national development objectives.

Conclusion

By 2017, South Africa had terminated 9 of the 20 BITs then in force: agreements with Denmark, Spain, Germany, Luxembourg, Switzerland, the Netherlands, the United Kingdom and Austria. Some have contended that the PIA does little more than affirm the government's regulatory authority rather than giving prospective foreign investors any assurance of a predictable regulatory environment that is conducive to investment. However, the PIA has not yet come into force because regulations still need to be finalized for the creation for a mediation facility for foreign investors.[15] The more recent move to incorporate the UNCITRAL Model Law into South African law appears to have provided a further stable mechanism to balance the two policy objectives of foreign investment and the promotion of legitimate public interest objectives, as set out in the Constitution.[16]

South Africa, like many countries in the Global South, was compelled to engage with investment regulation at a time when developing countries were competing for foreign capital to promote local economic development. As a young democracy, which had little local expertise in the area of foreign investment law given the decades of isolation caused by apartheid, it found itself confronted with an investment climate and economic discourse in which BITs were presented as essential tools to attract the vitally necessary foreign investment for a country that had experienced much deserved sanctions for two decades.

These local and global factors certainly provided an impetus for South Africa's signing these treaties without critically evaluating the negative consequences to the country's own regulatory space at the very time it was compelled to engage in the imperative of substantive redress of the consequences of its history. In its own review of the BITs into which it entered, South Africa concluded that there was no clear relationship between BITs and increased foreign investment inflows.[17]

It might be too early to determine decisively whether the South African legislative initiative is preferable to an attempt to amend the content of the BITs into which the country would have entered, absent the PIA. However, on the basis of the investment

---

[15] The draft regulations have been criticized, particularly because the mediation process prescribed does not comply with international best practice, such as the International Bar Association's Model Rules for Investor-State Mediation. See Peter Leon, "South Africa: How Safe for Investment?," Politicsweb, October 19, 2017.

[16] See Fabio Morosini and Michelle Ratton Sanchez Badin, eds., *Reconceptualizing International Investment Law from the Global South* (Cambridge: Cambridge University Press, 2018).

[17] Xavier Carim, "South Africa and Bilateral Investment Treaties" (presentation, 26th Annual Labour Conference, Sandton, South Africa, July 31, 2013). On file with author.

record following the introduction of the PIA, the South African experience shows that BITs may not be essential for encouraging investment and that investor protection can be provided domestically without being at the expense of the country's important constitutional values and developmental objectives.

Chapter Fifteen

RETHINKING THE RIGHT TO REGULATE IN INVESTMENT AGREEMENTS: REFLECTIONS FROM THE SOUTH AFRICAN AND BRAZILIAN EXPERIENCES

Fabio Morosini

The international investment regime is under attack, and reform proposals are receiving increased attention in international negotiations and in the literature. Existing debates have put a great deal of attention on dispute settlement alternatives, while leaving out other equally contested features of the regime, such as the need for rebalancing investors' and states' rights and obligations.[1] This essay intends to shift the discussion to one of these features by focusing on the countries' right to regulate (RTR). In international investment law, RTR can be defined as the policy space available in investment agreements for countries to regulate in the public interest. Because investment agreements were created to limit certain aspects of countries' RTR, the first wave of agreements inhibited regulatory experimentation harmful to foreign investors' rights.[2] Mounting domestic criticism and fear of challenges before arbitral tribunals against developed countries made them carve out some policy space within investment agreements under the rubric of RTR. This development in investment law has mostly benefited countries wanting more policy space in areas such as environment, health and safety. Investment tribunals have, by and large, accompanied these changes. Within this broad debate, however, other policy goals central to countries in the Global South have not received sufficient attention.

From the perspective of countries in the Global South, an honest reform to promote greater policy space should be able to accommodate policy experimentation in a variety

---

[1]   Fabio Morosini and Michelle Ratton Sanchez Badin, eds., *Reconceptualizing International Investment Law from the Global South* (Cambridge: Cambridge University Press, 2017).

[2]   Dani Rodrik has made a similar claim in relation to trade agreements after the World Trade Organization (WTO). For his most recent iteration of this claim, see Dani Rodrik, "The WTO Has Become Dysfunctional," *Financial Times*, August 5, 2018, https://www.ft.com/content/c2beedfe-964d-11e8-95f8-8640db9060a7 (arguing that the WTO "reached inside the border (of Members) to constrain domestic policies in subsidies, health and safety and intellectual property").

of areas.[3] In this essay, I propose to enlarge the notion of RTR in investment agreements to provide more flexibility for countries, an aspect that has been largely overlooked in the processes of reforming investment agreements and accompanying literature. An RTR approach to take account of other needs should allow countries to incorporate policy areas as diverse as redistributive justice and industrial policies.

I am focusing on the recent experiences of South Africa and Brazil in relation to RTR. While South Africa decided to terminate their bilateral investment treaties (BITs) and resort to domestic laws and institutions, Brazil chose to initiate an investment treaty program that moves away from standard investment treaty language that has the protection of foreign investment as the primary, or sole, subject matter. These two cases suggest that (1) there are alternative paths to match investors' rights with countries' RTR and (2) these alternatives face constant pressure to conform with the neoliberal-embedded BIT program from internal and/or external sources.

Investment Agreements and Policy Autonomy in South Africa and Brazil

South Africa: Rebalancing black economic empowerment and investors' rights

South Africa is currently the most unequal country in the world.[4] Even if the investment regime is not entirely to blame for this, it certainly plays a part. The difficult balance between correcting racial inequalities and preserving property rights (domestic and foreign) has been the South African society's major challenge since the end of the apartheid rule in 1994. It has proven to be a difficult balance to strike, given that protection of property rights is a central feature of the African National Congress's (ANC) commitment with the global capitalist system after apartheid. In this context, conflicts with foreign investors' rights are only one element of a much broader narrative, whereby the standard BIT formulation represents the interests of the global capital.

South Africa is highly reliant on foreign capital.[5] As part of its strategy to attract foreign direct investment (FDI), the country rushed into BITs with capital-exporting

---

[3] Gregory Shaffer (chapter 17, this volume) addresses the tension between WTO law and policy space in relation to labor standards and development strategies, offering concrete proposals to address these tensions. See also Alvaro Santos, "Carving Out Policy Autonomy for Developing Countries in the World Trade Organization: The Experience of Brazil and Mexico," *Virginia Journal of International Law* 52 (2012): 551–632.

[4] Data obtained from two different measurement systems are (1) the Gini index estimates from the World Bank, which looks at the distribution of a nation's income or wealth to measure financial inequality, and (2) the Palma ratio, an alternative to the Gini index that focuses on the differences between those in the top- and bottom-income brackets. *Guardian*, Inequality Index 2017, https://www.theguardian.com/inequality/datablog/2017/apr/26/inequality-index-where-are-the-worlds-most-unequal-countries.

[5] IMF Country Report no. 16/218, International Monetary Fund, July 2016, https://www.imf.org/external/pubs/ft/scr/2016/cr16218.pdf. See also Barend de Beer, "South Africa's Experience with Capital Flows Since the Financial Crisis," IFC-BCB-CEMLA Satellite

countries to suggest its commitment to global capitalism. The standard BIT formulation allowed very little policy space for host countries,[6] and certainly no room for the promotion of racially based policies potentially harmful to investors' rights. Curiously, the process of adhering to BITs occurred simultaneously with the process of drafting a new and transformative constitution, which acknowledged the need to correct racial inequalities as central to South Africa's development. Eager to join the global capitalist system after years of isolation and desperately needing capital, the country did not fully evaluate possible negative externalities of BITs on South Africa's policy space until much later, when a claim was brought against the state, opening a Pandora's box for similarly motivated disputes.

In the *Foresti* case, private investors challenged South Africa's Mineral and Petroleum Resources Development Act (MPRDA) and Mining Charter for allegedly expropriating investment while adjusting to the demands of the Black Economic Empowerment Act, a policy designed to transfer control of the economy from white South Africans to black ones. Attempting to encourage greater ownership of mining industry assets by historically disadvantaged South Africans (HDSA), the Mining Charter required mining companies to achieve 26 percent HDSA ownership of mining assets and publish employment equity plans directed toward achieving a baseline 40 percent HDSA participation in management. The parties ended up reaching an agreement whereby investors would be deemed to have complied with the Mining Charter by making a 21 percent beneficiation offset and providing a 5 percent employee ownership program for employees of the investors. In other words, the government of South Africa fell short of fully meeting the country's constitutional values of correcting the legacies of the apartheid rule.

This case has major domestic and systemic repercussions. Domestically, it tells South Africans that, despite constitutional provisions, corrections of past legacies of the apartheid rule will not easily happen, due to, inter alia, previous investment commitments. Systemically, it demonstrates that whatever room exists for countries to exercise their regulatory power, BITs may deter their policy space even in relation to core constitutional values.

South Africa reacted! In response to *Foresti* and fear of similar claims, the country has been undergoing a process of restructuring its investment regulation to align it with South Africa's Constitution and postapartheid promises, carving out policy autonomy to promote affirmative action programs. In 2009, South Africa issued a position paper to critically evaluate its investment policies, suggesting rebalancing investor rights and

---

Meeting, https://www.bis.org/ifc/events/sat_semi_rio_jul15/1_beer_presentation.pdf (noting that South Africa's domestic gross fixed capital formation, a key requirement for future growth sustainment, has become increasingly reliant on international capital inflows).

[6] The traditional BIT formulation is framed around one main goal: protecting foreign investors. Under this approach, treaties usually include broad definitions of investors and investment; expansive standards of treatment to investors, such as most favored nation, national treatment, fair and equitable treatment, umbrella clauses and full protection and security; stringent rules on expropriation (both direct and indirect) and compensation; free transfer of funds; and investor–state dispute settlement.

regulatory space, which served as the basis for the 2015 South African Protection of Investment Act.

The Act challenges mainstream formulations of investment regulation designed around the goal of protecting foreign investors, sets out the government's intention of not renewing the so-called first-generation BITs and restricts the country from entering into new BITs, unless there are compelling economic and political reasons for doing so. The Act embraces substantive changes, including limiting the definition of investment/investor and exclusion of fair and equitable treatment to foreign investors, and replaces investor-state dispute settlement (ISDS) for domestic courts. Most important, the Act subjects property rights to the Constitution of the Republic. The Constitution of South Africa guarantees property rights, but, like any other constitutional right, they are subjected to public purpose limitations. Specifically, Section 25(2) of the Constitution allows expropriation of property for public purpose subject to payment of equitable compensation. Another important aspect is the obligation to take measures to protect or advance historically disadvantaged persons, which is in the Act's preamble, in its RTR provision and as an exception to the national treatment obligation.

South Africa's intention to carve out policy autonomy on the basis of black economic empowerment faces external and internal challenges. The decision to not renew its investment agreements was a source of great concern to foreign investors, because it was read as South Africa's officially denouncing the treaties. For a country that relies heavily on foreign capital, these concerns cannot be easily dismissed. Second, the adoption of a new investment act that incorporates flexibilities to correct racial inequalities makes investors very apprehensive as to its actual impacts.[7]

At the time of this writing, new challenges are underway. As an additional feature of the Black Economic Empowerment policy, there is pending legislation and heated public debate on the possibility of land expropriation without compensation. This brings an additional element of tension to the debate in South Africa. While previous measures adopted by the government have centered around violations of BIT commitments, these new measures attempting to expropriate land without compensation also appear to conflict with Section 25 of the Constitution, which requires expropriation to be followed by compensation.

The success of South Africa's alternative in rebalancing Black Economic Empowerment with investors' rights is uncertain. It will depend on at least two elements: (1) how foreign investors respond to these regulatory changes and (2) if the South African government is able to uphold the Black Economic Empowerment policy in light of internal and external pressures. Despite these uncertainties at home, debates in South Africa are already influencing the Southern African Development Community (SADC), an intergovernmental organization composed of 15 Southern African states. South Africa was actively engaged in designing the 2012 SADC BIT Template, which, among others, contains a development dimension in its RTR provision and another specific provision on the rights of a state party to pursue development goals, which includes

---

[7] But see D. M. Davis (chapter 14, this volume).

taking "measures necessary to address historically based economic disparities suffered by identifiable ethnic or cultural groups due to discriminatory or oppressive measures against such groups."[8]

Brazil: Carving policy space in the shadow of BITs

Brazil's engagement with investment policies has varied from resisting standard BITs in the 1990s to developing a new model investment agreement in 2013, replacing the paradigm of investment protection with one based on investment cooperation and facilitation. In both occasions, the government was concerned with shielding Brazil's regulatory space from investment commitments.

In the 1990s, during the heyday of neoliberalism, Brazil resisted joining any investment agreement, although it signed 14 such agreements never to be ratified. During this period, Brazil was perceived, and perceived itself, not as an exporter but as a destination of FDI, which helps explain the country's resistance to investment agreements. These agreements, mostly with developed economies, replicated the same investor-protective BIT standards to Brazil. At the time, there was resistance to these agreements from different fronts of the Brazilian society, but mostly from the then-opposition party, the Workers' Party. Two particular clauses were seen as problematic. First, the method of compensation provided in these agreements conflicted with the Brazilian Constitution. Second, the government was adamant about rejecting ISDS. It refused to accept the idea that private arbitrators could decide matters of Brazilian public law. At the time, it echoed much of the same reactions that we now see emerging in the United States and Europe against ISDS: it bypasses local administrative bodies and courts and lacks democratic accountability. After much resistance, by the very end of Fernando Henrique Cardoso's neoliberal(ish) government, these agreements were discontinued. From an economic point of view, the decision not to ratify these agreements did not prevent Brazil from remaining as one of the top FDI recipients, challenging the neoliberal narrative that BITs are necessary to attract foreign investment.

In 2003, Luiz Inácio Lula da Silva was elected president and awoke a dormant developmental state, resuscitating Brazil's industrial policy with important spillover effects on investments.[9] Mostly through the Brazilian National Development Bank (BNDES) financing, the government targeted a group of national champions and fostered the emergence of a new constituency in the country: the Brazilian multinational corporation.[10]

---

[8] Southern African Development Community, SADC Model Bilateral Investment Treaty Template with Commentary, Article 21, July 2012, http://www.iisd.org/itn/wp-content/uploads/2012/10/SADC-Model-BIT-Template-Final.pdf.

[9] David M. Trubek, Helena Alviar Garcia, Diogo R. Coutinho and Alvaro Santos, *Law and the New Developmental State: The Brazilian Experience in Latin American Context* (Cambridge: Cambridge University Press, 2013).

[10] Edmund Amann, "Technology, Public Policy and the Emergence of Brazilian Multinationals," in *Brazil as an Economic Superpower? Understanding Brazil's Changing Role in the Global Economy*, ed. Lael Brainard and Leonardo Martinez-Diaz (Washington, DC: Brookings Institution, 2009), 187–220.

Such a policy had direct effects on the activities of these corporations in foreign markets. Between 2005 and 2010, Brazil's FDI outflow was multiplied by almost nine times.[11]

Although debatable in the literature, it has been argued that BNDES financing was a relevant factor to foster Brazilian investment outflows during that period. This policy could have been curtailed and negatively affected Brazilian multinationals if (1) Brazil was part of standard BITs and (2) competing foreign investors with local subsidiaries had BNDES funding denied. In this case, foreign investors could challenge Brazil's measures under the national treatment clause and other standard of treatment obligations. In the worst-case scenario, if Brazil was found in violation of the BITs, compensation would ensue and, most important, Brazil's development strategy could be compromised, if not discontinued. Outside this large government-financing program, Brazil could equally have had its RTR challenged by foreign investors in matters as diverse as fiscal policy to water supply, as some neighboring countries experienced. It is, however, beyond the scope of this essay to screen Brazil's policies in light of standard BIT provisions. Even if it could be argued that Brazilian investors could have also benefited from the protection of BITs when investing abroad—a positive externality of BITs for Brazil in the 1990s, when BITs were being considered by Brazil—Brazilian outward FDI was not really significant and concentrated in a few players who employed other legal arrangements, such as contracts and incorporating in foreign jurisdictions, to benefit from their laws, including their BITs.[12]

Following its vein of experimentation, in 2013 Brazil finalized a new model investment agreement, substituting the protection of investment narrative for a new one based on investment cooperation and facilitation.[13] Since March 2015 Brazil has signed nine Agreements on Cooperation and Facilitation of Investments (ACFI) with other developing countries (Angola, Chile, Colombia, Ethiopia, Malawi, Mexico, Mozambique, Peru and Suriname), as well as the intra-MERCOSUR (Mercado Común del Sur, or Southern Common Market) Investment Protocol. In addition, investment facilitation agreements, the kind supported by Brazil, are being discussed in multilateral fora, such as the G20 and the World Trade Organization (WTO), with the open support of China.[14]

---

[11] United Nations Conference on Trade and Development, UNCTADstat, 2018, http://unctadstat.unctad.org.

[12] I have dealt with this issue in Fabio Morosini and Michelle Ratton Sanchez Badin, "Petrobras in Bolivia: Is There a Rule of Law in the 'Primitive' World?," in *Global Private International Law: Adjudication without Frontiers*, ed. Horatia Muir Watt, Lucia Bizikova, Agatha Brandao de Oliveira and Diego P. Fernandez Arroyo (Cheltenham, UK: Edward Elgar, forthcoming).

[13] For a detailed analysis of Brazil's investment treaty program, see Michelle Ratton Sanchez Badin and Fabio Morosini, "Navigating between Resistance and Conformity with the International Investment Regime: The Brazilian Agreement on Cooperation and Facilitation of Investments (ACFIs)," in *Reconceptualizing International Investment Law from the Global South*, ed. Fabio Morosini and Michelle Ratton Sanchez Badin (Cambridge: Cambridge University Press, 2017), 244–45.

[14] Axel Berger, "What's Next for Investment Facilitation?," *Columbia FDI Perspectives* 224 (2018), http://ccsi.columbia.edu/files/2016/10/No-224-Berger-FINAL.pdf.

The presence of Brazilian multinational enterprises (MNEs) in the Global South, especially Latin America and Africa, pressured the government into creating an investment agreement that responded to the new demands of Brazil's private sector, especially the creation of communication channels inside the countries where Brazilian MNEs invest in order to serve as a dispute prevention mechanism. Unlike other investment agreements currently under consideration that focus on adjudication, the Brazilian model was designed to encourage more diplomacy through well-defined institutional channels. Another important factor that contributed to the development of a new investment policy in Brazil was the country's bureaucracy, which has kept the topic on their agenda since 2003. Debates concerning an alternative type of investment agreement took place in CAMEX, a permanent advisory body of the presidency in matters related to the formulation, adoption, implementation and coordination of trade/investment policies. But it was only in 2013, under the leadership of the Ministry of Development, Industry and Commerce (MDIC) Foreign Trade Secretariat (SECEX), that a final template of the ACFI was approved by CAMEX and bilateral negotiations started.

The new model investment agreement moves away from the standard investor-protective treaty by limiting the definition of investment/investor; excluding indirect expropriation and key standards of treatment clauses, such as fair and equitable treatment; and ruling out ISDS. The approach, based on investment cooperation and facilitation, puts emphasis on (1) creating mechanisms such as ombudspersons and joint committees to monitor investment relations and prevent disputes from happening and (2) creating open-ended/framework agreements that can be adapted over time to accommodate the parties' needs through thematic work programs, a living part of every ACFI and an important feature for policy experimentation and coordination.

The search for policy autonomy in the shadow of investment agreements and through alternative regulatory frameworks is on hold in postimpeachment Brazil. The administration has been taking specific measures doing away with or threatening many features of Brazil's developmental state.[15] In his inauguration speech as Brazil's foreign affairs minister immediately after the impeachment, José Serra set the tone of the country's foreign policy, even if he was swiftly substituted by another like-minded politician. Instead of what he termed as ideological alliances, Brazil should reengage with countries like the United States and the European Union. Implicit in his speech is the idea of abandonment of a resistance and experimentation project, and adoption of strategies that reinforce domination of hegemonic globalization.[16] At a more practical level, Brazil has been aggressively confronted with a neoliberal agenda for reforms led by the Ministry of Finance that includes (1) approving a 20-year budgetary cut affecting investment in education and health, (2) curtailing labor rights, (3) making attempts to approve pension funds reform and (4) requesting accession to the Organisation for Economic

---

[15] André Singer, *The Failure of the Developmentalist Experiment in Three Acts* (São Paulo: Critical Policy Studies, 2017).

[16] David Schneiderman, *Resisting Economic Globalization: Critical Theory and International Investment Law* (London: Palgrave Macmillan, 2013).

Co-operation and Development (OECD). Under this new agenda, Brazil's investment law and policy innovations, seen by some as a legacy of the previous administration, risk losing traction.[17]

Concluding Thoughts

South Africa's and Brazil's experimentation with investment law to promote policy autonomy in different areas faces challenges. Externally, their practices go against a mainstream regime based on more than 3,000 agreements designed in the shadow of neoliberalism. While there have recently been signs that BITs may allow some flexibilities, as in the case of certain environmental and health policies, they will less likely welcome formulations that challenge the rationale of investment protection, such as the ones promoted by South Africa and Brazil.

In addition, both South Africa and Brazil face domestic challenges to implement their investment policies. After President Jacob Zuma's resignation, it is now President Cyril Ramaphosa's responsibility to strike a balance between addressing the country's historical racial inequalities—the DNA of the ANC—and the global capitalist system in which BITs are embedded. Brazil's experimentation with heterodox policies, including on investment, to further an alternative development model is less clear in the wake of a neoliberal-driven administration. In such a context, the future of Brazil's investment policy will remain uncertain until a newly elected government comes into power in 2019.

Despite these challenges, the experiences of South Africa and Brazil demonstrate that there is room for heterodoxy and genuine reimagination of the investment regime, where the interests of investors are matched with the core values of states, such as those concerning redistributive justice or industrial policy objectives. To achieve a balance on potentially conflicting interests, countries need to be creative and design more flexible alternatives that go beyond safeguarding policy space on environment, health and safety and include other national economic priorities. If the investment regime at large does not acknowledge and address more flexibility in relation to RTR, investment treaties and tribunals will only serve to perpetuate global inequalities under the rule of law.

---

[17] Initial indications are that these trends will accelerate under the new government led by Jair Bolsonaro, further placing these innovations at risk.

Chapter Sixteen

MAKING LOCAL COMMUNITIES VISIBLE: A WAY TO PREVENT THE POTENTIALLY TRAGIC CONSEQUENCES OF FOREIGN INVESTMENT?

Nicolás M. Perrone

For decades, international investment law has focused on investor-state dispute settlement (ISDS). The academic and policy debate has polarized into two competing camps arguing in favor and against this dispute settlement mechanism. A fundamental issue is whether ISDS can be consistent with an appropriate interpretation of states' right to regulate. There is nothing surprising in this debate. The *private vs. public* or *international vs. domestic* tensions are recurrent topics nowadays. What is surprising, however, is how both promoters and critics of ISDS have managed to narrow down the complex and multi-faceted field of foreign investment governance to ISDS and how investment tribunals resolve certain high-profile cases, such as the famous tobacco saga. This limited view does not acknowledge the complexity of foreign investment relations and how the benefits, costs and risks of large investment projects are allocated. Also, international investment law makes some interests and their actors less visible—or even invisible—potentially reducing their benefits and increasing their costs and risks. The most paradigmatic case is that of local communities.

The literature on international investment law and policy has consistently avoided the role and interests of local communities. This is especially troublesome in natural resource and infrastructure projects, as local communities live near these projects and are often the most affected. Experience shows that foreign investment in natural resources can lead to overexploitation, environmental harm and, just as important, social conflict. However, there is little evidence that host states will necessarily use their regulatory powers to promote and protect local communities. Host states play an ambivalent role, facilitating foreign investment first and responding to local demands only when resistance escalates to unacceptable levels, such as in the case of Cochabamba, Bolivia (*Aguas del Tunari v. Bolivia*), which illustrates the potentially tragic consequences of a foreign investment and how difficult it is for local communities to find relief in either domestic or international jurisdictions.

This essay explores how the international investment regime makes things more difficult for local communities. This regime is not the sole reason for their problems, but it does deteriorate their situation vis-à-vis foreign investors and states. The good news is that there is no rationale for a narrow international investment regime. The crisis of ISDS can be an opportunity to move from foreign investment dispute settlement to foreign investment governance, ensuring local participation before, during and after the investment. Trust and cooperation are fundamental to avoid costly disputes and prevent the potentially tragic consequences of foreign investment.

Local Communities, Governments and the International Investment Regime

There are at least two sides to most large-scale natural resource and infrastructure projects. A few months ago I attended a presentation on a small country's economic achievements. The speakers were celebratory about the country's increasing domestic and foreign investment in tropical fruit production, essentially for export. This was positive on many levels. Focusing on tropical fruits allowed this small country to advertise itself as an environmentally friendly tourist destination. It also created many opportunities for its young people, from learning new languages to gaining insights into the business culture of the world's largest economies. The investment and exports in natural resources were, in other words, transformative of the economy and the people. This congratulatory narrative contrasted with a meeting later in the day, where civil society representatives denounced the consequences of the increasing production of tropical fruits: land grabs, overproduction, excessive use of water and uncontrolled use of pesticides and fertilizers. This example confirms that investment is a transformative force but that people's perceptions of the benefits, costs and risks can be markedly different.

Many disputes concerning investment in natural resources illustrate not only the complexity of these projects but also the ambivalence of governments toward the costs and benefits. Initially, governments are positive about the prospects of a project. They encourage domestic and foreign investors to consider establishing in the region or country and might even make specific regulatory decisions that signal their interest. Sometimes states themselves make the investment as part of public development projects, such as the Belo Monte Dam project in Brazil. This attitude, however, might change if local communities mobilize and resist the projects. Then states might take the local costs and risks more seriously and reconsider the project. But when foreign investors and an international investment treaty are involved, this behavior can create problems. Investment tribunals may look at government action as political, arbitrary or a violation of foreign investor legitimate expectations or due process. Many international investment disputes begin precisely because of this tension between the public function to promote and facilitate foreign investment and the states' obligation to maximize the benefits and minimize the costs for the population.[1]

---

[1] Nicolás M. Perrone, "The International Investment Regime and Local Populations: Are the Weakest Voices Unheard?," *Transnational Legal Theory* 7 (2016): 383.

Several high-profile investment disputes share a chronology where states facilitated a foreign investment at first only to change their minds later when local actors, after learning about the project, organized and resisted it. Such cases include *Pacific Rim v. Salvador, Bilcon v. Canada, Bear Creek v. Peru, Copper Mesa v. Ecuador* and, more recently, *Eco Oro v. Colombia*. In the latter, the government granted mining titles and explicitly acknowledged the possibility of mining in certain *páramos* (wastelands) in the country's 2014–18 national development plan. These measures prompted local resistance, and ultimately the Constitutional Court declared mining in *páramos* unconstitutional.

Governments can also express ambivalence during the life of an investment. They want to maintain a good relationship with foreign investors as a way to attract more investment. For example, in *Chevron v. Ecuador*, the Ecuadorian government signed and approved a remediation agreement that many people believed was deficient at best. The only public rationale for that decision was to facilitate new investments, but the local community resisted, initiating one of the most spectacular cases of transnational litigation, which was later supported by the then new president, Rafael Correa.

It is not news that states change their minds. In a way it is part of the democratic process. Modern democracies require tolerating some inconsistency as different actors pursue not only their interests but also their vision of community. For those who suffer the costs of foreign investment in natural resources, the problem is that international investment law makes certain changes more difficult than others. The standards of protection under investment law, particularly the fair and equitable standard of treatment (or minimum standard), are essentially about foreign investor calculability and legitimate expectations; changes in favor of local communities can only lead to trouble and disputes. This does not mean that investment tribunals reject the possibility of change. Arbitrators are receptive to reasonable and proportionate measures that respect due process and are backed by expert evidence. But they are much less open to considering the views of locals as a valid reason to modify foreign investor legitimate expectations or overhaul an entire regulatory framework. In their minds, local preferences are too political and unpredictable.

The real problem, however, is not that local preferences are too political—preferences are always subjective—but that the international investment regime has systematically ignored them.[2] Similarly, the study of the political economy of foreign investment looks at the benefits, costs and risks of foreign investment, but only from a foreign investor and state perspective—it rarely considers local actors or their interests.[3] Research on foreign investment and development is similar. It normally concludes that any positive effects on development depend on several factors. The role of governments is very relevant because foreign investment will not transform a country on its own. But the interplay between local communities, states and foreign investors is, at best, less clear. Locals are

---

[2]   Ibid.
[3]   Nicolás M. Perrone, "UNCTAD World Investment Reports 1991–2015: 25 Years of Narratives Justifying and Balancing Foreign Investor Rights," *Journal of World Investment and Trade* 19 (2018): 7.

not expected to have an active role. It is as if multinational corporations (MNCs) and states would prefer that locals adapt quickly to the changes brought about by the new economic activity, retraining if necessary to work on the project.

Most arbitral awards and scholarly work focus only on states and foreign investors. Books, articles and awards minimize or ignore local actors. Foreign investment in natural resources creates numerous and complex relationships, but investment law focuses on the interplay between foreign investors and host states—even the home state has been moved to a secondary place. This already narrow focus is also asymmetric as only foreign investors can sue states before an investment tribunal. Governments, at least, have the opportunity to tell their story and elaborate on their right to regulate, but local communities sometimes learn of the projects quite late and have no standing before investment tribunals—at best, arbitrators may accept their amicus curiae submissions.

In this way investment arbitration reflects a particular view of the facts of any foreign investment dispute. The narrative begins and centers on foreign investors, hence the significance of the moment of establishment, and focuses later on whether states' measures are arbitrary or unreasonable. States can prevail—and indeed do in many investment arbitrations—if they show that they acted proportionately and according to due process and existing technical evidence. But they do not win cases by relying on local values or preexisting private or communal rights. The latter is difficult if governments promote the foreign investment in the first place and change their minds later after increasing local pressure. For investment tribunals, the political decision was already taken, and governments are expected to behave in a consistent manner whether or not locals knew or were properly consulted about the project. In contrast, investment tribunals expect foreign investors to participate in any decision that might affect them.

By overlooking local views, the international investment regime distorts the perception of the benefits, costs and risks favoring certain use of the resources against others. Foreign investors, states and local actors have different opinions about what constitutes overexploitation of natural resources in terms of both space and time. Local communities live in the same space as the foreign investment. They cohabit with the project on a daily basis, unlike the states. Governments are absent from the local space but not indifferent to it. They may be less concerned about protecting each local community but often have a long-term vision for the nation, where development and economic prosperity play an important role. Foreign investors, on the other hand, establish themselves in a country with the perspective of an outsider or absentee owner. They care about the economic and social sustainability of a project because social unrest is bad for business, but they do not have any particular vision for a place—their vision is limited to the scope and length of the project, and most natural resource projects will end one day.

These different preferences are everywhere in foreign investment disputes, but the law does not recognize or protect them in the same way. Investment law is about the expectations of foreign investors, not those of states or, even less so, local communities. Arbitral awards embrace a commodity and fungible version of foreign investor rights whose main purpose is to facilitate wealth maximization through foreign investment. This interpretation suits foreign investors because it weakens local normative demands but contrasts with different versions of property that focus on personal and communal preferences.[4] These alternative versions recognize the importance of property for local and social life. Property is about social relations and deserves special protection as a keystone of the community. Unsurprisingly, these two versions of property are in tension. Foreign investors prefer to shape local aspirations to the size, form and shape of each project.

Taking Local Communities Seriously

To resolve the tensions and imbalances of the international investment regime, most literature suggests strengthening the right to regulate. The right to regulate is very important, but for local communities it is a source of both solutions and problems. States use the right to regulate to promote and facilitate foreign investment, overlooking local communities' preferences. The *Chevron v. Ecuador* dispute illustrates this well. Chevron's main legal argument is not that remediation was appropriate but that Ecuador consented and approved such remediation. Regulatory givings are a common practice as states compete to attract foreign investment. This pro-investment use of regulation, however, is never a problem for the international investment regime. If these regulations annihilate the locals' right to use water or produce food, this is outside the scope of this regime. But there seems to be no reason (or the reasons are not openly discussed) that foreign investor rights should be superior to other property interests.

The economic literature agrees that the most efficient solution to the under- or overexploitation of resources and social conflict—for example, the "tragedy of the commons"—consists of well-defined property rights.[5] This analysis is relevant to international investment law as it relates to the narrative of underuse of natural resources in the Global South. To facilitate investment, it is necessary to define stable and predictable property rights. Investment law can contribute to this goal, experts say. Investment treaties lock in certain investor-friendly policies, increase the cost of change and prompt countries to focus on the long-term economic goal of wealth maximization through foreign investment.[6]

But foreign investor rights, depending on how they are defined and interpreted, can also lead to overexploitation. When the incentive to invest is higher than the efficient environmental and social use of the resource, the chances of the tragedy of foreign investment increases dramatically. The evidence of land grabs, displacement, human abuse and environmental degradation confirms the risks related to foreign investment.[7]

---

[4]   Nicolás M. Perrone, "The Emerging Global Right to Investment: Understanding the Reasoning behind Foreign Investor Rights," *Journal of International Dispute Settlement* 8 (2017): 673.

[5]   Gary D. Libecap, "The Tragedy of the Commons: Property Rights and Markets as Solutions to Resource and Environmental Problems," *Australian Journal of Agricultural and Resource Economics* 53 (2009): 129.

[6]   For an analysis of the different rationales for granting special protection to foreign investors, see Rob Howse, "International Investment Law and Arbitration: A Conceptual Framework" (working paper, vol. 1, Institute for International Law and Justice, New York, 2017).

[7]   For evidence in the agriculture sector, see the work of Lorenzo Cotula, https://www.iied.org/users/lorenzo-cotula.

Overuse is worse than underuse because it disrupts the local way of life, and remediation is often impossible.

Invariably, when discussing foreign investment in natural resources and infrastructure, we are dealing not just with resources and investments but also with complex social relations between foreign investors, states and local actors. International investment law, however, is equipped with neither a vision nor a toolkit to shift the focus from investments to social relations. For one, this field is mainly about investment dispute settlement through arbitration. This view straitjackets many other forms of legal imagination. For another, tribunals have remained cognitively open but normatively closed to other preferences. Arbitrators are willing to accept changes in regulation that respond to expert knowledge, but they are extremely cautious about political and democratic mobilization. The outcome is a type of moral hazard. Foreign investors may decide not to worry about local politics, knowing that investment tribunals will compensate them if governments change their minds as a result of political mobilization.

To resolve these problems, the risks of overexploitation and local expectations could be internalized so that they are accounted for in foreign investment projects. Making local actors visible and granting them certain entitlements would ensure that investments take a form that would increase social welfare and a fairer distribution. Local actors are less willing to destroy their community and also want a better life and a reasonable level of prosperity. The recognition of local expectations or foreign investor obligations would constitute an important step in this direction. It is illusory to think that governments will always use their regulatory power in favor of those vulnerable to foreign investment. Modern democracies have problems, including the weakening relationship between citizens and their representatives.[8]

Some alternatives to incorporating foreign investor obligations and local expectations involve a stronger interface between human rights and international investment law or the inclusion of a chapter on local communities in international investment agreements, as happens in labor or gender. The problem with human rights obligations of nonstate actors, such as foreign investors, is that states are mainly responsible for human rights protection. While investment tribunals have recently recognized that foreign investors may have human rights obligations, it is difficult to pinpoint their specific responsibilities.[9] Furthermore, as Alvaro Santos and Kerry Rittich explain in their discussion of labor clauses in trade agreements, the mere inclusion of a special chapter or section in the investment agreements is not a good solution. Instead, the challenge is to reshape the international investment regime to make local communities visible and increase their participation. The economics literature also supports this approach and is wary about public regulation as there is no residual claimant to the social gains from the alternative

---

[8] Pierre Rosanvallon, *Counter-Democracy: Politics in an Age of Distrust* (New York: Cambridge University Press, 2013).

[9] *Urbaser S.A. v. The Argentine Republic* (ICSID Case No. ARB/07/26) Award, December 8, 2016, paras. 1193–1205.

use of the resources.[10] Making local communities the claimants of their communal rights seems, then, a fair and sensible move.

But this is not as simple as allocating private property or veto rights. Local communities are not always organized through private property rights and, even if they are, the main reason for resistance is usually a communal interest in their way of life that cannot be easily allocated. Moreover, local communities' interests, as any other interest, cannot be absolute. Community interests may be in conflict with legitimate state and other community objectives. Making local community interests visible does not mean that they should always prevail.

The work of Elinor Ostrom offers us a way to rethink foreign investment governance and gives local communities a meaningful role in the governance structure.[11] Some of Ostrom's recommendations for a successful cooperative platform are similar to those favored by investment treaties. The problem is that the international investment regime has implemented them in a one-sided manner. First, everybody needs clarity about rights, duties and obligations. Well-defined entitlements are not a new demand in international investment law. The emphasis on foreign investor rights, however, has created uncertainty for states and local actors. These entitlements also need to reflect a fair distribution of benefits, costs and risks. But while foreign investors are savvy actors who can extract benefits and incentives from states, local communities are in a much weaker position to maximize their benefits and minimize their costs. Foreign investors and states may offer local communities some incentives, for example, new roads or schools, but local actors rarely have enough information and capacity to negotiate appropriately.[12]

Furthermore, a fair distribution of benefits, costs and risks requires a mechanism to enforce this distribution and resolve disputes. This creates an additional imbalance. Although ISDS protects foreign investor rights, there is little in the current regime reassuring local communities. Foreign investor obligations need to be easily enforceable, but many communities lack effective access to a fast and flexible dispute settlement mechanism. It is unlikely that ISDS or a permanent investment court could protect local interests because of the large legal costs, the duration of the proceedings and the distance between the locality and the adjudicators—whether ad hoc arbitrators or permanent judges. Domestic courts might be better prepared to respond to local community needs, but their decisions can still be influenced by pro-investment governments and, in any case, remain subject to international investment law scrutiny.

Designing a dispute settlement mechanism that can resolve local claims in a timely and appropriate manner constitutes an important challenge. Part of the challenge is how to maintain the dispute close to the locality while offering foreign investors an acceptable forum. Promoting mediations between foreign investors and local communities

---

[10] Libecap, "The Tragedy of the Commons," 132.

[11] Elinor Ostrom, *Governing the Commons: The Evolution of Institutions for Collective Action* (Cambridge: Cambridge University Press, 2016).

[12] The five local communities who participated in the first meeting of the Local Communities and Foreign Investment project in Bogotá, August 1 and 2, 2018, highlighted the importance of capacity building at the community level.

could be a good strategy, but again, local actors need to have enough capacity and information to enforce a fair deal. The lack of clear options creates a space for domestic or international institutions to design a new dispute settlement mechanism that could operate close to the locality, reassuring local communities, but would also be acceptable to foreign investors. Any agreement between a local community, the state and a foreign investor could be subject to this jurisdiction, and decisions could be appealed before human rights courts, such as the Inter-American, African or European Courts of Human Rights.

In addition to well-defined rights and timely enforcement, cooperation and community participation are also significant, which, as Ostrom explains, do not simply happen. It is necessary to create the right institutional and social conditions. In the case of local communities, this would require defining who speaks on behalf of the local community and the timing and scope of this participation. The experience in public participation in zoning or environmental concerns illustrates the relevance and complexity of defining who participates.[13] Wide participation ensures representation but does not work when important decisions need to be made on a regular basis. In comparative administrative practice, the selection of local representatives in advisory committees is carried out by the public authorities, which normally invite existing organizations. This poses a series of challenges in plural urban contexts, but in rural areas or small towns, where most natural resources or infrastructure projects are located, some of these issues do not arise or are less relevant.[14]

Importantly, local communities are easier to identify and more homogenous than urban groups. They share a specific locality, a common cultural identity and previous experiences of resistance and organization. This applies not only to indigenous or ethnic communities but also to small towns. In Colombia, for instance, small towns have successfully self-organized referendums to ban mining and oil investments.[15] Experience also shows that many of these communities have put in place mechanisms to appoint representatives to defend their interests, particularly if they have been exposed to foreign investment projects—or the possibility of one.[16]

Respecting these local practices and mechanisms is fundamental to promoting trustworthy foreign investment relations and to the success of any consultation process or advisory committee. This does not mean that communities never have different opinions or that a decision made by a community may not affect another community or nearby cities. The challenge is to ensure the fair representation of these different voices according to their exposure to the costs and risks of a project. Participation should be calibrated to the transformations that a project would produce in the host locality. In this regard,

---

[13] See Thomas C. Beierle and Jerry Cayford, *Democracy in Practice: Public Participation in Environmental Decisions* (Washington, DC: Resources for the Future, 2002), 42–49.

[14] Ibid, 49.

[15] See https://www.eltiempo.com/colombia/otras-ciudades/resultados-de-consulta-petrolera-en-cumaral-meta-95396.

[16] The discussions during the first meeting of the Local Communities and Foreign Investment project show that local communities have a high level of organization and internal coordination.

international institutions or treaties could provide rules to ensure a balanced and appropriate representation of the different local interests.

The timing and scope of community participation are also fundamental. Local participation should begin as early as possible and continue throughout the project to ensure local willingness to consider not only the project's costs but also the benefits. The scope of participation, on the other hand, should vary depending on the stage of the project. Before establishment, local actors should be protagonists of the human and environmental impact assessment. This requires that the local community as a whole has enough and reliable information. In addition to public hearings, the right to be informed should include the possibility to request more information if necessary. This is fundamental to the effective compliance of states' and foreign investors' obligation to seek free, prior and informed consent (or consultation, depending on the applicable legislation). The organization of a consultation process, in addition, should be done in close coordination with local leaders and rely on existing practices and mechanisms.

During and after the investment, local communities should also have an important role in the governance of the project. This would require the establishment of advisory committees. The function and authority of these committees—and whether foreign investors and states need to consult them or seek their consent—would depend on the severity of the costs and risks for the local community. As noted earlier, the selection of local representatives for these committees is also a central issue; trusting existing local institutions seems to be the best strategy.

Enshrining this participatory model in the international investment regime is not easy, but it is feasible. The report of the expert meeting convened by the International Institute for Sustainable Development provides examples of specific clauses to be included in new investment treaties (e.g., the right of local communities to be informed before the project).[17] More important than the actual drafting, however, is to acknowledge that this would imply a shift from a regime based on the rule of law and dispute settlement to a more relational and participatory model. An international agreement could define the basis for this new framework following a procedure similar to the one used to create the new rules on transparency (the Mauritius Convention on Transparency) or to discuss the reform of ISDS and the potential creation of a multilateral investment court. After negotiating this framework, states would remain free to join the new agreement, and if they decide to ratify it, this new participatory model could apply only to their relations with other ratifying states. This framework, moreover, would not need to define every detail concerning local community participation but rather establish general principles that each country could adjust to its domestic context.

---

[17] International Institute for Sustainable Development, "Integrating Investor Obligations and Corporate Accountability Provisions in Trade and Investment Agreements," Report of the Expert Meeting held in Versoix, Switzerland, January 11–12, 2018 (the author participated in this meeting).

Making the Invisible Visible

Local communities have remained invisible in international investment law and policy. This is not only unfair but also increases the potentially tragic consequences of foreign investment. This essay has explained why and how this could be changed. Foreign investment in natural resources and infrastructure are complex economic transactions with large relational implications. A governance regime based on the rule of law and dispute settlement is too narrow and ill-equipped to deal with these challenges. These projects demand a governance model based on cooperation and participation. The obstacles to implement such a reform are not minor, but the benefits would be commensurable to the effort, considerably increasing local trust in foreign investment.

SECTION 4

SUPPORTING DEVELOPMENT

Chapter Seventeen

BARGAINING OVER POLICY SPACE IN TRADE NEGOTIATIONS[1]

Gregory Shaffer

The international trade law regime overseen by the World Trade Organization (WTO) faces two significant issues from the perspective of policy space: its failure to deal with imports produced under conditions that violate international labor norms and the restrictions it imposes on development strategies that deter legitimate experimentation. This essay proposes two reforms in trade law to address these two issues: (1) a hybrid antidumping/safeguard regime that would authorize increased tariffs when imported goods are produced under substandard labor conditions and (2) exceptions to the law on subsidies for legitimate industrial policy for development purposes. While there will be opposition to these measures since the Global North has an interest in the first and the Global South in the second, it may be possible to negotiate such a reform package with appropriate safeguards against abuse if political will can be mustered. Otherwise, countries may push the interpretation of existing WTO law to accommodate these policies, placing greater pressure on the WTO's judicial bodies.

Trade negotiations traditionally involve reciprocal bargaining to increase market access. In this way, they ratchet up trade liberalization over time. Yet democratic governments are interested in more than just one-way trade liberalization. They are also concerned about policy space, and thus negotiations can and should involve reciprocal bargains to ensure democratic legitimacy and responsiveness. One can envisage parallel trade negotiations over policy space between developed and developing countries. The negotiations could involve the provision of greater policy space for developed countries to uphold the domestic social contract by protecting labor against social dumping, on the one hand, and greater policy space for developing countries to adopt experimental industrial policies to move up the value-added production chain, on the other hand. In this way, they can address both the trade-labor problem involving the export of goods produced under working conditions that violate international norms and the trade-development problem involving WTO restrictions on industrial policies for development.

---

[1] This essay draws from Gregory Shaffer, "Reconceiving Trade Agreements to Address Social Inclusion," *Illinois Law Review* 1 (2019).

The challenge with these proposals is that they can impose significant externalities on outsiders. These externalities, however, can be subject to bargaining, as is the case with any rule. The challenge is to operationalize the concept of negotiating over policy space through new legal provisions while limiting the risks of protectionist abuse. Dani Rodrik has advocated the need for these policies to address distributional and development concerns.[2] What we need is complementary legal analysis regarding how they can be designed and operationalized. This essay sets forth a proposal.

Protection against Social Dumping

Claims of unfair trade proliferated following the election of neonationalist US president Donald Trump. The underlying problem from a social policy perspective, however, is not unfair trade as viewed through the traditional WTO lens of product dumping, because antidumping procedures tend to involve accounting ploys to show differences in pricing that may be economically justifiable and thus not unfair.[3] The real underlying concern should be social dumping of products—that is, products produced under exploitative labor conditions—that sell for less than domestically produced products, thus leading to concerns over wage suppression and reductions of labor protections in the North. These policies can undermine the domestic social contract and trigger political contestation against trade. A number of bilateral and plurilateral agreements include labor clauses pursuant to which countries agree not to obtain a trade advantage by failing to uphold national labor laws or (in some cases) minimum labor standards. These provisions, however, have proved insufficient in ways that this proposal aims to remedy.[4]

If provisions to safeguard against social dumping are incorporated into trade agreements, they should be subject to strict procedural, substantive and injury requirements to combat abuse. Many of the provisions could take from the current WTO antidumping regime. The procedural criteria could mirror or build on Articles 5 (Initiation and Subsequent Investigation), 6 (Evidence), 11 (Duration), 12 (Public Notice and Explanation of Determinations) and 13 (Judicial Review) of the WTO Antidumping Agreement. Most important, due process rights would be provided to affected parties,

---

[2] See Dani Rodrik, *Has Globalization Gone Too Far?* (Washington, DC: Peterson Institute for International Economics, 1997); Dani Rodrik, *The Globalization Paradox: Democracy and the Future of the World Economy* (Oxford: Oxford University Press, 2011); and Dani Rodrik, *Straight Talk on Trade: Ideas for a Sane World Economy* (Princeton, NJ: Princeton University Press, 2017).

[3] The issue of subsidies, such as from China, is more complicated. On the one hand, traditional economic analysis contends that foreign subsidies of traded goods benefit importing countries and their consumers. In particular, they increase a country's terms of trade because foreign governments make their subsidized exports cheaper for an importing country's consumers while that country's exports sell at the same price, bringing in the same amount of revenue. Nonetheless, there is significant evidence that subsidized Chinese products have harmed some US workers and communities. Existing WTO rules permit governments to countervail and directly challenge these subsidies. However, the WTO Appellate Body has been criticized for placing undue constraints on governments' ability to countervail and challenge them.

[4] See Kerry Rittich (chapter 19, this volume).

including exporters, importers, organized labor and other social groups, including consumer organizations. Similarly, injury criteria could reflect those set forth in Articles 3 and 4 of the WTO Antidumping Agreement, which require the showing of a "material injury," or threat thereof, to a "domestic industry." WTO jurisprudence provides significant guidance regarding these provisions' application.

The first challenge with implementing this proposal is to specify when violations of labor rights occur so that a country may impose increased tariffs. The criteria chosen would build from experience with existing labor chapters in trade agreements, including the original Trans-Pacific Partnership (TPP) and the new United States–Mexico–Canada Agreement, including its Annex on Worker Representation in Collective Bargaining in Mexico.[5] The norms would address labor rights violations and thus not undercut developing countries' comparative advantage in producing goods with lower-skilled labor in reflection of differences in productivity. The list of labor norms would include rights against forced labor, child labor, hazardous work and discrimination; establishment of maximum working hours and a minimum wage; and most fundamentally, rights to freedom of association and collective bargaining.[6] A country deciding to impose duties would need to show sustained violations.

A second challenge is obtaining evidence establishing labor rights violations. This can be and has been done.[7] Indeed, the United States prevailed on this issue in its challenge of Guatemala's labor practices under the US–Central America Free Trade Agreement (CAFTA).[8] To gather evidence of labor rights violations, governments can work with labor and civil society organizations, and recognize and incorporate evidence from reports of the International Labour Organization (ILO) on country practices, as the United States did in the *Guatemala* case.

A third challenge is to determine the number of tariffs that may be imposed on the imports in response to the labor rights violations. The WTO Antidumping Agreement provides detailed provisions for the calculation of antidumping duties based on a comparison of product prices in the country of production and the importing country to determine dumping margins. The result is high transaction costs for all sides, including for the administrative authority. Accounting for the price differential caused by social dumping, in contrast, would not be necessary. In the case of social dumping, duties could be limited to the

---

[5] See United States–Mexico–Canada Agreement, chap. 19, annex 23-A: Worker Representation in Collective Bargaining in Mexico, https://ustr.gov/trade-agreements/free-trade-agreements/united-states-mexico-canada-agreement/united-states-mexico.

[6] See, e.g., Mark Barenberg, "Sustaining Workers' Bargaining Power in an Age of Globalization" (report, Economic Policy Institute, Washington, DC, 2009). The minimum wage would have to be set near the market clearing rate, which will vary not only by country but also within countries. Countries should thus have discretion in setting a minimum wage, which may vary within them in light of differing labor market conditions.

[7] Discussion with a former official at USTR who worked on the case where the United States challenged Guatemala under the US–Central America Free Trade Agreement (CAFTA), March 1, 2018.

[8] See "In the Matter of Guatemala—Issues Relating to Obligations," CAFTA-DR, Article 16.2.1(a) (final panel report, 2017).

amount that would offset the injury that the increased imports from the country in question cause, or threaten to cause, to the domestic industry. Calculating such an amount would be more transparent and not involve the manipulation of pricing data, thus reducing administrative costs for firms and administrative agencies. It would be analogous to the calculations made in safeguard procedures conducted under the WTO Agreement on Safeguards.

There are two key differences between this proposal and trade agreements such as the CAFTA. First, under this proposal, a country can take direct action against imports produced under nonconforming labor standards. This proposal would shift leverage to the importing state to protect its social contract. No longer would it have to bring an international claim against the party violating the agreement. Rather, subject to procedural, substantive and injury requirements, the importing country could impose a social dumping duty, just as it currently can apply a traditional antidumping duty under existing antidumping law.

Second, the petitioner bringing the domestic social dumping action need not prove a causal link between the labor rights violations and increased imports. Rather, a petitioner would only need to show a correlation between the violation of the specified labor rights and an increase of imports of the products from the country in question that causes, or threatens to cause, material injury to a domestic industry. The analysis would be simplified. The focus would be on the existence of sustained labor rights violations, in combination with a percentage rise in imports relative to domestic production that causes, or threatens to cause, material injury to a domestic industry.

This proposal is a hybrid that combines antidumping procedures with a safeguard remedy—that is, it includes both a substantive law trigger based on labor rights violations and a safeguard remedy based on increased imports of products causing, or threatening to cause, material injury to a domestic industry. The rationale for this hybrid is at least twofold (and for many threefold). First, it is notoriously difficult to prove causation, and such difficulty should not work to the advantage of a producer that violates labor rights in a sustained manner. Second, a country should be able to safeguard its social contract by providing a remedy against products produced in such a manner. Third, for many people, sustained violations of international labor rights raise moral concerns, and a country should not be forced to open its market to products produced in violation of them.

In practice, as under the current antidumping regime, the initiation of the investigation would trigger negotiations with the party subject to the investigation. As under Article 15 of the Antidumping Agreement, "constructive remedies" could be explored. In this case, however, negotiations triggered by a threat of tariffs would focus on measures to enhance compliance with labor rights. Labor and civil society organizations would be granted access to the process. This proposal would thus more directly benefit the exporting country's workers.

Such a social dumping agreement can be subject to abuse and thus must be subject to legal discipline. To counter abuse, an analogue to NAFTA Chapter 19 could be incorporated so that an exporter could request the establishment of a binational panel to review the final determination issued by the relevant authority.[9] In addition,

---

[9] North American Free Trade Agreement, December 17, 1992, 32 I.L.M. 289, Article 1904.5. See also David A. Gantz, "Resolution of Trade Disputes under NAFTA's Chapter 19: The

or alternatively, the targeted country could bring a claim of noncompliance before the WTO dispute settlement system, just as under the existing WTO antidumping regime. Finally, as with all WTO agreements, compliance would be overseen by a WTO committee. In this case, however, representatives of the ILO could be granted official or observer status within it, leading to greater coordination of international labor rights policies.[10] If current antidumping law remains a parallel procedure (which would likely be the case given the political economy of trade negotiations and the need for a political safety valve), there would be rules against "double counting," just as there are when antidumping and countervailing duty investigations are currently conducted.

If countries fail to agree to such provisions, they could attempt to apply the provisions under existing WTO law by claiming a general exception under GATT Article XX(a), which permits countries to restrict imports where it is "necessary to protect public morals" so long as the measures do not "constitute a means of arbitrary or unjustifiable discrimination between countries where the same conditions prevail, or a disguised restriction of international trade."[11] Article XX(a), however, lacks this proposal's procedural, substantive and injury criteria and thus would be more subject to abuse. Moreover, the rationale for its use would have to be on moral grounds over the treatment of *foreign* workers, rather than economic and distributional grounds regarding protection of *domestic* workers and the domestic social contract. Thus, it should be much more difficult for a neonationalist government—such as that currently in power in the United States—to prevail compared to one whose policies are expressly outward looking.

Lessons of Extending the Binational Panel Process to Mexico," *Law and Policy in International Business* 29 (1998): 297, 298.

[10] For example, the ILO has official status regarding the implementation and supervision of the Bangladesh accord that followed in the wake of the Rana Factory fire. See Larry Catá Backer, "Are Supply Chains Transnational Legal Orders? What We Can Learn from the Rana Plaza Factory Building Collapse," *UC Irvine Journal of International, Transnational, and Comparative Law* 1 (2016): 11, 13. In the WTO context, the International Monetary Fund (IMF) is granted official status within the WTO Committee on Balance of Payments Restrictions. See Gregory Shaffer and Michael Waibel, "The (Mis)alignment of the Trade and Monetary Legal Orders," in *Transnational Legal Orders*, ed. Terence Halliday and Gregory Shaffer (Cambridge: Cambridge University Press, 2015): 187, 195, 198–201 (formal analysis required from IMF before the WTO committee). In contrast, the World Intellectual Property Organization is granted observer status in the WTO Council for Trade-Related Aspects of Intellectual Property Rights and the United Nations Environment Programme holds such status in the WTO Committee on Trade and Environment. See World Trade Organization, "International Intergovernmental Organizations Granted Observer Status to WTO Bodies," https://www.wto.org/english/thewto_e/igo_obs_e.htm.

[11] The WTO Appellate Body recognized the application of this defense for an EU ban on the importation of seal products in response to and in reflection of public morals regarding animal welfare. Restrictions on imports of goods produced in violation of human rights should also be permitted on "public morals" grounds.

Industrial Policy Space for Developing Countries

Considerable policy experimentation is needed to catalyze economic development since no one knows in advance what works. This is particularly the case given the vastly differing contexts that countries face. Rodrik and others critique WTO rules for taking industrial policy options off the table for developing countries.[12] Industrial policy experimentation for development could be expressly authorized by amending existing WTO agreements, which already provide a framework. Developing countries could demand enhanced policy space for their development initiatives in return for provisions authorizing social dumping measures, again subject to legal discipline.

Since one country's industrial policy will have externalities on others, criteria need to be specified as part of a bargain. In the case of industrial policy, rules could be set forth in a separate agreement or in a revision of the WTO Agreement on Subsidies and Countervailing Measures (SCM Agreement). They would include general principles, substantive criteria, time limits, and reporting and transparency obligations. The general principle would be that the plans must aim to increase productivity and set forth clear criteria for success so that they can be evaluated.[13] The substantive criteria would aim to constrain potential abuse.

The SCM Agreement initially provided exceptions pursuant to which three types of subsidies would not be actionable: subsidies for research, subsidies providing assistance to disadvantaged regions, and subsidies for adaptation of facilities to meet environmental requirements, provided in each case they met specified criteria.[14] Those provisions lapsed, but they could be revamped and updated to include development-related industrial policies. For example, they could cover experimentalist policies to develop infant industries, which were initially permitted under GATT Article XVI (on Subsidies) and Article XVIII (on Governmental Assistance to Economic Development) but are now subject to challenge under the SCM Agreement.

Under a revamped SCM Agreement, special authorization for industrial policy experimentation for development could be made available under agreed terms. For example, it could be limited to developing countries that meet defined World Bank criteria in terms of per capita income, and it could be further subject to industry competitiveness criteria. The criteria could build from national programs under the existing Generalized System of Preferences (GSP) that provide for preferential tariff treatment of developing-country imports, subject to the denial of benefits once an industry becomes competitive.[15] Under

---

[12] See Rodrik, *The Globalization Paradox*; Rodrik, *Straight Talk on Trade*.

[13] Ricardo Haussman, Dani Rodrik and Charles Sabel, "Reconfiguring Industrial Policy: A Framework with an Application to South Africa" (working paper no. RWP08-031, Harvard Kennedy School, Cambridge, MA, 2008); Dani Rodrik, "Industrial Policy for the Twenty-First Century," UNIDO (2004), http://www.vedegylet.hu/fejkrit/szvggyujt/rodrik_industrial_policy.pdf.

[14] Agreement on Subsidies and Countervailing Measures, Article 8.2, April 15, 1994, Marrakesh Agreement Establishing the World Trade Organization, Annex 1A, 1869 U.N.T.S. 14.

[15] The provisions could also build on the concept of "export competitiveness" under Article 27.6 of the SCM Agreement (3.25 percent share of world trade for a product for two consecutive years) and the carve-out for export subsidies provided under Annex VII of the SCM

the European Union's GSP program, for example, once countries become listed as high- or upper-middle-income economies (using World Bank criteria based on per capita income) for three consecutive years, they cease to benefit from the program.[16] Similarly, countries lose GSP preferences for their highly competitive export sectors.

Analogous criteria could define beneficiary countries and sectors entitled to benefit from preferential treatment for industrial policy experimentation for development. In this way, countries like China would graduate from the system. Under the proposed system, the criteria for graduation would be agreed multilaterally and thus not left to countries' discretion.

Time limits would be agreed so that ineffective programs are abandoned. The WTO Agreement on Safeguards provides an example of imposing time limits. Under it, a safeguard measure may be maintained without being subject to a withdrawal of concessions for three years.[17] Similarly, an industrial policy measure could be limited to a set number of years without being subject to retaliation, provided it met the agreed criteria and the country complied with the other obligations relating to it.

The country adopting such a measure would have to report its program. The SCM Agreement already requires that members notify their subsidies each year to the WTO Committee on Subsidies and Countervailing Measures. However, the record of industrial subsidies notification is poor, with more than half of WTO members not notifying them.[18] China's failures have particularly irked the United States, which has proposed sanctions against countries that fail to notify, such as a suspension of certain WTO benefits.[19] Under this proposal, a country's failure to report its obligations could trigger a suspension of the ability to use the policy until compliance occurs. Such a sanction would incentivize reporting in ways that the current SCM Agreement does not.

Transparency and reporting are public goods. They are important not only for trade relations but also for domestic governance to limit rent seeking. They reduce information asymmetries, enabling firms, citizens and trading partners alike to know what governments are doing. Even if an industrial policy measure is legitimate, the public has a right to know, and other governments must be assured that it is not abused. In particular, domestic stakeholders must be able to monitor and hold experimental industrial policy programs accountable. Otherwise, the results of experiments would not be known,

---

Agreement (for least developed countries and a list of developing countries until they reach a per capita GNP of $1,000).

[16] See *GSP Handbook on the Scheme of the European Union*, UNCTAD/ITCD/TSB/MISC.25/Rev.4 (2016), http://unctad.org/en/pages/PublicationWebflyer.aspx?publicationid=1470.

[17] Agreement on Safeguards, Article 8, April 15, 1994, Marrakesh Agreement Establishing the World Trade Organization, Annex 1A, 1869 U.N.T.S. 154.

[18] Gregory Shaffer, Robert Wolfe and Vinhcent Le, "Can Informal Law Discipline Subsidies?" *Journal of International Economic Law* 18 (2015): 711.

[19] Communication from the United States, "Procedures to Enhance Transparency and Strengthen Notification Requirements under WTO Agreements," World Trade Organization JOB/GC/148, October 30, 2017.

and the risks of cronyism would increase. In the process, governments can learn from one another's experiences.

This proposal too would be subject to risk of abuse. To counter abuse, just as under WTO agreements generally, policies that fail to meet the criteria would be subject to traditional trade dispute settlement. In addition, to the extent that such policies cause material injury to a domestic industry in an importing country, that country could still impose countervailing duties, as under the current SCM Agreement. The ability to bring countervailing duties against such policies would, of course, limit the impact of industrial policies. Yet such provisions would be required to address potential externalities on producers in Third World countries. This proposal would represent a return to the trade policies under the GATT where developing countries could subsidize infant industries, but their products could be countervailed when imported into a developed country where the subsidies caused, or threatened to cause, significant injury to a domestic industry.

Once again, if no agreement is reached, developing countries could initiate them and claim that they are not prohibited "specific subsidies" under the SCM Agreement and are thus permissible. This proposal, however, provides criteria that would help combat abuse in ways that are important both for trading partners and for domestic stakeholders.

Feasibility

Negotiation of these provisions would not be easy. Developing countries are wary of granting authorization to developed countries to block imports on social dumping grounds, and developed countries are suspicious of emerging economy industrial policies. Emerging economies would demand some benefit from the negotiations to the extent that they could be excluded from the industrial policy exceptions and be a target of social dumping measures. Similarly, to the extent that many developing countries do not feel constrained by the SCM Agreement, they may find that they have less to gain from these negotiations than developed countries.

Here is where bargaining comes in. Subject to bargaining, provisions can be structured to combat abuse so that they would be subject to no more (and arguably much less) abuse than current WTO rules on unfair trade, such as antidumping and countervailing duty rules. For example, developing countries could be granted compensation when prevailing in a WTO challenge against a social dumping measure. In addition, bargaining could incorporate other issues of interest to countries, whether involving market access or other forms of policy space. Finally, the difficulties faced should be compared with the real-life alternative of existing challenges to the trading system. These issues should be frontally discussed so that the underlying social and development issues are addressed transparently. A multilateral institution such as the WTO provides an important forum for doing so. Negotiations can advance in parallel in plurilateral and bilateral fora. The conceptualization of trade negotiations in all fora should explicitly address policy space concerns.

Conclusion

These are politically challenging times. They present severe risks as well as opportunities. It is time to put forward proposals that retool trade agreements so that they directly address the challenges of social dumping and industrial policy experimentation for development. To address these issues, this essay proposes the creation of an antidumping system that directly addresses labor exploitation and new rules that permit industrial policy experimentation for development, in each case subject to defined criteria.

Lawyers and economists provided the intellectual constructs and designs for the existing trade legal order. John Maynard Keynes, for example, called lawyers the "poets" at Bretton Woods for their imagination in helping to craft the agreements.[20] Now economists and lawyers must do the same for the regime's redesign so as to save it from imploding.

---

[20] John Maynard Keynes, *The Collected Writings of John Maynard Keynes,* ed. Donald Moggridge, vol. 26 (London: Royal Economic Society, 1980), 102.

Chapter Eighteen

TRUMPING THE IMF: TRADE AND INVESTMENT TREATIES AND THE REGULATION OF CROSS-BORDER FINANCIAL FLOWS

Kevin P. Gallagher

The trade and investment treaty regime has largely closed the opening in the Articles of Agreement of the International Monetary Fund (IMF) that allow nations to regulate cross-border capital flows. The lack of policy space for regulating cross-border capital flows conflicts with prevailing economic theory and new policy at the IMF that encourages nation-states to regulate cross-border capital flows in certain circumstances. This essay suggests reforms to the treaty system that could make it more conducive to fostering financial stability.

The Need to Regulate Capital Flows

Cross-border financial investments that are not foreign direct investments—such as bonds, stocks, derivatives and other instruments—can be essential parts of government, banking and corporate finance. Indeed, many developing countries may lack the savings or financial institutions that can help finance business activity. Capital from abroad can fill that gap. Therefore, under normal circumstances, the more capital flowing into a developing country, the more the country benefits. However, cross-border capital flows tend to be procyclical: too much money comes in when times are good, and too much money evaporates during a downturn.

A key characteristic of the global financial instability has been mass swings of capital flows across the globe. Indeed, international investment positions now surpass global output. Developing and emerging markets are no strangers to these flows. When the crisis hit, capital rapidly left the developing world in a flight to the safety of the US market. In an attempt to recover, many industrialized nations, including the United States, resorted to loose monetary policy with characteristically low interest rates. Relatively higher interest rates and a stronger recovery triggered yet another surge in capital flows to the developing world. The result has been an increasing concern over currency appreciation, asset bubbles and even inflation.

The East Asian Financial Crisis is a case in point, where surges of short-term capital flows led to upward pressure on exchange rates in a region where competitiveness was the cornerstone of national export-led growth strategies. When global investors speculated that those countries would no longer be able to maintain their competitive exchange rates, there was a sudden stop that caused the region's currencies to collapse and a major crisis to ensue. Malaysia largely avoided the worst of those impacts (and having to go to the IMF) after imposing capital controls on outflows—though they were threatened with an investor-state dispute settlement (ISDS) case under a bilateral investment treaty (BIT).

Under these circumstances, regulations on cross-border financial transactions can help smooth the inflows and outflows of capital and protect developing economies. Most existing regulations target highly short-term capital flows, usually conducted for speculative purposes. For example, Colombia's 2007 regulations required foreign investors to park a percentage of their investment in the country's central bank, which helped that nation escape some of the damage from the global financial crisis. Chile and Malaysia successfully regulated capital flows in the 1990s to avoid the worst of the damages during crises in that decade. That said, in 2011, when Chile was considering controls to avoid a surge in inflows triggered by abnormally low interest rates in the United States, the Central Bank of Chile cited the country's free trade agreement (FTA) with the United States and refrained from the measure fearing that hostile ISDS cases would ensue.

In the aftermath of the global financial crisis, an IMF study found that in the past such regulations have helped developing nations stem currency appreciation and asset bubbles. Moreover, the study found that capital controls helped buffer some of the worst effects of the financial crisis in some developing countries. In lieu of these findings, the IMF now endorses the use of capital account regulations as a part of the macroeconomic policy toolkit.

In fact, as Jagdish Bhagwati noted in his famous 1998 essay, "The Capital Myth,"[1] there is not a coherent theory of the liberalization of capital flows, and Bhagwati has long argued that the inclusion of transfers provisions in trade treaties was not justified. Where capital flows can be beneficial is filling savings gaps in emerging-market and developing countries and creating microeconomic spillovers into the local economy. A comprehensive review of the literature on the subject by Olivier Jeanne and colleagues, *Who Needs to Open the Capital Account?*,[2] revealed, however, that capital account liberalization has been associated not with growth in emerging-market and developing countries but rather with banking crises.

Quantifying the Reach of Trade Treaties and Cross-Border Investment Flows

As part of the World Bank's Deep Integration project, a team convened by Boston University's Global Development Policy Center and Deborah Siegel, former senior legal

---

[1] Jagdish Bhagwati, "The Capital Myth: The Difference between Trade in Widgets and Dollars," *Foreign Affairs*, May/June 1998.

[2] Olivier Jeanne, Arvind Subramanian and John Williamson, *Who Needs to Open the Capital Account?* (Washington, DC: Peterson Institute for International Economics, 2012).

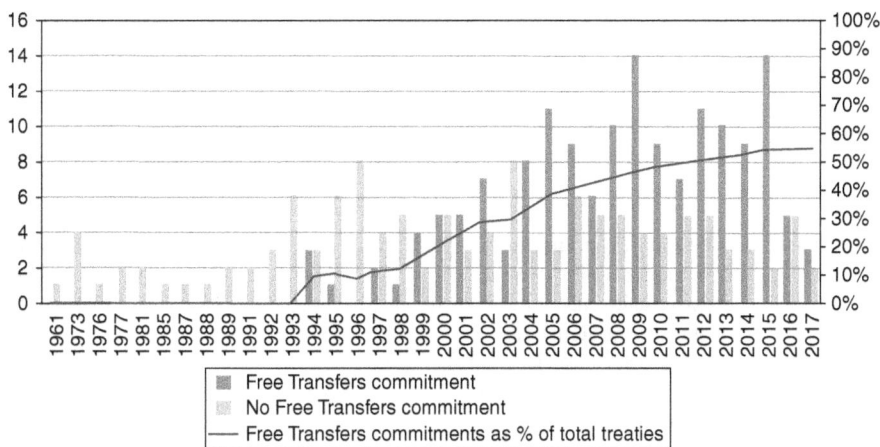

Figure 18.1 Free transfers commitments in trade and investment treaties (1961–2017)

counsel at the IMF, coded 284 trade and investment treaties with 90 questions to measure the extent to which these treaties restrict the ability of nation-states to regulate cross-border capital flows. In that research, we found that free transfers commitments are found in just fewer than half of all treaties, but the share of treaties including such commitments has increased significantly over time, as shown in Figure 18.1.[3] We also found that, in general, free transfers commitments tend to be located in North–North treaties and North–South treaties, but are less likely in South–South trade and investment treaties.

In our research for the World Bank, we found that 119 treaties that included free transfers commitments had some form of safeguard to mitigate a financial crisis (putting controls on outflows), and 95 treaties had a prudential exception that might allow for restrictions on inflows to prevent financial instability. In subsequent research, we have expanded on this coding effort to create a composite score of the overall degree of restrictiveness of a particular treaty on its ability to regulate capital flows. The score ranged from zero (no commitments to free transfers) to 9 (highly restrictive commitments in this area). We colored those from green (plenty of room to maneuver) to bright red (highly restrictive).

When simply looking at the number of treaties, there appears to be a significant amount of flexibility in the trading system to regulate capital flows (see Figure 18.2).

More than 120 treaties allow for regulating capital flows (green), and almost another 100 treaties allow for regulation with fairly broad safeguards and exceptions (yellow, orange). Indeed, only 60 treaties are in the "red" category, the most restrictive cases. Figure 18.3, however, shows that looking at the number of treaties may be deceiving.

---

[3] See Deborah Siegel, Kevin P. Gallagher and Rachel Thrasher, " 'Deep Integration' Database: Transfers and Capital Controls in Preferential Trade Agreements" (Washington, DC: World Bank, 2018); see Kevin P. Gallagher, *Ruling Capital: Emerging Markets and the Reregulation of Cross-Border Finance* (Ithaca, NY: Cornell University Press, 2015), for many of the other arguments and citations in this essay.

Table 18.1 Quantifying flexibilities for cross-border financial regulations

Color Scale	Description	Number Scale	Examples
GREEN	Treaties with no commitments to liberalize capital flows	0	Andean Community (CAN) (1988), Argentina–Brazil Partial Scope Agreement (2016)
YELLOW	Treaties with free transfers commitments with a very limited scope (usually only in the context of investment, sometimes services), which usually contain safeguards for capital controls in the event of macroeconomic crises, though they are not always listed, and no investor-state dispute settlement process	1.2	European Free Trade Area (2002), EU–Palestinian Authority (1997)
ORANGE	Treaties with *either* broader free transfers commitments with safeguards for macroeconomic crises and no investor-state dispute settlement, *or* narrow free transfers commitments with investor-state dispute settlement	3.4	ASEAN–China (2007), EU–Republic of Korea (2011), Japan–Vietnam (2009)
RED	Treaties with broad free transfers (2–3) commitments, and lack general safeguards for macroeconomic crises *or* contain investor-state dispute settlement. Some may contain specific annexes with carve-outs for capital controls, usually unilaterally. These may contain a limitation on the "prudential reasons" exception under Financial Services.	5, 6, 7	ASEAN–Australia-New Zealand (2010), Costa Rica–Colombia (2016), MERCOSUR (2005)
BRIGHT RED	Treaties with broad free transfers (2–3) commitments, and lack general safeguards for macroeconomic crises *and* contain investor-state dispute settlement. Some may contain specific annexes with carve-outs for capital controls, usually unilaterally. These may contain a limitation on the prudential reasons exception under Financial Services.	8, 9	Canada–Peru (2009), DR–CAFTA (2006)

Figure 18.1–18.3, Table 18.1 and discussion of new research are derived from Kevin Gallagher, Sarah Sklar and Rachel Thrasher, "Trading Away Financial Stability: Estimating the Flexibilities for Regulating Capital Flows in Trade and Investment Treaties" (working paper, Global Development Policy Center, Boston University, Boston, 2018).

Treaties by Restrictiveness

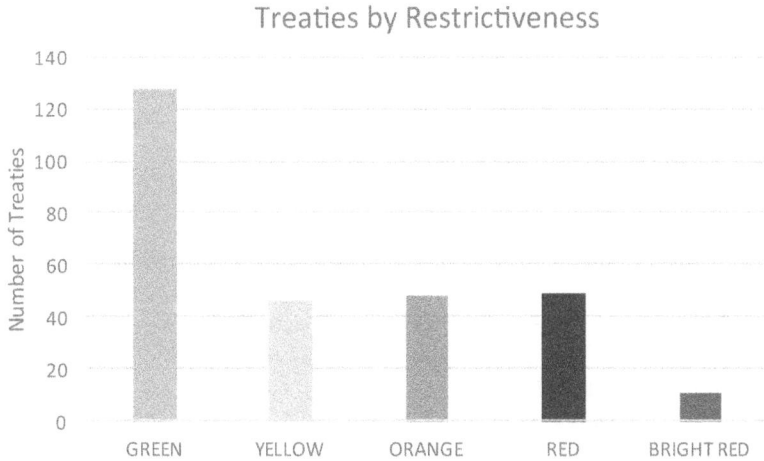

Figure 18.2 Restrictiveness of treaties to cross-border financial regulation

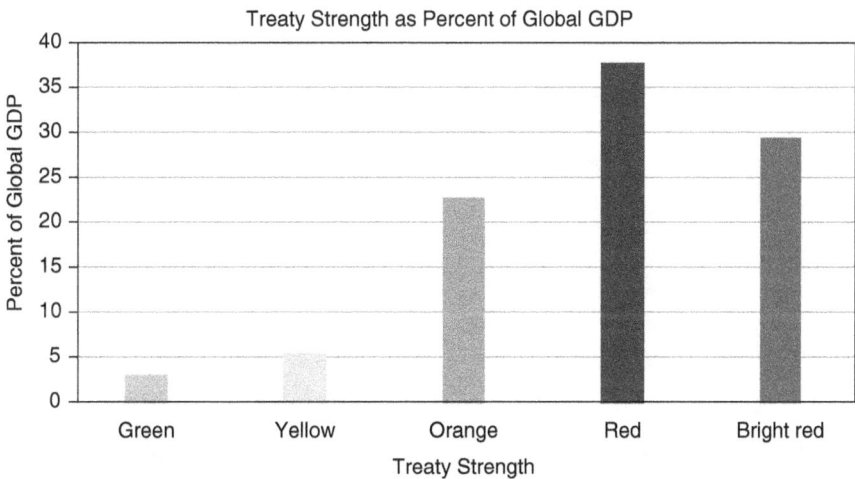

Figure 18.3 Number of treaties in each category weighted by the amount of GDP covered by members of the treaty

Figure 18.3 shows that those treaties that cover the largest amount of foreign investment in the world tend to also have free transfers commitments that are highly restrictive in terms of allowing nation-states to regulate capital flows—more than 80 percent of the world economy is orange, red or bright red.

US Trade Policy and the Regulation of Cross-Border Finance

Our quantitative research mirrors legal analyses that show how the treaties of one particular country have the most restrictive posture on regulating capital flows—the United

States.[4] In contrast with the treaties of many other industrialized nations, the template for US trade and investment treaties does not leave adequate flexibility for nations to use or regulate capital flows to prevent and mitigate financial crises. At their core, US treaties see restrictions on the movement of speculative capital as a violation of their terms. Moreover, the safeguards in US treaties were not intended to cover the regulation of capital flows.

US trade and investment treaties explicitly deem regulations of cross-border financial transactions as actionable measures that can trigger investor-state claims. The transfers provisions in the investment chapters of trade treaties, or in stand-alone BITs, require that capital be allowed to flow between trading partners "freely and without delay." This is reinforced in trade treaties' chapters on financial services, which often state that nations are not permitted to pose "limitations on the total value of transactions or assets in the form of numerical quotas" across borders.

In the financial services chapters of US trade treaties, and in US BITs, there is usually a section on "exceptions." One exception, informally referred to as the "prudential exception," usually has language similar to the following from the US–Peru trade treaty:

Financial Services chapter: Article 12.10: Exceptions

1. Notwithstanding any other provision of this Chapter or Chapter Ten (Investment), Fourteen (Telecommunications), or Fifteen (Electronic Commerce), including specifically Articles 14.16 (Relationship to Other Chapters) and 11.1 (Scope and Coverage) with respect to the supply of financial services in the territory of a Party by a covered investment, a Party shall not be prevented from adopting or maintaining measures for prudential reasons, including for the protection of investors, depositors, policy holders, or persons to whom a fiduciary duty is owed by a financial institution or cross-border financial service supplier, or to ensure the integrity and stability of the financial system. Where such measures do not conform with the provisions of this Agreement referred to in this paragraph, they shall not be used as a means of avoiding the Party's commitments or obligations under such provisions.

Under this exception, capital account regulations are not seen as permissible. This has been communicated by the Office of the United States Trade Representative and, in 2003, testimony by the Under Secretary of Treasury for International Affairs to the US Congress.[5] In general, this is because the term *prudential reasons* is usually interpreted in a much narrower fashion, pertaining to individual financial institutions. Concern has also been expressed that the last sentence is self-canceling, making many measures not permissible.

Nothing in this chapter or Chapters Ten (Investment), Fourteen (Telecommunications) or Fifteen (Electronic Commerce), including specifically Articles 14.16 (Relationship to Other Chapters) and 11.1 (Scope and Coverage) with respect to the supply of financial services in the territory of a Party by a covered investment, applies to non-discriminatory

---

[4]   Siegel et al., "'Deep Integration' Database"; Gallagher et al., "Trading Away Financial Stability."

[5]   See Gallagher, *Ruling Capital.*

measures of general application taken by any public entity in pursuit of monetary and related credit or exchange rate policies. *This paragraph shall not affect a Party's obligations under Article 10.9 (Performance Requirements) with respect to measures covered by Chapter Ten (Investment) or under Article 10.8 (Transfers) or 11.10 (Transfers and Payments).*

These provisions were very controversial with the US–Chile and US–Singapore trade treaties in the early 2000s. US trading partners have repeatedly asked for a safeguard that would include capital controls, but the United States has denied those requests. In a few instances, US negotiators granted special annexes that allowed US trading partners to receive an extended grace period before investor-state claims can be filed with respect to capital controls, as well as limits on damages related to certain types of controls.

These annexes are still inadequate in the wake of the financial crisis for at least four reasons. First, the annexes still allow investor-state claims related to capital controls— they just require investors to delay the claims for compensation. An investor has to wait one year to file a claim related to capital controls to prevent and mitigate crises, but that claim can be for a measure taken during the cooling-off year. The prospect of such investor-state cases could discourage the use of controls that may be beneficial to financial stability. Second, many other nations' treaties allow for capital controls. Indeed, the Canada–Chile FTA, the EU–Korea FTA, the Japan–Peru BIT and the Japan–Korea BIT (just to name a few) all grant greater flexibility for capital controls. This gives incentives for nations to apply controls in a discriminatory manner (applying controls on European Union investors but not on US investors). Third, the IMF has expressed concerns that restrictions on capital controls in US agreements, even those with the special annexes, may conflict with the IMF's authority to recommend capital controls in certain countries' programs, as they have done in Iceland and several other countries. Finally, the special dispute settlement procedure included in the US–Chile and Singapore FTAs did not become a standard feature of US agreements. It is not in the Central America Free Trade Agreement (CAFTA), any US BIT or the pending US–Korea FTA.

The IMF has also expressed concern about US treaties. In late 2012, the IMF officially endorsed an institutional view on the management of capital flows. Although the IMF will continue to urge nations to eventually liberalize all capital transfers, henceforth the IMF will advise nations, under certain circumstances, to deploy capital controls on inflows and outflows of capital. In its new view the IMF pointed out that such advice may conflict with obligations that nations have under trade and investment treaties and offered to provide a forum for reconciliation.

The IMF is aware that they may recommend capital controls to nations that do not have the policy space to deploy such instruments because they would be deemed actionable under a trade agreement or investment treaty. A 2012 IMF board report states,

> The limited flexibility afforded by some bilateral and regional agreements in respect to liberalization obligations may create challenges for the management of capital flows. These challenges should be weighed against the agreements' potential benefits. In particular, such agreements could be a step toward broader liberalization. However, *these agreements in many*

cases do not provide appropriate safeguards or proper sequencing of liberalization and could thus benefit from reform to include these protections.[6]

Indeed, the IMF suggests that the new IMF institutional view could help guide future trade treaties and that the IMF could serve as a forum for such discussions:

> In particular, the proposed institutional view could help foster a more consistent approach to the design of policy space for CFMs under bilateral and regional agreements. Recognizing the macroeconomic, IMS and global stability goals that underpin the institutional view, *members drafting such agreements in the future, as well as the various international bodies that promote these agreements, could take into account this view in designing the circumstances under which both inflows and outflows CFMs may be imposed within the scope of their agreements. Similarly—and depending on the stages of development of the relevant signatories—the sequenced approach to liberalization under the integrated approach could be taken into account to guide the pace and sequencing of liberalization obligations, and the re-imposition of CFMs due to institutional considerations.*[7]

Reforming US Treaties for Financial Stability

It is in the broader interests of the United States and its trading partners to have adequate policy space to prevent and mitigate financial crises. The larger benefits to society from financial stability outweigh the static losses to certain interest groups. This last section outlines a number of possible (nonexclusive) options.

With respect to regulating cross-border financial flows, some IMF officials have gone so far as to recommend that speculative capitals in the form of derivatives and other financial "innovations" be omitted from the definition of investment in treaties. Another option, more recently advocated by the IMF, is to come up with a uniform safeguard language that all nations can use. More specific to US treaties, the exceptions language in US treaties could be broadened to explicitly allow for the flexibility to deploy controls and other measures now recognized as prudential to prevent or mitigate a crisis. After many discussions and lobbying efforts by Chile, Malaysia and independent experts, the Trans-Pacific Partnership agreement included such flexibilities. Finally, regulators of party states, not private investors, could settle disputes over these matters.

The global financial crisis has made it obvious that granting our trading partners the flexibility to use legitimate policies to prevent and mitigate financial crises is also good for the United States. When its trading partners fall into financial crisis, the United States loses export markets and subsequently jobs in the export sector. Capital controls can help stabilize exchange rates, which is good for long-term investors and for exporters and importers from the United States. When countries abroad cannot control financial bubbles that drive up currency values, American consumers may be hurt by rising prices on imported goods. As we have learned all too well, financial instability in a globalized world can be contagious and quickly come back to the United States.

---

6   International Monetary Fund, "Liberalizing Capital Flows and Managing Outflows," 8.
7   International Monetary Fund, "The Liberalization and Management of Capital Flows: An Institutional View."

SECTION 5

REINFORCING SOCIAL PROTECTION: SPREADING THE BENEFITS OF TRADE, DEALING WITH LOSSES AND EXPLORING THE TRADE–IMMIGRATION NEXUS

Chapter Nineteen

TRADE AGREEMENTS IN THE TWENTY-FIRST CENTURY: RETHINKING THE TRADE–LABOR LINKAGE

Kerry Rittich

Work represents one of the major vectors connecting trade regimes to social welfare goals or objectives. Because work is a central marker of social status and because labor markets function as key nodes or transfer points in the diffusion of economic gains, for most people, access to work and the terms and conditions on which it is available are central to the promise of trade liberalization. To the extent that this relationship holds, in either direction, issues of work are inseparable from the general issues of welfare and distributive justice that trade agreements engage. For the same reason, debates around trade–labor linkage can be understood as a subset of the general inquiry into a fair—that is, ethically and politically defensible—globalization.[1]

Notwithstanding its importance, the suggestion here is that the principal way we have approached the relationship between trade and labor so far—seeking to make trade regimes more worker friendly through the inclusion of labor standards and rights at work—has been unduly limited. Other possibilities of trade–labor linkage remain, accordingly, unexplored, and the goals of labor-focused trade agendas have been some-what mistargeted as a result.

Yet whatever the limits of conventional standards-focused strategies in achieving the goals of better work and greater worker empowerment, trade agreements do play a critically important role, both in affecting the terms and conditions of work and in determining workers' general fates in the labor market. This is because of the myriad direct and indirect channels through which trade agreements influence domestic rule and policy choices; alter social, industrial and organizational norms and practices; affect the presence and viability of economic activities; and thereby alter the distribution of gains and losses among the actors involved.

Imagining trade regimes in this alternative way points to a broader trade and labor agenda, one that connects labor issues to a host of trade rules and concerns beyond rights at work. Rather than a point of irretrievable division, moreover, such an agenda

---

[1] Christian Barry and Sanjay Reddy, *International Trade and Labor Standards: A Proposal for Linkage* (New York: Columbia University Press, 2008).

potentially joins workers and citizens in the Global North and Global South on many issues, even in the face of ongoing conflict among states.

The Case for Linkage

During the 1990s, an international consensus developed that global market integration and increasingly dense flows of goods, services and people across borders—globalization—had an undesirable counterpart in the form of a growing social deficit, one that was especially marked in respect of labor standards and workers' rights.[2] For many labor scholars, advocates and academics, the dispute resolution mechanism provided by the newly formed World Trade Organization (WTO) appeared to be the most promising route for the redress of this deficit for the indefinite future. The case for linkage was not limited to issues related to work: many other groups framing social justice concerns in the language of human rights expressed similar hopes for a productive integration of their agendas into the global trade regime. The entire "trade and" agenda was driven by the idea that trade agreements provided an opportunity to put muscle behind international norms and standards that were widely understood to be weakly respected, if not routinely flouted, and, at the same time, ensure that social concerns were properly addressed in the adjudication of cross-border economic disputes. The argument, in brief, was that international norms in respect of such issues should (or already did) form part of the substance and structure of trade agreements—for example, under Article XX of the General Agreement on Tariffs and Trade (GATT)—a scenario that would render them enforceable through dispute resolution procedures and expose malfeasors to the possibilities of sanctions under the trade regime.[3] It seemed to make independent sense to link protections for workers to regimes that were catalyzing profound changes to global labor markets and the terms, conditions and organization of work.

Linkage nonetheless ran into blockages almost immediately. As all trade scholars know, the proposal was rejected at the first Singapore Ministerial meeting, the final declaration warning against the use of labor standards for protectionist purposes, underscoring that the comparative advantage of countries "should in no way be called into question"[4] and establishing that the International Labour Organization (ILO) was the competent international body to both set and deal with questions of labor standards.[5] That declaration

---

[2] United Nations, Copenhagen Declaration on Social Development, A/CONF.166/9, March 14, 1995.

[3] Robert Howse and Makua Mutua, "Protecting Human Rights in a Global Economy: Challenges for the World Trade Organization," in *Human Rights in Development Yearbook 1999/2000: The Millennium Edition*, ed. Hugo Stokke and Arne Tostensen (The Hague: Kluwer Law International, 2001), 51–82.

[4] Singapore Ministerial Declaration, December 13, 1996, https://www.wto.org/english/thewto_e/minist_e/min96_e/wtodec_e.htm.

[5] David M. Trubek and Lance Compa, "Trade Law, Labor, and Global Inequality," in *Law and Class in America: Trends since the Cold War*, ed. Paul Carrington and Trina Jones (New York: New York University Press, 2006).

was followed in relatively short order by the ILO Declaration on Fundamental Principles and Rights at Work (the ILO Declaration).[6] Yet notwithstanding the rejection of labor standards at the WTO, the vast majority of bilateral, regional and megaregional trade and investment agreements now *do* include labor standards and rights at work, and those standards and rights are becoming more convergent all the time. Equally noteworthy, such agreements increasingly deploy common vernaculars and terms of art when it comes to the content, enforcement and adjudication of those standards. Labor provisions are typically an amalgam of two basic models—the North American Agreement on Labor Cooperation (NAALC), a side agreement to the North American Free Trade Agreement (NAFTA), which obliges states not to derogate from domestic labor standards to gain a competitive advantage in trade—plus the four core rights set out in the ILO Declaration: freedom of association and the effective right to collective bargaining, freedom from discrimination, freedom from child labor, and freedom from forced labor. These are now commonly supplemented by provisions concerning health and safety, minimum standards and nondiscrimination, for example, in respect of working conditions and/or migrant workers.[7] Across a range of agreements, the lineaments of global trade-related labor standards are now fairly easy to discern and describe.

The Inclusion of Labor Standards Matters Less Than We Hope or Think

Trade itself affects workers and labor standards in diverse and complex ways. Trade may be the conduit for the diffusion of higher standards, especially to the extent that firms from higher-wage jurisdictions export their human resource practices along with their modes of production and service delivery. But the development of more far-flung supplier networks that trade enables is just as likely to normalize low labor standards and reliance on precarious forms of work.[8] The changing, often-transitory contractual relations that organize the operation of supply chains provide well-documented mechanisms to destandardize the terms under which workers labor.[9] Insulating lead firms from the costs and legal responsibilities associated with employment, they typically exacerbate distributional inequities among labor and capital as well.

The inclusion of labor standards in trade agreements, however, is fundamentally irrelevant to these developments or, at minimum, much less relevant than might seem at first glance. Both what has and hasn't happened in respect of the recognition of workers'

[6] International Labour Conference, ILO Declaration on Fundamental Principles and Rights at Work and Its Follow-Up, June 18, 1998, http://ec.europa.eu/trade/policy/in-focus/ceta/ceta-chapter-by-chapter/.

[7] EU–Canada Comprehensive Economic and Trade Agreement (CETA), Article 23.3, September 21, 2016, http://ec.europa.eu/trade/policy/in-focus/ceta/ceta-chapter-by-chapter.

[8] Guy Mundlak and Kerry Rittich, "The Challenge to Comparative Labor Law in a Globalized Era," in *Comparative Labor Law*, ed. Matthew Finkin and Guy Mundlak (Cheltenham, UK: Edward Elgar, 2015).

[9] David Weil, *The Fissured Workplace: Why Work Became So Bad for So Many and What Can Be Done to Improve It* (Cambridge, MA: Harvard University Press, 2014).

rights and labor standards in trade regimes has little to do with the state of work and working conditions on the ground.[10] There are good reasons to think that this will continue to be the case, even if more disputes were litigated through trade dispute resolution mechanisms, which for the most part in the future, as in the past, they will not.

Labor advocates share many of the general concerns that have been identified with the arbitration of trade and investment disputes: conflicts of interests on the part of the arbitrators, the lack of standing for parties who might have interests in the dispute, the absence of means to bring forward matters of public policy, to which they might add the ongoing asymmetry in the adjudicative mechanisms available to labor and capital. However, the adjudication of labor standards also engages a distinct set of concerns; here the problems are legion.

In order to make labor standards operative in dispute resolution, it is necessary to specify them with some degree of precision; otherwise, there is no means to adjudicate noncompliance and, by extension, no basis for imposing sanctions.[11] This might be done in a variety of ways: by reference to international standards as determined by the relevant United Nations (UN) and ILO committees, on the basis of a state party's own labor standards or with reference to terms determined by collective agreements. In theory, labor standards might also be established by dynamic processes of norm generation emerging through knowledge garnered and practices established in particular industries and workplaces as well.[12]

However, labor standards within trade and investment agreements are stated at such a high level of generality and abstraction that it is unclear whether they could be litigated successfully: the newly signed Comprehensive and Progressive Agreement for Trans-Pacific Partnership (CPTPP), for example, makes reference only to the rights stated in the ILO Declaration rather than those established by the ILO conventions. Those rights are, in any event, capable of supporting widely divergent interpretations of the legal obligations of states when it comes to protections and entitlements for workers.[13] Nonderogation provisions do not compel states to adopt any particular level of labor standards, merely to refrain from lowering those they already have to gain competitive advantage. Moreover, they often contain exceptions and qualifications that further limit their strength and reach. For example, the CPTPP requires parties to commit not to waive or derogate from their own statutes and regulations "in a manner affecting trade or investment," but limits the obligation concerning working conditions to special economic

---

10 Staff of Sen. Elizabeth Warren, "Broken Promises: Decades of Failure to Enforce Labor Standards in Free Trade Agreements," 2015, https://www.warren.senate.gov/files/documents/BrokenPromises.pdf.

11 Mark Barenberg, "Sustaining Workers' Bargaining Power in an Age of Globalization" (report, Economic Policy Institute, Washington, DC, 2009).

12 Jonathan Zeitlin and David M. Trubek, eds., *Governing Work and Welfare in a New Economy: European and American Experiments* (Oxford: Oxford University Press, 2003).

13 Kerry Rittich, "Core Labour Rights and Labour Market Flexibility: Two Paths Entwined?," in *Labor Law Beyond Borders: ADR and the Internationalization of Labor Dispute Resolution: The Permanent Court of Arbitration/Peace Palace Papers* (The Hague: Kluwer Law International, 2003).

areas and export processing zones.[14] Other agreements contain still weaker provisions, requiring only that the state "strive to ensure that it does not waive or otherwise derogate from [...] such laws."[15] Agreements often explicitly recognize state discretion over enforcement and the allocation of enforcement resources as well.[16]

To the extent that the included provisions index a new normative consensus around global rights at work, that consensus provides very weak protection for workers and grants states and employers immense latitude to set workplace practices and standards as they wish. Just as important, they are arguably not responsive to some of the central problems of work enabled by liberalized trade itself. Two brief examples, both from the recently signed CPTPP and both touching on the nature and structure of transnational production, will serve to illustrate.

Forced labor is used in the production of a range of common consumer goods, and it occurs routinely at the tail ends of global supply chains.[17] To the extent that forced labor is relevant to trade and investment agreements, trade in goods with inputs procured through forced or coerced labor is arguably the central issue of interest. Yet despite the fact that norms against forced and child labor are identified as "core" and included in all trade-related labor standards, the CPTPP merely requires that each party "discourage, through initiatives it considers appropriate, the importation of goods from other sources produced in whole or in part by forced or compulsory labour, including forced or compulsory child labour."[18] The level of commitment when it comes to the most uncontentious of labor standards is telling.

The second related problem is the regulatory deficit and lacunae concerning labor standards and workers' rights within transnational value and supply chains. Violations of workers' rights and low labor standards are endemic in supply chains, in part because of the opportunities that these contractual networks provide lead firms to avoid legal responsibilities associated with employment and to structure production so as to shift risks and costs to other, weaker parties lower down on the chain. Yet even though the expansion of such organizational practices is a principal effect of trade agreements themselves, recent agreements give only the weakest possible nod toward private ordering as a solution to the problems for workers that they routinely engender. For example, the CPTPP states that each party shall "endeavor to encourage enterprises to voluntarily adopt corporate social responsibility initiatives on labor that have been endorsed or supported by that party."[19]

---

[14] Comprehensive and Progressive Agreement for Trans-Pacific Partnership (CPTPP), Article 19, February 2, 2018, http://wtocenter.vn/tpp/full-text-comprehensive-and-progressive-agreement-trans-pacific-partnership-cptpp.

[15] Dominican Republic–Central America FTA (CAFTA-DR), Article 16.2.2, https://ustr.gov/trade-agreements/free-trade-agreements/cafta-dr-dominican-republic-central-america-fta/final-text.

[16] CPTPP, Article 19.5.

[17] International Labour Organization, "A Global Alliance against Forced Labour."

[18] CPTPP, Article 19.6.

[19] Ibid., Article 19.71.

Even where violations are satisfactorily made out, complainants must typically establish that the violation ensued from a failure on the part of the state "to effectively enforce its labor laws, through a sustained or recurring course of action or inaction" and "in a manner affecting trade."[20] How would a tribunal make a determination about such a recurring failure, assuming no cooperation from the responsible state? Establishing this link often requires that the panel be open to accepting evidence, whether from the ILO, other international organizations, trade unions, NGOs or labor scholars, about broader patterns of workplace or industry practice; the panel would also need to take cognizance of the full effects of employer malfeasance, such as violence or reprisals against union organizers, on labor standards and workers' rights.[21] While such adjudicative practices are well accepted, even routine, in national labor courts and labor arbitrations, they cannot be assumed in trade and investment panels. As the recent *US–Guatemala* decision,[22] the only labor standards case so far to reach the stage of formal dispute resolution, illustrates, the complaining state may not put such information forward; the panel might decide to discount it if it does; or the panel may conclude that evidence presented in a manner designed to shield workers' identities and protect against the possibility of employer reprisals has less probative value for that very reason. Even more challenging is establishing that the specific violation has an impact on trade. In the typical case, there will simply be no data available; here too, in order for the complaint to succeed, the panel must be open to making a determination on the basis of the foreseeable and expected economic effects of employer behavior.

This raises a general issue. It is widely recognized that specialized tribunals cognizant of the causes and character of labor disputes are required to effectively assess and dispose of complaints about alleged violations of rights and standards at work. However, there can be no expectation that trade and investment tribunals will rule on complaints—or even appreciate the nature and scope of the complaint before them—as labor tribunals would, because panel members are not required to have specialized knowledge of labor (as distinct from trade) disputes. It is also well established that neither compliance with labor standards nor respect for workers' rights can be assessed objectively from afar or after the fact by disinterested observers. Rather, close and consistent monitoring of work and worksites over time is required to accurately determine the status of standards and rights on the ground and to prevent any violations from recurring.[23] This makes labor standards and workers' rights complaints somewhat distinct as a class of disputes, and it imposes fairly well-known conditions on their successful resolution.

---

[20] CAFTA-DR FTA, Article 16.2l.

[21] See, e.g., Paul Weiler, "Promises to Keep: Securing Workers' Rights to Self-Organization under the NLRA," *Harvard Law Review* 96 (1983): 1769.

[22] "In the Matter of Guatemala—Issues Relating to the Obligations under Article 16.2.1(a) of the CAFTA-DR," panel report, June 14, 2017.

[23] Mark Barenberg, "Toward a Democratic Model of Transnational Labour Organizing?," in *Regulating Labour in the Wake of Globalisation*, ed. Brian Bercusson and Cynthia Estlund (Oxford: Hart Publishing, 2008).

To avoid what we might think of as a Heisenberg effect on workers' rights and labor standards, monitoring must be done by workers or their associations (unions) at the work-site level; in addition, there needs to be some institutionalized means of channeling the information that they possess or obtain into any dispute resolution process. In short, making trade-related labor standards even minimally effective would seem to require the construction of institutional mechanisms and adjudicative apparatuses that, if not precisely akin to those that support domestic labor standards, replicate some of their key features. Finally, to avoid merely licensing employer violations and to be at all useful to the workers themselves, disputes need to be resolved quickly.

Stating even the basic operational requirements of the successful implementation of labor standards illustrates the profound institutional challenges involved. But other basic design features of trade and investment regimes mean that hopes for nonarbitrary, nondiscretionary enforcement of their labor standards are destined to be frustrated in any event. Put simply, trade dispute resolution just does not work this way. Because workers, unions and their advocates have no independent means to launch complaints, the state must be enlisted to do so; this means that labor standards complaints will be sub-ject to the normal political and economic calculus that governs the management of other state-to-state disputes. Layered on top of this general challenge are additional consider-ations that may well restrain states from moving forward on labor standards complaints, or at least reduce the number they feel moved to litigate. It is not difficult to imagine the conflicts and competing interests in play—within as well as between labor and capital—especially for those states desperately seeking investment, including to provide jobs to their citizens. Indeed, states can be expected to be mindful of the conflicts that citizens harbor within themselves—as consumers who may benefit from trade on the one hand and as workers who may both gain and lose on the other—when deciding whether to launch a complaint.[24]

Ongoing concerns about the covert use of labor standards for protectionist purposes may also induce tribunals to be unusually cautious when establishing violations of labor standards, despite the undoubted interpretive scope in the provisions themselves.

As with other trade disputes, the adjudication of labor standards complaints may engage competing aims understood to be integral to the treaties themselves, as well as specific rights of benefit to employers. But adverse results for workers may also result from the ordinary biases operating within regimes and tribunals, biases that might incline human rights or labor courts, for example, to give greater weight to workers' rights and interests while those of their employer prevail under trade and investment arbitration.[25] The famous cases of *Viking* and *Laval*, decided by the European Court of Justice in 2007, illustrate both the problems of conflicting rights and the risks to workers when their

---

[24] Robert Reich, *Supercapitalism: The Transformation of Business, Democracy and Everyday Life* (New York: Knopf, 2007).

[25] International Law Commission, "Fragmentation of International Law: Difficulties Arising from the Diversification and Expansion of International Law," UN Doc A/CN.4/L.682, April 13, 2006.

rights are adjudicated within regimes principally designed to promote market integration and protect investor rights; put simply, it didn't go well for the unions or their workers. Moreover, one of the risks of losses at the supranational level appears to be downward pressure on labor standards at the national level—preemptive as well as remedial alterations for fear that they will come under successful attack by employers.[26] This is hardly the effect that advocates for linkage envisioned.

While labor standards provisions might aid in sanctioning outlier employers and practices in extreme circumstances (although given the track record so far, even that possibility seems optimistic), states have been unable to converge on anything beyond highly general norms that permit widely varying levels of protection, underpinned by lengthy and highly uncertain adjudicative procedures that present as many risks as benefits to workers, particularly in those states that already possess relatively high levels of labor standards. It is not at all clear why linkage in this form should be counted as a win for workers.

Reconceiving Linkage

The conventional response to the deficits identified is to call for more and stronger rights for workers and better enforcement of those rights. There are good reasons to resist this approach, at least as a general conclusion. On the one hand, included labor standards are not responsive to many of the most pressing predicaments for workers, even those that trade agreements enable or directly underwrite. On the other, many issues that *do* matter to workers are found in provisions other than labor standards.

Popular grievances around trade and labor in the Global North are mostly centered around job losses, declining wages and growing economic insecurity associated with trade liberalization and market integration. Complaints from workers in the South range from brute subjection to violence, and even death, at the hands of employers or their allies to the routine inability to extract recognition of their associations and better terms and conditions from those who control, and ultimately benefit from, their work.

These complaints are more often linked than they first appear. Work itself is now linked transnationally through automation and technological innovations, new forms of intellectual property protecting firms from competition, and the vertical disintegration of firms and consequent outsourcing of work. Three other developments are putting pressure on the number of jobs and the terms and conditions of work as well. One is declining levels of growth. A second is the emergence of jobless, or even "job-loss," growth. Yet a third is the feminization of work: the massive entry of women into the global labor force, accompanied by the normalization of terms, conditions and wages approximating those always endured by those at the margins of the labor market.[27]

---

[26] Mark Freedland and Jeremias Prassl, eds., *Viking, Laval and Beyond* (Oxford: Hart Publishing, 2014).

[27] Guy Standing, "Global Feminization through Flexible Labour: A Theme Revisited," *World Development* 27 (1999): 583–602.

While states remain preoccupied with how they can win in the global competition for investment,[28] wage increases no longer reliably track economic growth and productivity gains, and workers are capturing less of the returns to investment, production and trade. This development is intimately related to the general concentration of economic gains that is such a noteworthy feature of the current economic landscape.[29] Compare, for example, the immense profits realized by Apple in virtue of the global reach of its markets with the famously bad working conditions of those who make its products.[30] Both are enabled by trade, yet the asymmetry in gains between the parties is impossible to miss.

This points to the more fundamental issue: the reallocation of labor resources, axiomatic to market integration, has the potential to provide, and does in fact provide, jobs and other economic opportunities for many workers. These opportunities cannot be discounted. But nor are they enough on their own. Moreover, the very same process is also a threat to other workers. And due to other factors and forces—skills and experience mismatch, geographic and familial constraints on mobility, labor market stratification and discrimination, as well as ongoing protectionism enabled by trade regimes themselves—those who are displaced do not automatically find better work. In the context of the increased competition for work that trade facilitates and the diminished bargaining power for workers that predictably ensues, many workers must settle for lower levels of income and economic security; some leave the labor force altogether; others turn to informal or illegal activities; and many migrate in search of work. Even the apparent winners often gain less than they might, and their benefits almost invariably pale in comparison to those accruing to the parties who ultimately control their access to work. Moreover, their gains may well be accompanied by local trade-related losses. For example, those engaged in subsistence agriculture may find their economic activities no longer viable, due to the combined effects of competition from more efficient (or subsidized) foreign providers and reforms that promote commodification for export and/or favor large over small commercial actors.[31] Their fates are part of any complete accounting when it comes to work, too.

In most states, certainly those in North America, there has never been a robust commitment to compensate the losers, still less to redistribute the gains realized from market integration in any general way. Instead, we largely let the gains and losses lie where they fall, despite the fact that we might expect the opportunities provided by trade liberalization to go disproportionately to those with superior skill and access to capital,

---

[28] United States Trade Representative, "TPP—Made in America," https://ustr.gov/sites/default/files/TPP-Chapter-Summary-Labour-1.pdf.

[29] Branko Milanovic, *Global Inequality: A New Approach for the Age of Globalization* (Cambridge, MA: Harvard University Press, 2016).

[30] Brian Merchant, "Life and Death in Apple's Forbidden City," *Guardian*, June 18, 2017, https://www.theguardian.com/technology/2017/jun/18/foxconn-life-death-forbidden-city-longhua-suicide-apple-iphone-brian-merchant-one-device-extract.

[31] See Chantal Thomas, *Disorderly Borders: How International Law Shapes Irregular Migration* (Oxford: Oxford University Press, forthcoming).

credit and networking opportunities while the disadvantages fall on those without. Many of these risks and predicaments, moreover, now extend to those imagined as the principal beneficiaries of liberalized trade: workers in developing countries. Whatever the reasons for our lack of interest in the past, this path seems less attractive and less available going forward. Economic insecurity engendered by increased trade is a real prospect or reality for many workers, and not only those in the industrialized world.

Popular discontent around trade agreements is often received with alarm by those who fear the return of protectionism or a rejection of globalization *tout court*. Much less remarked upon is elite tolerance of the equilibrium in which we have settled: the real issue is that for many workers the link between trade and welfare gains has either come apart or never materialized to the degree advertised. Ongoing labor market disruption is unavoidable and inseparable from the risks and opportunities generated by liberalization. But much of the disadvantage to workers, along with the correlative advantage to those who employ them, flows from contestable regulatory and policy decisions about how to organize economic activity. What claims the losers should have in a system that, in theory, generates gains sufficient to compensate them is a conundrum that can no longer be avoided.

What Should We Advocate in This Complex Terrain?

It is simply magical thinking to imagine that adding labor standards and workers' rights to trade agreements will fix, or even dent, the complex problems at work to which trade liberalization is intimately connected. Social dumping clauses may address some of the concerns identified with the adjudication of labor standards, but it remains unclear how they would avoid the longstanding fear associated with labor standards themselves: that they will be used for protectionist purposes. Moreover, such clauses would enable hard sanctions, such as antidumping duties on the goods produced; in so doing, they risk punishing workers, as well as their employers, through loss of work. Given the current normative baseline for international labor standards, their utility for most workers may be extremely limited in any event. But the more profound problem is also more basic: problems at work are already fueled and supported by many other rules, regimes and policy choices, domestic as well as international. The limits of labor standards provisions suggest not that trade agreements don't matter but rather that we should pay more attention to the impact of other trade provisions than we now do, both on workers' opportunities, resources and bargaining endowments and on their capacity to further empower capital, including in its encounter with labor.

Even within countries, trade provisions will affect workers in varied ways, combining with domestic legal institutions and economic formations to different effect in different contexts. Rather than merely respond after the fact, we should attempt to anticipate these different fates and futures for workers and citizens, scrutinizing the impact of proposed provisions and/or resisting their implementation, or even further liberalization entirely, until the risks and challenges are addressed.

The deinstitutionalization of labor standards and collective bargaining and the weakening of public services and social protection schemes, visible across the

Anglo-American world in particular, have undercut workers' collective power to mitigate trade-related income losses and secure more of the gains from trade. Part of the remedy involves breaking the current regulatory consensus that associates higher domestic labor standards and more robust workers' rights with suboptimal economic performance and the impairment of competitive advantage. This will require more than simply respect for workers' fundamental rights or agreement on an expanded list of worker entitlements and protections, however. Rather than simply argue over the correct basket of rights or baseline for labor standards, we should both maintain that labor market institutions are a normal part of the institutional fabric in which trade occurs *and* defend a degree of necessary diversity in those rules at the national and regional levels. This is especially important given the varied situations in which workers now find themselves and the diverse forms that work itself now takes. The rules and policy that might alternatively enable or impede more effective organizing and better wages and working conditions are destined to take different forms in different places. When it comes to work, even the relevant site of regulatory attention is likely to vary; for some workers in developing countries and informal markets, for example, changes to property, land use and commercial rules may turn out to be more important than labor standards.

Given the range of ways that markets can be designed, the profound impact of those design choices on different groups at the local and national levels and the expectation that whatever the initial choices in the future as in the past trade liberalization will reliably produce problems to be managed, particularly for workers and small producers and traders, it seems important to reduce the extent to which trade and investment regimes constrain state policy space in general. These same considerations militate in favor of careful attention to the metrics by which any policy and regulatory decisions *are* ultimately assessed. Here, a central concern is to ensure that distributive considerations are not demoted or foreclosed in the regulatory calculus. Consider, for example, how, notwithstanding the recognition of sovereign regulatory authority, the regulatory impact assessments under the CPTPP might affect state regulatory choices, given the mandated assessment of the need for covered regulations, alternatives and their costs and benefits; why the "selected alternative achieves the policy objectives in an efficient manner"; and a demonstration that they rely on "the best reasonably obtainable existing information."[32]

For the same reasons, states might well want to consider renewed emphasis on industrial policy and/or state developmental capacities, with an explicit focus on making them job-centric. This will require, inter alia, careful evaluation of how trade provisions such as public procurement intersect with models and strategies for development, especially where, as in the case of infrastructure investment, they affect local or national employment prospects.

Due to the growing risk that employers will choose to replace jobs with automation, another task is to delink at least some benefits and entitlements, including assistance for trade-related job losses, from employment. But because trade is only one factor transforming the nature of, and returns to, work and because it is often difficult

---

[32] CPTPP, chap. 25.

or impossible to disentangle trade from non-trade-related labor market disruption, distinguishing trade-related assistance from other forms of adjustment assistance seems unwise; hence the importance of protecting, and expanding, the general policy and regulatory mechanisms—including job stimulus measures and public procurement—available to (re)allocate economic opportunities and redistribute income.

Because so much production and service delivery is now transnationally organized, finding ways to reallocate costs and risks, benefits and burdens, across global value chains is also a central challenge. Along with more effective taxation of worldwide corporate income, what is needed are legal rules that more effectively bind lead firms to the debts and obligations of their contractors and subcontractors, as well as rules and regimes that permit workers to organize more easily across borders and thereby capture more of the gains of their labor. Whether trade negotiations can be used to advance these objectives is uncertain, but it is an avenue worth exploring.

At the end of the day, trade liberalization is a social as well as economic project. The form and substance of trade agreements have profound implications for questions of equality, solidarity, citizenship and justice at the domestic as well as transnational levels. We can continue to focus on labor standards and social clauses hoping they will address, if not entirely fix, the complex distributive problems in which trade regimes as a whole are implicated. But if we move beyond imagining trade regimes simply as devices to set the ground rules of economic competition and begin to view them instead as mechanisms for allocating risks and immunities, powers and disabilities, including among workers and those that employ them, we might well start to make some different choices about their design and content. We will certainly argue more clearly about what trade regimes are for and how they work.

Chapter Twenty

THE NEW FRONTIER FOR LABOR IN TRADE AGREEMENTS

Alvaro Santos

In the spring of 2015, I took my students of international trade law to visit the World Trade Organization (WTO) in Geneva. It was a two-day trip, organized around lectures and discussions with staff from different divisions of the organization, the Advisory Centre of WTO Law and the permanent missions of two countries. None of my students had been there before, and even though I had taught international trade law for several years, it was also my first time visiting the headquarters of the organization. We were excited and curious. The building looked big and majestic. The backside opened to a spacious park overlooking Lake Geneva. It made for a pleasant tour on a cool, sunny morning. The WTO was celebrating its twentieth anniversary, and there were banners hanging from the walls in the internal atrium marking the occasion, as well as announcements of events to come.

In our second session, we were led to a room with wooden panels and a colorful mural that spanned the four walls. It depicted industrial workers—strong men making a car, miners, shipbuilders, men using heavy equipment, but also women, seamstresses, teachers and a few children. In the center a bare-chested man between two goddess-like women was holding a torch. The mural struck me as an ode to work, to achievement and to emancipation. A tale of the human race transforming the world through physical and intellectual labor. The painting, by Dean Cornwell, reminded me of the frescos of Mexican artist Diego Rivera in its depiction of industrial workers, although this one had no reference to exploitation or the confrontation between capital and labor. It was an incredibly optimistic image of work and human progress.

I was surprised to see a mural of workers in the WTO. The painting seemed not only vintage but also out of place. What was it doing here? We learned that the mural had been hidden for years and it was only in 2007 that it was discovered and unveiled. It turned out that the building had been the headquarters of the International Labour Organization (ILO), and when the ILO moved to another building in Geneva in 1975, the General Agreement on Tariffs and Trade (GATT) moved in. When the WTO was created in 1995, it took its place. In a different hall, we saw another painting with a construction worker front and center, surrounded by the text of the preamble of the Treaty of Versailles establishing the ILO. Below, a plaque memorialized its donation by the International Federation of Trade Unions. I had the impression that I was visiting the ruins of a bygone era. And I imagined what a different world that was, when labor was prominent and had power and money. When workers' organizations sat at the table. When they were "in the room where it happened." It was a feeling like the one I had when visiting the ruins of a Mayan city and imagining it in all its splendor, no doubt with a similar dose of romanticizing. How could labor have fallen so hard that it surprises me that they could have been hosted in a building like this, that they could have inspired such a narrative of triumph and that yet, today, it does not make sense? There was something ironic about these images of labor reappearing in the walls of the WTO, where the linkage of trade and labor had been both discussed and resisted.

There was also something humbling at seeing that countries had set up an international organization to address labor and the social question almost 100 years before. Coming out of the first world war, the winning countries set up the ILO because they believed that peace could "be established only if it is based upon social justice" and because "the failure of any nation to adopt humane conditions of labour is an obstacle in the way of other nations which desire to improve the conditions in their own countries." There was a clear sense of interdependence and the need for coordination and collective action so as not to undermine each other. They set out to improve conditions of people by regulating

> hours of work, including the establishment of a maximum working day and week, the regulation of the labour supply, the prevention of unemployment, the provision of an adequate living wage, the protection of the worker against sickness, disease and injury arising out of his employment, the protection of children, young persons and women, provision for old age and injury, protection of the interests of workers when employed in countries other than their own, recognition of the principle of freedom of association.[1]

Many of these laws were seen as unthinkable or as unnecessary in the era of classical legal thought where private contract law regulated relations among individuals in the market. Labor laws were the product of a legal imagination that defied the dominant legal constructs and upset the established order. The twentieth century witnessed many countries adopting national labor regulations, often in fits and starts, following their own domestic struggles and political processes. At the time of our visit, the WTO was suffering from a sense of growing irrelevance amid the hype for other megaregional agreements. The great powers were seeking for deals, and for shaping global trade rules elsewhere. Although the WTO's dispute settlement system was busy and in high demand, the WTO as a forum for multilateral action seemed stagnant. Now, the WTO seems under threat, with the United States bluntly enacting measures that flout its rules and undermining the proper staffing of its Appellate Body. Labor, jobs, wages and conditions of work have reemerged with force in the opposition to trade. Can we reimagine the shape of legal institutions and agreements, such as the WTO and other trade agreements, to usher in a

---

[1] Treaty of Versailles, Part XIII, http://www.ilo.org/public/libdoc/ilo/1920/20B09_18_engl. pdf.

different kind of globalization geared toward improving the lot of workers and benefiting those who have been left behind? What would that architecture look like?

Farewell to Globalization's Gold Standard

The United Kingdom's decision to leave the EU and the US decision to withdraw from the Trans-Pacific Partnership (TPP) and initially threaten to leave the North American Free Trade Agreement (NAFTA) gave a serious blow to the hopes that opposition to globalization would dwindle once political campaigns gave way to governing. A string of nationalist, populist parties who are critical of globalization are gaining strength in Europe. Moreover, the Trump administration's recent imposition of tariffs on steel and aluminum, and then on China more generally, along with Chinese retaliation, has led many commentators to declare a trade war and warn about the potential unraveling of the world trading system. In the face of the Trump administration's actions, many commentators evoke, somewhat nostalgically, the WTO's accomplishments and rules-based multilateral character. Responses to the current crisis urge a defense of existing institutions and a return to the underpinning international commitments that ushered in the current global economy. The hope seems to be to contain the Trump administration in action, even if the combative and inflammatory rhetoric continues. These responses assume that all would be well if we could simply respect and enforce the existing agreements. I argue that the attempt to preserve liberal globalization as we knew it is wrongheaded. It ignores that the current retrenchment to nationalism and the opposition to international trade is a reaction to the effects of liberal globalization. Preserving the existing architecture won't dissipate, and may even increase the discontent.

Consider the TPP. It is symbolically important because the Obama administration and TPP supporters advanced it as the gold standard of globalization. I would contend that just as in the twentieth century, when the United States abandoned the gold standard for global monetary policy, the gold standard for international trade agreements has, too, been abandoned. Recently, however, the remaining 11 members of the TPP, now called the Comprehensive and Progressive Agreement for Trans-Pacific Partnership (CPTPP) without the United States, have resurrected it and are charging ahead. Unfortunately, they are not seizing the moment for charting a new path. The challenge is precisely to resist the temptation to preserve the existing trade agreements as they are in the hopes that the nationalist turn can be contained. The task is to design an alternative to both liberal globalization as we know it and the nationalistic turn currently seen in various governments around the world.

The Rise and Fall of Labor Chapters

The standard response to concerns about labor has been to include a labor chapter in trade agreements. Starting with NAFTA, gradually evolving in a multitude of trade agreements and then reaching its apex in the TPP, labor standards have been strengthened substantially and procedurally. Whereas in NAFTA countries agreed to enforce their own domestic labor laws, the TPP incorporates internationally recognized labor standards contained in the ILO's Declaration of Fundamental Principles and Rights at Work. Similarly, whereas in NAFTA labor obligations were contained in a side agreement, in the TPP they are a constitutive part of the agreement, like any other area. Whereas sanctions in NAFTA were limited, the TPP contains a dispute settlement system that may lead to trade sanctions.

So, if the TPP contained the most advanced of the labor chapters ever, why did the labor organizations in the United States oppose it? They argued that the substantive obligations did not go far enough. The rights often were vague, aspirational, or their implementation was left to the discretion of the governments, rendering them ineffective. Moreover, the chapter did not improve on the procedural hurdles any claim needed to jump in order to succeed. It still requires the state to bring up the claim, unlike the investment chapter, where private parties have standing. Moreover, it preserved the requirements that labor violations be systematic and "in a manner affecting trade" to trigger action. In the only labor case ever decided in a trade agreement, eight years after the United States brought the case against Guatemala under the Dominican Republic–Central America Free Trade Agreement (CAFTA-DR), the 2017 panel decision interpreted the term "in a manner affecting trade" as requiring that a labor standard violation conferred a competitive advantage on employers engaged in trade between the parties. This interpretation, in addition to the requirement that the violation be "sustained or recurring," imposed a very high threshold and made the panel decide that Guatemala had not breached its commitments. Labor unions understandably asked, unsuccessfully, that such requirement be removed from the labor chapter.

Proponents of the TPP, however, made so much of the labor chapter that it seemed more a mechanism for legitimating the agreement than anything else. If the parties to a trade agreement wanted to address concerns about jobs, wages and working conditions, how would they do that? How would they make these concerns structurally central to the design of the agreement rather than *formally* relevant with a chapter that talks about labor? The point here is that by pretending that the labor chapter addresses these questions, the design and liberalization ethos of trade agreements is left otherwise unchanged. I propose that we invert the assumption and instead conclude that labor chapters, as currently proposed, will not address the concerns of organized labor. What, then, would be the tools to address these concerns? To put it bluntly, if we were to eliminate the labor chapter, what instruments would there be in the trade agreements to improve working conditions and benefit workers?

The New Frontier for Labor

Our current legal and institutional imagination seems seriously constrained when the hopes to improve working conditions are pinned on an accommodation to labor with a special chapter in a trade agreement. The more useful question may be how to rebalance key levers for distribution of power and wealth at international and domestic levels to reach a different equilibrium. Reform may be directed both at international rules that shape the existing global market and at the domestic level, where the effects of those global rules are felt by market actors. At the international level, labor advocates may gain by focusing on legal regimes, such as investment, government procurement, tax and immigration. At the domestic level, labor groups may gain from focusing on labor-related initiatives, like minimum wage and collective bargaining. But they may have much to gain, too, by focusing on background policy regimes that greatly affect workers, such as safety nets traditionally associated with good, stable jobs like health insurance, maternity leave and child care; investment in human capital such as education and training; and compensatory mechanisms such as unemployment insurance, income support and job placement programs.

This list is more a map than an agenda. Any one of these, or a combination of several, may hold promise depending on the context. The current regulation of *investment* affords foreign investors a standard of protection unknown in any other trade domain where the baseline is national treatment. In this regime, foreign investors are given greater protection than national investors. Labor organizations in the United States worry that this treatment may be encouraging outsourcing, although the empirical evidence seems to cast doubt on a direct relationship between an investment treaty and foreign direct investment. Nevertheless, investment rules may considerably constrain the regulatory autonomy of host countries in areas of public interest such as health and safety, the environment and labor. Investor rights are defined too broadly and too generously, making the state liable for actions that would be perfectly fine under many countries' legal orders. Granting investors standing to sue states in transnational panels, thereby circumventing national courts, empowers investors vis-à-vis the state and gives corporate interests a privileged position in relation to the public interest.

Finally, scholars have pointed out the potential conflict of interest of ad hoc arbitrators, who often serve as litigators in other cases and who have an interest in being appointed to subsequent arbitral panels given reputational and financial rewards. Substantively, critics have proposed reducing the scope of investor protection. Procedurally, some have proposed establishing a permanent court, including an Appellate Body staffed by judges and other jurists not drawn from the investment arbitration circuit, which could review judgments, better balance corporate and public interests, and bring consistency to the regime. The Canada–EU investment chapter moves clearly in this direction, and initial proposals to eliminate NAFTA Chapter 11 went a step further.

Labor organizations have sought to stop the further liberalization of or to scale back the *government procurement* rules in trade agreements. The objective would be twofold: first, to use public procurement as a mechanism for job creation domestically, via local content requirements, and second, to use government procurement as a deliberate tool for economic stimulus in times of economic downturn. This cuts against the trends of megaregional agreements, like the TPP, which bind governments to nondiscrimination rules in their procurement. The WTO has created an agreement on government procurement that opens procurement to all members of the agreement. However, government procurement exists only as a plurilateral agreement in the WTO binding only countries that have expressly agreed to join it. Of the current 164 WTO members, only 47 are members. This would be an important area for countries to experiment and exercise flexibility. It would not even have to translate into an absolute required preference for domestic goods but into an advantage, using certain benchmarks as discipline. Conversely, government procurement rules can be designed to impose requirements related to compliance with robust labor standards, subject to certification. Given that public investment in infrastructure seems to be one of the very few areas where liberals and conservatives agree on the need of an active role of the state, this may even be a plausible area to carve out from future trade agreements.

Other scholars have proposed a new *anti–social dumping remedy*, modeled after the existing antidumping remedies, where countries may impose tariffs on products made in violation of labor standards. The idea here would be to protect a domestically established social norm (respect for fundamental labor rights) in the market of the importing country from erosion due to competition with nonconforming states. Thus, importing countries would deem those imports as social dumping and, given their unfair character, subject to remedies. In designing such a legal remedy, proponents would need to elaborate details as to what standards would count as the baseline. For example, would it be their own? Internationally recognized labor standards? The bare minimum such as prohibition on forced labor, discrimination and child labor, and freedom of association and collective bargaining? Or more robust standards such as a living wage? Would the violations need to constitute a systematic pattern? Would there be a comparison with effectiveness of labor standards in the importing country? How would injury to the domestic industry of like products be determined? And what would the requirement for a causal link be? These are criteria that would need to be spelled out, but the principle is appealing because it would bring the labor conditions under which products are made to the center of the trade regime.

The *existing space in the WTO* should be used and expanded for the imposition of tariffs on goods produced under conditions that violate basic labor standards. Using existing mechanisms in the WTO would include distinguishing products on the basis of how they were made, under the GATT III national treatment obligation, invoking the public morals exception under GATT XX (a), as well as exploring the use of technical regulations, such as labeling under the Agreement on Technical Barriers to Trade (TBT Agreement). These avenues would need to be explored by a country willing to enact a measure, but the time seems ripe.

Finally, we can draw a lesson from the TPP negotiation that has gone largely overlooked. This consists in the significant *domestic labor law reforms* set in motion by Vietnam, formally agreed in a US–Vietnam Labor Consistency Plan, and by Mexico, informally, via US pressure. Vietnam agreed to end the monopoly of the government-controlled official union by allowing the formation of independent unions, enabling them to collect membership dues and allowing technical assistance and training by international workers' organizations, among many other changes. Mexico passed a constitutional reform that would dismantle entrenched vices of its corporatist system, which had been demanded for years by independent unions and civil society but resisted by the government, employers and official unions. The reform sought to change the dispute settlement system, eliminating the tripartite Arbitration and Conciliation Board controlled by the Executive and giving jurisdiction over labor matters to the courts. Similarly, it would transfer the authority to register unions and collective agreements away from the Ministry of Labor and into a new autonomous institute, which would also guarantee free and secret elections in disputes between unions. These reforms were scaled back (Vietnam) or derailed (Mexico) once the United States withdrew and the original TPP failed. It seems that the period *during* the negotiation of international trade agreements and *before* they enter into force provides the greatest leverage for influencing domestic reforms, considerably more than the operation of any labor chapter or future state vs. state litigation based on labor rights. This was confirmed in the negotiations over NAFTA (see "Epilogue" below).

This moment is ripe for rethinking. The legal and political architecture that shaped liberal globalization in the last three decades—the WTO, EU, NAFTA, myriad preferential trade agreements and bilateral investment treaties—has come under attack in the industrialized world. We should resist the temptation to defend these institutions wholesale, as if they represented the last line of defense against the ugly side of nationalism, populism and unilateralism in favor of prosperity and freedom. This opening to reshape the global institutions is an opportunity to remake the global markets and their effects, to change the equilibrium between capital and labor, to make globalization more attuned to domestic political processes and to make it work for those who have been left behind. To be sure, we cannot go back to the utopia of the industrial workers depicted in the WTO mural—a lost paradise that perhaps never was. The nature of work, production and organization has changed dramatically since then. But we can attempt to rediscover work, in all its forms, as central to our global market institutions.

Epilogue

After completion of this essay and beginning in July 2018, I had the privilege to serve as the deputy chief negotiator for the elected government of Mexico in the last stage of the NAFTA negotiation. The requisite reminder applies: the views expressed here are solely my own, and I make them as an academic long interested in the relationship between trade and labor. The United States–Mexico–Canada Agreement (USMCA), as it is now known in English, contains important changes beyond the labor chapter, anticipated by the American labor movement's critiques of the TPP.

The USMCA contains changes to the rules of origin, which increased the regional value content for a product to be considered North American and thus able to enjoy the Agreement's duty-free tariff. The most important of these changes took place in the auto sector, which increased the regional value content from 62.5 percent to 75 percent for passenger vehicles. In addition, seven central parts should originate in the region (meeting a minimum percentage threshold) for the vehicle to be considered originating, and the Agreement requires specific regional value percentages for other principal and complementary parts. Moreover, 70 percent of steel and aluminum used in autos should be regional in origin. For the first time in a trade agreement, 40 percent of labor value content must be produced with wages of $16 per hour. The new rules are ostensibly designed to increase production in North America—and away from other regions like Asia. The rules were announced by the Trump administration as a way to incentivize auto companies to invest and stay in the United States, favoring US workers.

The new rules will require adjustments by the auto industry in the region and would be particularly challenging for Mexico. Its effects for Mexican automakers and workers will depend on how the industry, in combination with government policies, adjusts. Mexico could become an attractive investment destination for foreign companies interested in selling in the now more restricted US market. But the Mexican government, working with the auto industry, can also try to expand the product range originating in Mexico and promote engineering, design and development in order to add greater value.

The labor chapter contains some changes when compared to the TPP. For a labor violation to be actionable, the text still requires that the violation be systematic and in a manner affecting trade. However, this latter clause is deliberately interpreted more loosely, to avoid a stringent interpretation that would require that the violation be shown to create a competitive disadvantage, as was required by the US–Guatemala panel. A violation would be considered to be "in a manner affecting trade" if it involves an export product or a domestic product that competes with imports. The chapter also contains a new provision on labor rights for migrant workers and an obligation to prevent violence against workers for exercising their rights.

Undoubtedly, the most important contribution to labor rights in the USMCA is the Labor Annex, in which Mexico commits itself to passing legislation ensuring freedom of association and collective bargaining. This legislation will implement the constitutional reform passed during the TPP negotiations. The reform stipulates the creation of an independent institute in charge of registering unions and collective bargaining agreements, as well as giving courts jurisdiction to solve labor disputes, thus ending the tripartite labor conciliation and arbitration boards, which have been a mainstay of Mexican corporatism and government control. A key part of the reform is the requirement of free, personal, direct and secret elections in the selection of union leadership and support for collective bargaining agreements. These changes have long been demanded by independent unions and proposed by progressive parties in Mexico. The Labor Annex's commitments now coincide with the new government's agenda, but, international commitments as they are, they lock in these obligations for the future independent of the agenda of the government in power.

Critics of the Agreement have pointed out that the labor chapter does not go far enough on a number of fronts. Perhaps the most important criticism is that enforcement action continues to rely on a state-to-state dispute settlement mechanism that is essentially the same as in NAFTA and has proven not to be effective when one of the parties is unwilling to solve the dispute. If the parties wanted to ratchet up enforcement of potential labor violations or any other commitments in the Agreement, this would be an important area to focus on.

Now that the Agreement has been signed and the ratification process commences with a new Congress in the United States, a number of Democratic legislators have urged for changes that can ensure enforcement of labor rights. This will be an important and probably contentious process, given that the Agreement already reflects a compromise between the parties. We will have to see the content of the domestic labor reform to be implemented in Mexico and its own enforcement mechanisms. This legislation is, in any case, a condition for the entry into force of the Agreement.

However imperfect, the USMCA has signaled a new direction in thinking about labor concerns in trade agreements, going well beyond the labor chapter. It has also made use of bargaining power during negotiations to push for domestic labor reforms, although these reforms focused only on Mexico. These are welcome developments, and it may be reasonable to expect changes in these and other areas of future trade agreements if labor concerns remain in the foreground.

Chapter Twenty-One

RE-EMBEDDING LIBERALISM: INTRODUCING PASSPORTING FEES FOR FREE TRADE

Thomas Streinz

Trade liberalization has proceeded on the assumption that eventual aggregate welfare gains will exceed the losses. While compensatory mechanisms exist in most countries, they tend to be underfunded and ineffective. To begin to address this problem, the direct beneficiaries from trade liberalization need to pay more than they do now. This essay proposes to introduce passporting fees to generate more public revenue.[1] Transnational business actors would be required to obtain a free trade passport to receive the excludable benefits that a free trade agreement provides. This would change the political economy of trade radically and allow for the creation and expansion of compensatory mechanisms necessary to re-embed economic liberalism in systems of social protection.

In his seminal article on "embedded liberalism," John Ruggie argued that to maximize the combination of free trade and social welfare, nation-states must have the power to buffer their populations from trade shocks.[2] The compensatory mechanisms—whether directly targeted at trade-related effects ("trade adjustment measures" such as transfer payments or retraining efforts directly linked to trade-related dislocations) or in the form of general economic and social policies (such as unemployment insurance)—are funded through nation-state–based systems of tariffs and taxation. Post–World War II trade

---

[1] The idea for passporting fees was sparked in a brainstorming session with my colleagues in the IILJ's MegaReg project: Benedict Kingsbury, Paul Mertenskötter and Richard B. Stewart (more information about the MegaReg project at www.iilj.org/megareg). The idea was first publicly discussed at the MegaReg workshop on TPP and Megaregionalism at NYU Law on November 29, 2016, and again at the conference Trade Law in the Trump Era: A Transatlantic Perspective, organized by Chantal Thomas and Daniela Caruso, at Boston University on September 9, 2017. Thanks to the participants in these meetings and to Gráinne de Búrca, Dan Ciuriak, Daniel Francis, Harlan Cohen, Nicolas Lamp, Alvaro Santos, Dave Trubek and Johann Justus Vasel for valuable comments, questions and suggestions. Special thanks to Frank Garcia, whose proposal (developed with Timothy Meyer) to restore trade's social contract by introducing a financial transaction tax shares many features and sensibilities of the passporting fees idea.
[2] John Ruggie, "International Regimes, Transactions, and Change: Embedded Liberalism in the Postwar Economic Order," *International Organization* 36, no. 2 (1982): 379.

liberalization through the now almost universal General Agreement on Tariffs and Trade (GATT), which continues to be the bedrock of the World Trade Organization (WTO), has successfully brought down tariff levels significantly. In the past two decades, an ever-increasing number of bilateral, regional and, most recently, megaregional free trade agreements (FTAs) has further expanded the freedom under which businesses operate transnationally. However, despite their extended scope and supposedly comprehensive nature, not even the most recent trade agreements address public revenue generation, instead maintaining the traditional separation of trade and tax.[3] This has contributed to an unsustainable "disembedded liberalism" in which transnational business actors enjoy the gains that trade agreements create while successfully avoiding state-based systems of taxation. The lack of funding is one reason the architects of the contemporary global economic order have failed to develop compensatory mechanisms commensurate with increased trade liberalization.

Disembedded liberalism found two unexpected political outlets when in 2016 a slim but decisive majority of the British people voted in the Brexit referendum to leave the European Union (EU), the most integrated transnational economic area in the world, and Donald J. Trump, running on a protectionist antiglobalization platform, was elected president of the United States. To be sure, both the Brexit and Trump campaigns were fraught with factual misinformation, nationalistic propaganda and economic nonsense. But their success at the ballot box made the question of whether something is systematically wrong with transnational economic integration and global trade hard to ignore.

At the same time, the UK and US governments' policy responses illustrate the lack of imagination that is characteristic of the trade debate, pitting free traders against protectionists and globalists against nationalists. While the UK government is engaged in futile efforts to offset the projected aggregate economic welfare loss from leaving the EU with gains through increased global trade, the Trump administration is trying to scale back transnational economic integration by renegotiating existing trade agreements and by protectionist policies in violation of WTO rules (e.g., by unilaterally imposing tariffs on flimsy national security grounds).[4] Neither has a credible strategy to redistribute the aggregate welfare gains from trade to domestically compensate the losers of globalization, not even domestically, let alone globally.

This essay proposes a new way to re-embed economic liberalism. Instead of trying to scale back transnational economic integration, this essay argues for a *transnational* mechanism to be embedded in future trade agreements to generate the revenue necessary for trade adjustment measures and other social policies. More concretely, it proposes to condition certain benefits transnational business actors receive from FTAs on obtaining a free trade passport in exchange for a fee.

---

[3] This is true, e.g., for the EU–Canada Comprehensive Economic and Trade Agreement (CETA) and the Comprehensive and Progressive Trans-Pacific Partnership (CPTPP).

[4] The renegotiations of the North American Free Trade Agreement (NAFTA) culminated in the US–Mexico–Canada Agreement (USMCA). The Korea–US (KORUS) agreement was adjusted at the margins. The tariffs on steel and aluminum are being challenged in the WTO (see WTO DS 564/2018, US–Steel and Aluminum Products (Turkey)).

In doing so, this essay challenges three common beliefs about international trade law. The first is the belief that international trade rules exclusively advance economic liberalization. This essay will show that they can also be designed to tame it by internalizing social cost. The second is the belief that international trade rules always constrain domestic policy space. This essay will indicate how they can enhance it by generating public revenue for social policies. The third is the belief that redistribution mechanisms in general, and public revenue generation (taxes) in particular, are not a matter for international trade law but for domestic policy. This essay will argue that transnational revenue generation via international trade law is a necessary supplement to domestic taxation in a globalized economy.

For reasons of time and space, this essay will bracket entirely a series of important questions raised by its proposal: Who would receive, manage and eventually spend the revenue that would be generated by passporting fees? What kinds of policies are best equipped to re-embed liberalism and to compensate the losers from increased trade? How would the passporting fees be calculated and collected? Rather, the main contribution this essay is trying to make is conceptual. The claim is that introducing passporting fees into trade agreements would shift the dynamics in the political economy of trade significantly—and for the better. It would give trade policymakers a new tool to recalibrate international trade and to generate the revenue necessary for compensatory policies to re-embed and thereby sustain transnational economic liberalism. To achieve this aim, one needs to reconceptualize FTAs as instruments granting transnational businesses certain excludable benefits that can be conditioned on obtaining a free trade passport against a fee.

Reconceptualizing FTAs

The founding of the WTO in 1995 institutionalized and solidified the global trading system that became quasiuniversal with the subsequent accessions by China (2001) and Russia (2012). But this system provides only the floor and not the ceiling for contemporary transnational economic integration. Indeed, states have made expansive use of the exceptions under GATT Article XXIV and General Agreement on Trade and Services (GATS) Article V to create preferential trade regimes for goods and services.

The conventional view sees these agreements as instruments of public international law, treaties under the Vienna Convention on the Law of Treaties (VCLT) that are binding (only) on the parties, that is, the states that have signed and ratified them. Furthermore, most jurisdictions, including the leading trading powers, deny the self-executing character of international trade law, thereby reinforcing the notion that international trade law is exclusively an interstate affair. Transnational business is strangely absent in this orthodox account of international trade law that obfuscates the realities of contemporary international trade. Without the tariff reductions, market-access expansions and regulatory alignment that international trade law has brought about, multinational corporations could not have created the complex regional supply chains that Richard Baldwin has described as the "second unbundling" of globalization.[5] Furthermore, recent FTAs

---

[5]   Richard Baldwin, *The Great Convergence: Information Technology and the New Globalization* (Cambridge, MA: Harvard University Press, 2016).

contain a whole range of provisions requiring states to modify their domestic administrative rule- and decision-making to allow for increased participation by "interested
persons." Transnational business actors are most likely to use these provisions to exercise
"remote control" abroad.[6]

In contrast to the conventional international trade law view, contemporary FTAs are
better understood as tools to expand firms' freedom to operate transnationally.[7] Take the
revived Trans-Pacific Partnership (TPP) agreement, which creates a transoceanic economic megaregion in which tariffs are to be gradually phased out, multicountry production networks benefit from cumulative rules of origin, states' interference with the market
is disciplined and domestic rule- and decision-making has to comply with common
(global) administrative law standards of transparency, participation, reason giving and
review.[8] Assessing such a comprehensive economic agreement purely from the conventional perspective of international trade law with its focus on the participating states
misses the point.

This is best exemplified by the US withdrawal from the TPP. Even though the United
States will (at least for the time being) not be a party to the agreement, "US" corporations
will benefit from the TPP's expanded economic freedom to operate in at least three ways:[9]
First, to the extent to which TPP parties fulfill their obligations under the agreement
by changing their laws wholesale—for example, without differentiating between entities
associated with TPP parties on the one hand and non-TPP parties on the other hand—
US corporations will be subject to the (uniformly) TPP reformed laws favoring transnational business. Second, even if the remaining TPP parties choose to create laws that
differentiate between TPP and non-TPP parties, US corporations' subsidiaries registered
in the TPP countries—benefiting from liberal laws for business incorporation—will have
all rights and obligations under the respective domestic laws, as reshaped by the TPP,
including the investment protection rights that the TPP accords. Third, US corporations
orchestrate sophisticated regional value chains in the TPP region; even though they
will not be able to import goods and services into the United States under the preferential TPP rules, their suppliers' regional production networks in the TPP region will
benefit from reduced tariffs, increased market access and gradually enhanced regulatory
alignment, which will ultimately also benefit the heads of the chain even though they are
headquartered outside the TPP region.

The result is a misalignment of international trade law, traditionally conceived,
with the reality of a globalized economy. While economists (associated with "new trade

---

[6]   Paul Mertenskötter and Richard B. Stewart, "Remote Control: Treaty Requirements for
      Regulatory Procedures," *Cornell Law Review* 104 (forthcoming).

[7]   Dan Ciuriak, "Generalized Freedom to Operate" (MegaReg Forum Paper, Institute for
      International Law and Justice, New York, 2016), www.iilj.org/megareg.

[8]   Benedict Kingsbury et al., eds., *Megaregulation Contested: Global Economic Ordering after TPP* (Oxford:
      Oxford University Press, forthcoming).

[9]   The scare quotes around US are meant to signal that the link between (multinational)
      corporations and the states they are registered and/or headquartered in is fraught.

theory") have shifted their attention to the vastly increased intrafirm trade in inter-mediate goods and corresponding services input, international trade law and the related political and economic discourse continues to frame the benefits of trade as accruing on a national level, benefiting (or, as the case may be, harming) a national economy. But the reality is that contemporary FTAs are sophisticated and insufficiently understood instruments of economic governance that create excludable and nonexcludable benefits for transnational businesses. The idea behind passporting fees is to subject the excludable benefits not just to an artificial and relatively easy-to-manipulate nationality requirement but to the obtaining of a transnational FTA passport against an appropriate fee.

Introducing Passporting Fees

Somewhat ironically, the idea to introduce passporting fees—that is, to require businesses to pay for a license to operate under the preferential conditions of an FTA—draws inspiration from an episode of the Brexit saga. The outcome of the June 2016 Brexit referendum raised the question whether the British finance industry, concentrated in London, would retain the passporting rights that financial service providers authorized anywhere in the European Economic Area (EEA) enjoy under EU law. The fundamental economic freedoms of the EU's single market and specific EU legislation—that the United Kingdom is bound to leave and cannot replicate unilaterally—allow the financial industry to operate throughout the EEA under a single license ("passport"). The British financial sector failed to convince the British government to soften its hard Brexit stance and stands to lose its passporting rights as a consequence of leaving the EU's single market. Reportedly, the British finance industry expressed indignation when confronted with the UK government's inquiry about how much continued passporting rights would be worth to the sector.

The question of "how much is it worth to retain a given benefit of transnational economic integration" should be asked mutatis mutandis when the expansion of inter-national trade liberalization is at issue. The best way to ask this question is to concep-tualize the excludable benefits that transnational business actors receive under a given FTA as passporting rights for which they ought to obtain an FTA passport against a passporting fee. Trade negotiators would have considerable leeway to decide whether a given FTA provision would be subject to the passport requirement or not. They might need to reconsider, or indeed consider for the first time, who actually benefits from any given provision (and their interaction) in an FTA and whether the benefits should be exclusive or not. Candidates to be subjected to the passport requirement are not only tariff reductions, increased market access (including to public procurement) and cumulative rules of origin, but also investment and intellectual property (IP) protec-tion. Provisions aimed at wider domestic law reform, involving changes to constitutive rules about administrative rule- and decision-making, are less suitable as a passport requirement would lead to frictions, especially once several FTAs (with or without passporting fees) layer onto one another. For related reasons, future TPP-style multi-party agreements consolidating existing bilateral FTAs appear to be the most suitable instruments into which passporting fees could be embedded. They also happen to be best geared toward facilitating multicountry production networks. But theoretically any FTA (including small-scale bilaterals) and even future WTO agreements could consider passporting fees.

Introducing passporting fees realigns the benefits created from economic integration with the costs by requiring the beneficiaries to pay a certain fee for the benefits they receive to generate revenue that could be used for compensatory policies. Instead of relying on an underspecified, undertheorized and widely debunked trickle-down theory of trade, leaving every national economy to its own devices, passporting fees constitute a novel transnational mechanism of public revenue generation (leaving open, for now, the question of whether the compensatory policies should also be managed transnationally). In this sense, the passporting fee idea shares some commonalities with Miguel Poiares Maduro's proposal to reform the EU by taxing transnational economic activity facilitated by the EU's single market.[10] While passporting fees in trade are meant to re-embed liberalism by funding compensatory policies, Maduro is trying to find a solution to Europe's economic governance crisis by capturing some of the welfare gains that are being generated by European economic integration via a transnational tax instead of relying on domestic taxation and ensuing transfers from rich to poor member states. The passporting fee idea also chimes with proposals to restore trade's social contract by introducing a financial transaction tax to fund domestic compensatory policies.[11] The key difference is that the passporting fee idea establishes a direct link between trade benefits and costs: receiving the benefits of economic integration would be *conditional* on obtaining a free trade passport.

It is important to emphasize a crucial difference between passporting fees and tariffs. Unlike tariffs, which are set by each country individually—within the constraints of international trade law, most notably the WTO's basic most-favored-nation (MFN) requirement from which further tariff reductions via FTAs are exempted—passporting fees, especially in multicountry settings, would not "distort" trade between the parties. The fees would apply uniformly across the economic area governed by a given FTA. This is one key advantage of a *transnational* rather than a *domestic* mechanism for public revenue generation. There are other reasons why public revenue generation via domestic taxes and tariffs is inferior to passporting fees. Transnational business actors in Western democracies have been largely successful in convincing the political establishment that a low-tax environment for corporations is a necessary precondition for successful transnational competition. What is more, multinational corporations, especially in IP-heavy industries, have found sophisticated ways to avoid domestic taxation altogether by shifting profits offshore into tax havens. The Organisation for Economic Co-operation and Development (OECD) efforts to tackle the pervasive practice of base erosion and profit shifting (BEPS) have been ineffective and do not challenge the increasingly questionable dogma that tax

---

is not a trade issue. The opposite is true: increased trade raises the question of effective transnational taxation even more acutely. Future comprehensive trade agreements should be truly comprehensive by addressing public revenue generation. Introducing passporting fees is one rather radical way to do this. It would dramatically change the political economy of trade.

Changing the Political Economy of Trade

With passporting fees, trade policymakers would have a new tool at their disposal to fine-tune trade agreements. For instance, they could be tailored to deliberately favor small- and medium-sized enterprises (SMEs) over large companies (e.g., by exempting microenterprises entirely from the fees). Encouraging SMEs to operate transnationally is a staple of free trade advocates, with renewed prominence in the debate around electronic commerce. But evidence that the dedicated SME chapters included in many recent FTAs actually achieve what they purport to do is lacking.[12] Passporting fees might be one way to actually level the playing field between large multinational corporations and SMEs.

Policymakers could use the revenue from passporting fees for redistributive measures and other social policies to mitigate the effects of transnational trade liberalization. Instead of relying on unspecified trickle-down effects, a portion of the increased aggregate welfare would be appropriated via passporting fees and could be used to compensate those who suffer the negative consequences of trade. In this context, the antiglobalization movement that tends to reject any effort to liberalize transnational trade further might need to reconsider its opposition to *any* new FTA in light of a mechanism that would increase revenue generation for socially beneficial aims.

Conversely, states that have so far resisted efforts to create more effective transnational mechanisms to sustain public revenue generation might eventually come to realize that a coordinated effort by nation-states is most likely the only way to effectively counterbalance the ability of multinational corporations to avoid domestic taxation. Making public revenue generation part of the trade conversation might lead to new national and transnational coalitions helping governments withstand the predictable corporate opposition to passporting fees.

It is true that passporting fees are a pay-for-play scheme. They make transparent that certain entities benefit from trade. Realistically, this will be used to portray trade agreements as a corporate power grab. But this conversation is already happening, cannot be avoided and is ultimately worth having. The key difference would be that passporting fees would put a price tag on the expansion of firms' privileges to operate transnationally.

Businesses would need to reassess the costs and benefits of conducting transnational business. Trade lawyers and economists would be highly incentivized to determine and

---

[12] Dan Ciuriak, "TPP's Business Asymmetries: Megaregulation and the Conditions of Competition between MNCs and SMEs," in *Megaregulation Contested: Global Economic Ordering after TPP*, ed. Kingsbury et al. (Oxford: Oxford University Press, forthcoming).

calculate the excludable benefits from a given trade regime. In the medium term, this would significantly improve our understanding of the realities of global trade and its winners and losers. Instead of continuing to play what Dani Rodrik has called the trade numbers game,[13] we could make progress on re-embedding liberalism by asking the right questions: Who benefits from trade liberalization? At what cost? And how are those who are suffering the consequences being compensated?

---

[13] Dani Rodrik, "The Trade Numbers Game," *Project Syndicate*, February 10, 2016, https://perma.cc/2KYF-FXB6.

Chapter Twenty-Two

RESTORING TRADE'S SOCIAL CONTRACT IN THE UNITED STATES

Frank J. Garcia

The current crisis in trade policy affords an important opportunity to reexamine the quality of consent (and its absence) in trade law and policy today. Consent is an essential, constitutive element in trade—without it, we engage in some form of predation, coercion or exploitation, whether or not we call it "trade."[1] Consent is not only an element in trade between states, however—it is equally important in understanding the internal political and social bargains political communities make when they undertake trade liberalization policies, or what I call the "social contract of trade."[2] In exchange for pursuing free trade as a policy, a society has an obligation to compensate those within the polity who are vulnerable to trade's downside risks. One way this social obligation is met is through a collection of specialized labor support policies called trade adjustment assistance (TAA), which in the United States is explicitly linked to securing congressional support for free trade negotiations.

In trade terms, the 2016 US presidential election was a wake-up call for many. A significant element within the US polity feels betrayed by our current trade policies and believes that free trade is being imposed on them for others' benefits, but at a cost for them. This reflects in part the widely acknowledged failure of TAA as it is currently designed and implemented. To restore trade's social contract, TAA needs to be significantly transformed to guarantee effective retraining, relocation support and adequate wage insurance benefits. Funding for a revamped TAA could come from incorporating a financial transaction tax (FTT) into all trade agreements, which would support domestic adjustment assistance programs. This reform will be an effective way to honor the social contract of trade and make it self-sustaining.

---

[1] See Frank Garcia, *Consent and Trade: Trading Freely in a Global Market* (Cambridge: Cambridge University Press, 2018).

[2] See Frank J. Garcia and Timothy Meyer, "Restoring Trade's Social Contract," *Michigan Law Review Online* 116 (2017): 78, 82, http://michiganlawreview.org/restoring-trades-social-contract/.

Trade and the "Country within the Country"

The social contract of trade

The social contract of trade involves the decisions we make as a society to pursue a free trade policy and, as part of those decisions, the commitments we make to vulnerable groups within our own society who are at risk when we engage in free trade. The choice to enact a free trade regime forms part of what John Rawls calls the "basic structure of a society": a set of institutions, policies and practices that fundamentally shape the allocation of social resources and the life prospects of a community's members.[3] It is choosing a set of social arrangements that we hope collectively brings us the benefits of social and economic cooperation—in this case, trade. However, these arrangements may also bring substantial costs in the form of lost jobs or lost wages for particular members of our society.

The social contract of trade, as I am using the term here, consists of the obligation we have toward those vulnerable workers to hold them free from harm or, more precisely, to ensure they are no worse off than they would have been had we not embarked on a free trade policy. This obligation has deep roots in both liberal theory[4] and the economic justifications for free trade.[5] If we fail in this obligation, our trade policies become a kind of theft, or nonconsensual economic extraction, on those subject to them insofar as the promises made to secure their consent are betrayed.

In an advanced capitalist welfare society, a key area for investigating the state of this social contract is adjustment assistance for displaced workers. Adjustment assistance consists of a package of enhanced benefits that the Organisation for Economic Co-operation and Development (OECD) and other governments offer to workers who have lost their jobs as a result of trade. It is designed to support displaced workers as they face unemployment or underemployment, as well as to provide the retraining and relocation necessary to rebuild their lives and their communities. For many social welfare democracies, this is considered to be part of the basic social contract of the welfare

---

[3] See John Rawls, *The Law of Peoples: With "The Idea of Public Reason Revisited,"* 4th ed. (Cambridge, MA: Harvard University Press, 1992), 42–43 (linking the trade regime to the social choice for markets and the need for fair background conditions as part of the basic structure). On the relationship between free trade and Rawls's earlier views in *A Theory of Justice*, see Frank J. Garcia, *Global Justice and International Economic Law: Three Takes* (Cambridge: Cambridge University Press, 2013), 70–95.

[4] Aaron James calls this the "Duty of Collective Due Care," one of the three equitable principles he finds inherent in the collective social practice he calls mutual reliance on markets, or mutual market reliance, for short. Aaron James, *Fairness in Practice: A Social Contract for a Global Economy* (Oxford: Oxford University Press, 2012), 17–18.

[5] See Garcia and Meyer, "Restoring Trade's Social Contract," 82 (the importance of domestic adjustment policies in fairly distributing gains from liberalized trade). See generally, C. Michael Aho and Thomas O. Bayard, "Costs and Benefits of Trade Adjustment Assistance," in *The Structure and Evolution of Recent US Trade Policy*, ed. Robert E. Baldwin and Anne O. Krueger (Chicago: University of Chicago Press, 1984), 157–60 (a review of economic justifications for adjustment assistance).

state and has been linked to calls for a broader welfare response to globalization's economic risks.[6]

In the United States, adjustment assistance (called trade adjustment assistance, or TAA) is explicitly linked to securing congressional support for free trade negotiations (trade promotion authority, or TPA) going as far back as the Kennedy administration.[7] In the United States, we have a special or specific social contract of trade, whatever the nature of the larger, more general social contract we maintain with workers. The domestic political and legal process of granting the Executive Branch TPA—and, in the process, agreeing to TAA—forms an internal or domestic analog to transnational mechanisms for securing and protecting consent in forming true trade agreements. How we deliver (or not) on our commitment to TAA benefits following a decision to engage in trade is key for assessing the consensual nature of our trade agreements and trade policy, yet it is virtually invisible in the public debate once TPA has been granted.[8]

Betraying the social contract of trade

The current political crisis in the United States has revealed that many consider the process of formulating a consensus for trade to be broken and the commitment to deliver meaningful TAA to have been violated.[9] In the United States, we have in fact defaulted on the core promise of effective TAA for people whose jobs are at risk due to our decision to pursue trade. Despite TAA's broad ambitions when announced by the Kennedy administration in 1962, the benefits were limited to training programs to promote reemployment and some income support during the training period. Eligibility was also much more limited than under contemporary TAA programs, and many of the initial applications were denied.[10] By 1974, when Congress next revisited trade policy, support within organized labor for TAA had collapsed and the unions dismissed TAA as nothing more than "burial insurance."[11] In the 1980s the Reagan administration proposed abolishing TAA completely, and the program lapsed briefly.[12]

---

[6]   See US Library of Congress, Congressional Research Service, *TAA and Its Role in US Trade Policy*, by J. F. Hornbeck, R411922 (2013), 1–3 (summarizing equity arguments); Aho and Bayard, "Costs and Benefits of Trade Adjustment Assistance," 154–57 (reviewing in-depth equity-based arguments for TAA in the context of either a general or trade-specific social contract between government and workers).

[7]   See Garcia and Meyer, "Restoring Trade's Social Contract," 85.

[8]   See Stephen Kim Park, "Bridging the Global Governance Gap: Reforming the Law of Trade Adjustment," *Georgetown Journal of International Law* 43, no. 3 (2012): 797 (TAA often misunderstood and overlooked).

[9]   See Garcia and Meyer, "Restoring Trade's Social Contract," 82–84 (citing 2016 presidential campaign poll data).

[10] The first application accepted for benefits did not take place until November 1969. See ibid., 508.

[11] Ibid., 509.

[12] Hornbeck, *TAA and Its Role*, 9.

Since then, the renewal of TAA has always been tied to new rounds of trade negotiations and has in principle outlined a commitment to a broader and more nuanced approach. Congress has renewed or extended TAA each time it has granted the president TPA or approved a new round of trade agreements, reinforcing the connection between decisions to trade and decisions to compensate at-risk workers but underscoring its political vulnerability as well.[13] However, once TPA is granted or the agreements ratified, TAA funding has tended to diminish, further reinforcing the many defects inherent in the TAA design and leading to widespread acknowledgment that TAA as currently constituted is a failure.[14]

This has rendered TAA a political football rather than a consensual agreement. With TAA's design and funding failures, our execution of this commitment has only undermined the social contract of trade.

Restoring trade's social contract

The core element in any attempt to restore the social contract of trade is to ensure that any promises made in the process of securing consent for trade are in fact honored. This means, in the United States, that if we care about honoring consent in our domestic trade policy, we should reform how TAA is designed and delivered in the United States.[15] The key to a successful TAA program is worker retraining toward sustainable reemployment. European states have successfully demonstrated that TAA works if one is serious about the commitment. By investing in worker retraining as a percentage of GDP (I shall have more to say about this below), as well as offering a more effective training and apprenticeship process that better matches training to market needs, rewards early intervention (sometimes before unemployment even occurs) and offers thorough and effective job counseling, a significant number of trade-displaced workers can find alternative meaningful employment.[16]

For a country as large as the United States, relocation support is another key element to effective reemployment assistance, perhaps even more important than training.[17]

---

[13] Ibid., 10–12.

[14] See Garcia and Meyer, "Restoring Trade's Social Contract," 87. See also Timothy Meyer, "Saving the Political Consensus in Favor of Free Trade," *Vanderbilt Law Review* 70, no. 3 (2017): 985.

[15] These suggestions also have implications for other countries as they consider how best to design effective compensation programs. Tim Meyer has argued that for this reason the commitment to undertake domestic adjustment policies should itself be internationalized in the form of commitments within trade agreements, thus binding all parties to a collective decision to support the social contract of trade throughout the free trade zone they collectively create. See Meyer, "Saving the Political," 985.

[16] These successful cases are being studied widely and are starting to be emulated in other OECD countries. See Organisation for Economic Co-operation and Development, *Connecting People with Jobs: The Labour Market, Activation Policies and Disadvantaged Workers in Slovenia* (Paris: OECD, 2016), 116–18.

[17] Jun Nie and Ethan Struby, "Would Active Labor Market Policies Help Combat High US Unemployment?," *Economic Review* (Federal Reserve Bank of Kansas City, Third Quarter 2011), 44–46.

However, current job search and relocation allowances are woefully inadequate and should be increased.[18] Moreover, in a country with a high cost of living like the United States, wage-insurance-benefit caps should be raised to acknowledge the costs of a secure middle-class life and the difficulties faced by workers supporting families in finding equivalent postdislocation work.[19] Without more public investment, TAA as configured will only ensure that more families enter the "working poor" rather than continue in their "pretrade" middle-class life.

The bottom line is that a well-designed and well-executed TAA program would fulfill the social contract of trade both formally and substantively.[20] However, meeting this obligation would require a deeper and more consistent commitment to funding, and this is TAA's most spectacular failure. Overall, there has been no effort to link funding levels to the levels of demand or need for the program.[21] As a result, TAA funding has consistently been set too low and has fluctuated due to political trends rather than political commitments.[22] Moreover, the United States is consistently near the bottom of all OECD countries in terms of adjustment spending.[23] Restoring trade's social contract must address funding, not simply program design and delivery.

Properly funding trade's social contract

Supporting the domestic consensus for trade means that adjustment assistance funding must be consistent with its overall role in the social contract. In my view, it should be most consistent with the social contract of trade as a promise from all of us that the funding to support those most vulnerable to trade comes from trade itself. While this could be

---

[18] Currently job search and relocation allowance is capped at $1,250, which is wholly inadequate. See Park, "Bridging the Global," 816; Garcia and Meyer, "Restoring Trade's Social Contract," 88.

[19] The median US income is approaching $60,000 a year, and survey data suggests this closely tracks what US consumers feel is necessary for a living wage for middle-class families today, and even this would not be enough in many parts of the United States. See Aimee Picchi, "How Much Money Do US Families Need to Get By?," *CBS News*, August 26, 2015, https://www.cbsnews.com/news/how-much-money-do-us-families-need-to-get-by/ [https://perma.cc/5LG2-YNQ8]. The median salary for a middle-class manufacturing job for a middle-aged worker is $75,000. See Patrick Gillespie, "$75 a Day vs. $75,000 a Year: How We Lost Jobs to Mexico," *CNN Money*, March 31, 2016, http://money.cnn.com/2016/03/31/news/economy/mexico-us-globalization-wage-gap/index.html [https://perma.cc/2YAC-B3HK].

[20] Nie and Struby, "Would Active Labor Market Policies," 43, 48, 51–54.

[21] Park, "Bridging the Global," 847–48.

[22] For example, the most recent TAA reauthorization was in 2015, extending TAA through 2021 and capping the annual funding at $450 million, a *reduction* from the amounts authorized in 2009 and 2011. Department of Labor, Employment and Training Administration, *Side-by-Side Comparison of TAA Program Benefits under the 2002 Program, 2009 Program, 2011 Program, and 2015 Program*, November 9, 2015, https://www.doleta.gov/tradeact/pdf/side-by-side.pdf [https://perma.cc/3YA8-MNVA]; Meyer, "Saving the Political," 1010–11.

[23] Nie and Struby, "Would Active Labor Market Policies" (demonstrating that the United States is third from the bottom of 21 OECD countries studied); Department of Labor, "Side-by-Side

accomplished through traditional legislative redistribution of the gains from trade, the history of trade politics, at least in the United States, shows that we cannot rely on this for anything as constitutive as the basic bargain underlying trade's social contract.

Instead, as a key element in restoring trade's social contract and honoring consent throughout domestic and foreign trade policy, we should consider incorporating a FTT into all new or renegotiated trade agreements. This will directly harness the wealth creation of FTAs themselves toward supporting domestic adjustment assistance programs. An FTT with revenue earmarked for adjustment assistance would place entities that benefit tremendously from trade liberalization—major financial institutions—in the role of assisting those who suffer most from the same.[24]

FTT proposals are not new, and a number of them have been adopted or proposed around the globe.[25] While a comprehensive review of the extensive literature on FTTs, and a detailed exposition of the features of an FTT such as I am proposing, are beyond the scope of this essay,[26] the essence of the arrangement is as follows: parties to an FTA would agree that each party shall impose an incremental tax on specified financial transactions (such as securities, derivatives and currency trades) of anywhere from 0.01 percent to 0.1 percent (the rate to be the same in each member state). Focusing exclusively on finance and keeping the rate low would ensure the tax does not discourage productive investment transactions but is sufficient to generate hundreds of millions of dollars for adjustment assistance for workers who share the risks but do not get the benefits of trade's joint venture.

In terms of scope and jurisdiction, a social contract FTT should be designed to tax wholesale capital market transactions (stocks, bonds, derivatives and currency trades) among major financial institutions such as banks, investment firms, insurance companies, pension funds and hedge funds, not retail transactions such as home mortgages and business loans.[27] Taxing capital market transactions and not, for example, trade-related finance helps ensure the tax does not has a discouraging effect on traditional commerce and productive investment.

Jurisdictionally, the tax should be tied to the geographic territory of the FTA itself. This could be achieved by defining taxable transactions as those between counterparties

---

Comparison" (demonstrating that the United States currently ranks second from the bottom among the 35 OECD countries in its level of TAA as a percentage of GDP, ahead of only Mexico).

[24] For an earlier call to shift TAA funding to a transnational model, see Park, "Bridging the Global," 862 (arguing that the TAA should be delivered by transnational worker payments through a global adjustment fund supported by state budgetary contributions). However, Park's model failed to link TAA support directly to the trade benefits enjoyed by others.

[25] See Garcia and Meyer, "Restoring Trade's Social Contract," 94–95.

[26] Ibid., 95–98.

[27] See generally European Commission, *Proposal for a Council Directive Implementing Enhanced Cooperation in the Area of Financial Transaction Tax* (Brussels: European Commission, February 14, 2013), 17, 36 (weighing the costs and benefits of taxing various transactions and institutions, and concluding that certain institutions, including refinancing institutions, should not be taxed with an FTT). It is important for political as well as normative reasons that the tax not apply to ordinary consumers at the retail level. See Len Burman and William G. Gale, "The Pros and

when at least one counterparty is a resident within the free trade area, like the EU does,[28] although in the context of FTAs, one should consider whether the proposal should require both counterparties to be resident.[29] Outside a highly integrated system such as the EU, with strong central institutions and arguably its own social contract, the states that are party to an FTA would have to negotiate among themselves how the tax would be collected and allocated between each state, subject to guidelines agreed on in the FTA itself.[30]

Even with jurisdictional and scope limitations, such a tax could generate considerable revenue toward funding TAA obligations. The EU Commission calculated that its earlier 2011 FTT proposal could generate as much as €57 billion with a tax rate of 0.1 percent on all wholesale stock and bond transfers and 0.01 percent on all derivatives trades, with all 27 member states participating.[31] An FTT with the same tax rate and jurisdictional structure, if applied in the North American Free Trade Agreement (NAFTA) zone today, could yield as much as $64 billion toward adjustment costs.[32] To put this in perspective, in 2015, the combined annual budget for *all* active labor market policies (TAA included) among the United States, Canada and Mexico totaled $25 billion.[33] Not only would an FTA-based FTT cover the cost of TAA as currently configured, but it would also allow for the necessary reforms and expansions without burdening the public.

Creating a trade-related FTT, however it is implemented and allocated, would be a breakthrough in trade adjustment financing and, more broadly, in mechanisms to address the social costs and inequality effects of trade. Linking such a tax to transactions within the economic zones that FTAs create would directly harness their wealth-creating potential and tie the funding for TAA to financial parties that benefit tremendously from the agreements themselves. Such a mechanism would be rooted directly in the social contract

Cons of a Consumption Tax" (Washington, DC: Brookings Institute, March 3, 2005), https://perma.cc/WA73-KXJJ.

[28] European Commission, *Proposal*, 18.

[29] Particularly when the FTA zone would include a major financial center such as New York in the case of a US FTA, or the city in the case of an EU or (potentially) UK FTA, it is easy to object that applying the tax when only one counterparty is resident risks an unjustifiably large tax base.

[30] There are a number of autonomous to more collaborative options. See Garcia and Meyer, "Restoring Trade's Social Contract," 99.

[31] European Commission, *Commission Proposal for a Council Directive on a Common System of Financial Transaction Tax and Amending Directive* (Brussels: European Commission, September 21, 2001), 1102–03. This would calculate to a tax yield of 0.3 percent of total EU nominal GDP for 2011 (€18.3 trillion), using GDP as a proxy for the tax base, although other measures such as total EU volume of wholesale capital market transactions could be more accurate. See "European Union GDP," *Trading Economics*, November 10, 2017, https://perma.cc/3UQW-8FBV.

[32] Assuming the same 0.3 percent calculation on a 2016 combined NAFTA GDP of $21.4 trillion. See "Report for Selected Countries and Subjects," International Monetary Fund, April 2017, https://perma.cc/R94U-J2S8. Apportionment of these revenues would of course have to be worked out among the FTA participants.

[33] "Public Expenditure and Participant Stocks on LMP," Organisation for Economic Co-operation and Development, https://perma.cc/99WY-HT27.

of trade itself and not more general calls for transnational wealth redistribution, however justified (or not) the latter may be for other reasons. Implementing such a reform would fulfill the social contract of trade and render it self-sustaining rather than subject to the vicissitudes of budgetary politics. Something as essential as consent in trade deserves no less, and as we are learning, we neglect this at our peril.

Chapter Twenty-Three

MIGRATION AND INTERNATIONAL ECONOMIC ASYMMETRY

Chantal Thomas

The world is on the point of a stunning reversal. Nationalism and isolationism have surged against the global laws and institutions that have advanced economic liberalization and integration for half a century. Hostility is rising against international trade and international migration, both of which the new cadre of self-styled antiglobalists see as interrelated and threatening to national security and economic stability.

In the case of immigration that is not authorized, this anathema has slipped into a toxic stew of xenophobia and scapegoating, and has fed much of the political and ideological antiglobalist backlash and accompanying orientation toward border militarization that have become increasingly salient in the years since the 2008 global financial crisis.[1] Those who cross borders without authorization in search of economic opportunity are, within this discourse, portrayed as morally culpable by virtue of their transgression of national immigration laws, particularly in the Global North. Less well-understood are the ways in which international law, itself significantly framed by the governments of the Global North, has helped shape the phenomenon of irregular migration.[2] This includes the international law of trade, which forms one part of a larger architecture of globalization that over the past quarter-century has brought governments into liberalized arrangements vis-à-vis world markets.

This essay examines both the explanatory and the normative implications of the relationship between international trade, and international economic liberalization more generally, and irregular migration. It focuses on a detailed case study of the relationship between Mexico and the United States in the years leading up to and following the adoption of the North American Free Trade Agreement (NAFTA). While of course characterized by historical specificities, the broad contours of this dynamic pertain in many other instances of undocumented migration from countries in the Global South to destinations in the Global North.

---

[1] For a discussion of the phenomenon of "reterritorialization," see Chantal Thomas, "Trade and Development in an Era of Multipolarity and Reterritorialization," *Yale Journal of International Law* Online Symposium (November 25, 2018).

[2] Chantal Thomas, *Disorderly Borders: How International Law Shapes Irregular Migration* (London: Oxford University Press, forthcoming).

The argument is the following: increased migration from Mexico to the United States, following NAFTA, was a function of (1) increased trade *in the context of* (2) significant wealth disparity between the two countries *coupled with* (3) adoption by the Mexican state of neoclassical measures that independently increased economic volatility and prevented the establishment of measures necessary to support both economic growth and stability. International trade liberalization is but one feature of an asymmetric world order that creates pressures for emigration from poor countries to rich countries. The asymmetry in international economic regulation, privileging movement of goods and capital over movement of people, is mirrored by a lack of focus on addressing the effect of international economic shocks on domestic employment. In the first section, "Open Markets, Closed Borders: An Asymmetric Globalization," I link international economic arrangements to irregular migration flows, and in particular to the asymmetry between people, goods and capital. Then, in "Looking Forward: To Close Markets or to Open Borders?," I argue that this asymmetry must be addressed and that the way forward is to do so by increasing openness in migration flows rather than retreating to a more pervasively nationalistic economic model.

When I first began to develop this analysis, it was intended to unseat the conventional wisdom at that time supporting the status quo embrace of asymmetric economic liberalism in the international order. I sought to show that those shaping the global economic order could not tenably pursue liberalization on some fronts—goods and capital—but not on others—movement of people. To do so would not prevent the movement of people so much as relegate it, and them, to the informal economy. As I write now, the political winds have shifted dramatically away from the neoclassicism of the status quo ante in a new and perhaps even more dangerous direction toward unreconstituted nationalism. The way forward cannot be to retreat from the international economic order, as many in politics currently hold, but rather to remake it to better comply with norms of equity and equality.

Open Markets, Closed Borders: An Asymmetric Globalization

International trade law was established to coordinate intergovernmental policy and to effectuate the substantial reduction of trade barriers.[3] At the same time that governments established legal institutions like the World Trade Organization (WTO) and NAFTA to maximize openness to flows of goods and flows of capital, they resisted enabling the movement of people. The world order designed by international economic law at the end of the twentieth century reflected an asymmetrical vision of globalization. It was, to a significant extent, a world vision of "open markets" but "closed borders."[4]

---

[3]   Preamble to the General Agreement on Tariffs and Trade, now part of the World Trade Organization.

[4]   I associate this terminology with Peter Andreas, "U.S.–Mexico: Open Markets, Closed Border," *Foreign Policy* 103 (Summer 1996): 51–69.

NAFTA, for example, established requirements to eliminate almost all tariffs on goods traded between Canada, Mexico and the United States, and to remove barriers to foreign investment. Yet NAFTA simultaneously excluded almost all labor movement from its purview, making only relatively narrow exceptions to permit some kinds of professional and business visas. The WTO reflected the same imbalance, adopting wide-ranging protocols liberalizing trade in goods and services but only limited measures on movement of people.

Trade experts have long decried this feature of asymmetry within international economic law, asserting two important critiques. The first critique points out that this asymmetry runs contrary to the logic and theory of economic liberalization. Labor constitutes, along with land and capital, one of the essential factors of production. As such, the same rationale as to why economic liberalization would increase aggregate social welfare should pertain to it as much as the other two. Yet international institutions pursuing economic liberalization have relaxed national regulatory controls on the ownership and exchange of land and capital (investment reforms and treaties meant that foreign direct investment, capital markets and land ownership were opened up to foreign actors), while leaving barriers to entry for labor markets largely in place. This internal contradiction, as the law and economics scholars Joel Trachtman and Howard Chang have observed, flouts the logic of free markets and the welfare they are meant to engender.[5]

The second established critique focuses on the deleterious consequences in particular for developing countries of this asymmetry. Hence the observations by international economists such as Dani Rodrik and Branko Milanovic that cross-border movement, or the lack thereof, constitutes the most impactful feature of the global economic landscape with respect to the prospects for poverty reduction. Rodrik writes that there "is practically nothing that would do more to [...] improv[e] the global distribution of income" than to lower "barriers to international labor mobility."[6] The continued existence of such barriers constitutes a primary reason why, as Milanovic has shown, global geographical location now forms the single most important factor in determining individual economic prospects.[7]

I offer a third reason why asymmetry is untenable, which centers on irregular migration as an unintended[8] consequence of broader institutions and policies of liberalization. The governments who crafted international agreements to achieve the liberalization of

---

[5] Howard F. Chang, "Migration as International Trade: The Economic Gains from the Liberalized Movement of Labor," *UCLA Journal of International Law and Foreign Affairs* 3 (1998): 371–414; Sungjoon Cho, "Development by Moving People: Unearthing the Development Potential of a GATS Visa," in *Developing Countries in the WTO Legal System* (Oxford: Oxford University Press, 2009), 457–74; Joel P. Trachtman, *The International Law of Economic Migration: Toward the Fourth Freedom* (Kalamazoo, MI: W. E. Upjohn Institute, 2009).

[6] Dani Rodrik, "It's Time to Think for Yourself on Free Trade," *Foreign Policy*, January 27, 2017.

[7] See Branko Milanovic, "Global Income Inequality in Numbers: In History and Now," *Global Policy* 4, no. 3 (2013): 198–208 (204).

[8] Many authors, including myself, have pointed out that there is a strong argument that irregular migration can be understood as an intended, rather than unintended, consequence of economic liberalization policies. Undocumented workers provide a source of highly pliable and exploitable labor and in that sense may well be both desired and sought by employers.

goods and capital seriously miscast the relationship between these dimensions of economic liberalization and migration patterns, particularly between countries of dramatically different income and poverty levels. In what follows, I present the empirical case for irregular migration as a consequence of international economic asymmetry, followed by a consideration of the normative implications of this relationship.

Trade and displacement: the evidence for a causal relationship to migration

Around the time that NAFTA's adoption was being debated, one of its extolled virtues was that it would cause a decline, rather than a rise, in Mexico–US migration. Anti-immigration politics were marshaled to build support for NAFTA on the argument that international economic integration between Mexico and the United States would reduce immigration from the former to the latter.[9] This argument was enabled by a widely accepted economic theorem (the "Heckscher–Ohlin" theorem)[10] that trade and migration would act as substitutes between countries that had different factor endowments—different levels of abundance of the main factors of production (land, labor and capital). With respect to trade between a relatively labor-abundant country and a relatively capital-abundant country, labor-intensive production would move to the former and capital-intensive production would move to the latter. This theorem provided the basis for the argument, circa the adoption of NAFTA, that liberalizing trade between Mexico (the relatively labor-abundant economy) and the United States (the relatively capital-abundant economy) would mean that Mexican workers, instead of crossing the border to look for employment physically inside the United States, would stay home and take advantage of increased opportunities to produce goods and services that could be traded with the United States. At the same time, the movement of capital-intensive production to the United States would form the basis for the creation of more "good-paying American jobs," to use the parlance employed by President Clinton in urging the passage of NAFTA.[11]

Certainly, this vulnerability to exploitation holds true whether the presence of these workers was intended or not.

[9] Kevin Johnson has provided an extensive discussion of the political debate surrounding the passage of NAFTA in the United States and how proponents of NAFTA steered controversy around illegal immigration to shore up support for, and counter opposition to, NAFTA's implementation by arguing that NAFTA would reduce illegal immigration by boosting economic growth in Mexico. Kevin R. Johnson, "Free Trade and Closed Borders: NAFTA and Mexican Immigration to the United States," *Immigration and Nationality Law Review* 16 (1994–95): 465–506 (489 and n. 92).

[10] Eli F. Heckscher and Bertil Ohlin, *Heckscher-Ohlin Trade Theory*, trans. and ed. Harry Flam and M. June Flanders (Cambridge, MA: MIT Press, 1991).

[11] "Presidential Address: Clinton Urges Passage of Free-Trade Pact," in *CQ Almanac 1993*, 49th ed., 46-D-47-D (Washington, DC: Congressional Quarterly, 1994), http://library.cqpress.com/cqalmanac/cqal93-844-25162-1104274.

For this reason, I refer to the Heckscher–Ohlin theorem below as the "substitutionist" line, because it argued that trade and migration acted as substitutes for each other, and therefore NAFTA would reduce migration by augmenting trade. Even around the time NAFTA was debated, however, migration specialists pointed out that, contrary to the Heckscher–Ohlin model, trade and migration can very well act as complements instead of substitutes.[12] The substitutionist line depends on a number of assumptions, in particular that production conditions across the two modeled countries are identical, save for differences in their factor endowments. If other variables are introduced across the countries, such as differences in available production technology or differences in economies of scale, then trade and migration can complement, rather than substitute for, each other.[13]

This latter, antisubstitutionist prediction more accurately described the movement of Mexican labor into the United States that began to be observed not long after NAFTA was implemented, in particular to work in agriculture. The much higher economies of scale and levels of technology of US agribusiness meant that, once lower post-NAFTA tariff prices were factored in, as the University of California agricultural economist Philip Martin put it in 1995, "it turned out that it was cheaper to produce lettuce here [in the United States] using Mexican labor than in Mexico."[14] Martin continued, "But the perverse effect of that is that it has increased the demand here for Mexican workers [who are willing to do this tough, low-wage work] [...] We're still sucking in workers to export these commodities."[15] In other words, the introduction of NAFTA increased both trade and migration across the Mexico–US border. The effect in agriculture was reproduced in numerous other industries, not only in rural sectors but also in urban ones, such as construction and food services.

Increased Mexico–US migration, including irregular migration, after NAFTA

A 1995 news report noted that the phenomenon of increased farmworker migration from Mexico to the United States "contradict[ed] the Clinton Administration's claims that NAFTA would reduce the floodtide of illegal immigrants."[16] This report acknowledged the fact that much of the labor movement between Mexico and the United States to supply farmworkers has been unauthorized. Indeed, in the years since NAFTA's implementation, both regular and irregular migration to the United States increased

---

[12] For a discussion of this literature, see Patricio Aroca and William F. Maloney, "Migration, Trade, and Foreign Direct Investment in Mexico," *World Bank Economic Review* 19, no. 3 (2005): 449–72 (449 and n. 1).

[13] Assaf Razin and Efraim Sadka, "International Migration and International Trade" (working paper no. 4239, National Bureau of Economic Research, Cambridge, MA, December 1992): 1–44 (19–25).

[14] James Sterngold, "NAFTA Trade-Off: Some Jobs Lost, Others Gained," *New York Times*, October 9, 1995, A1.

[15] Ibid.

[16] Ibid.

significantly. From 1994 to 2000, the annual number of Mexican citizens migrating to the United States jumped by 79 percent.[17] A little fewer than half of those were present without authorization, with the proportion of irregular migrants climbing to just above half by 2009, when overall net migration from Mexico to the United States peaked.[18]

Thus, migration from Mexico to the United States more than doubled during the 10 years between the mid-1990s, when NAFTA entered into force, and the late 2000s, when the overall number started to decline with the global financial crisis.[19] The estimated number of unauthorized immigrants from Mexico to the United States also more than doubled, from 2.9 million in 1995 to 6.9 million in 2007.[20] Rural migration from Mexico to the United States—where much of the farmworker population would come from—grew at two-and-a-half times the rate of the overall increase in Mexico-to-US migration.[21]

Competing causal accounts of the NAFTA–trade–migration relationship

Although the fact of increased migration from Mexico to the United States in the late twentieth century and early twenty-first century is well established, commentators have disagreed on what that fact conveys about the relationship between trade and migration. Critics of NAFTA have argued that increased trade significantly contributed to migration to the United States due to the displacement of economic production, especially agricultural production, and the concomitant loss in employment. Those taking a more favorable view have stated that NAFTA contributed a net increase to employment and that the economic situation in Mexico, with its related effects on Mexico–US migration, would have been worse without NAFTA.[22] On this view, NAFTA, and especially its substitutionist effects, helped abate, rather than exacerbate, migration from Mexico to the United States.

So where does the truth lie? My argument is that, even if the substitutionist model could theoretically have unfolded so that NAFTA could in fact potentially have operated

---

[17] Mark Weisbrot, Stephan Lefebvre and Joseph Sammut, "Did NAFTA Help Mexico? An Assessment after 20 Years" (Washington, DC: Center for Economic Policy Research, February 2014): 2.

[18] Ibid. (citing the total number of Mexican migrants in the United States as 9.4 million in 2000 and 12.6 in 2009 when migration peaked); Ana Gonzalez-Barrera, "More Mexicans Leaving Than Coming to the US" (Washington, DC: Pew Research Center, November 2015), 12 (citing 4.5 unauthorized migrants in 2000, and 6.9 in 2009).

[19] Gonzalez-Barrera, "More Mexicans Leaving Than Coming to the US," Figure 2 ("Mexican Immigrant Population in the U.S. in Decline"), 7.

[20] Ibid., 12.

[21] Francisco Meré, "Rural Migration in Mexico," Agricultural Outlook Forum, 2007: 5 (reporting a 200 percent increase in migration from rural Mexico to the United States between 1994 and 2000).

[22] John J. Audley, Demetrios G. Papademetriou, Sandra Polaski and Scott Vaughan, *NAFTA's Promise and Reality: Lessons from Mexico for the Hemisphere* (Washington, DC: Carnegie Endowment for International Peace, 2004), 53.

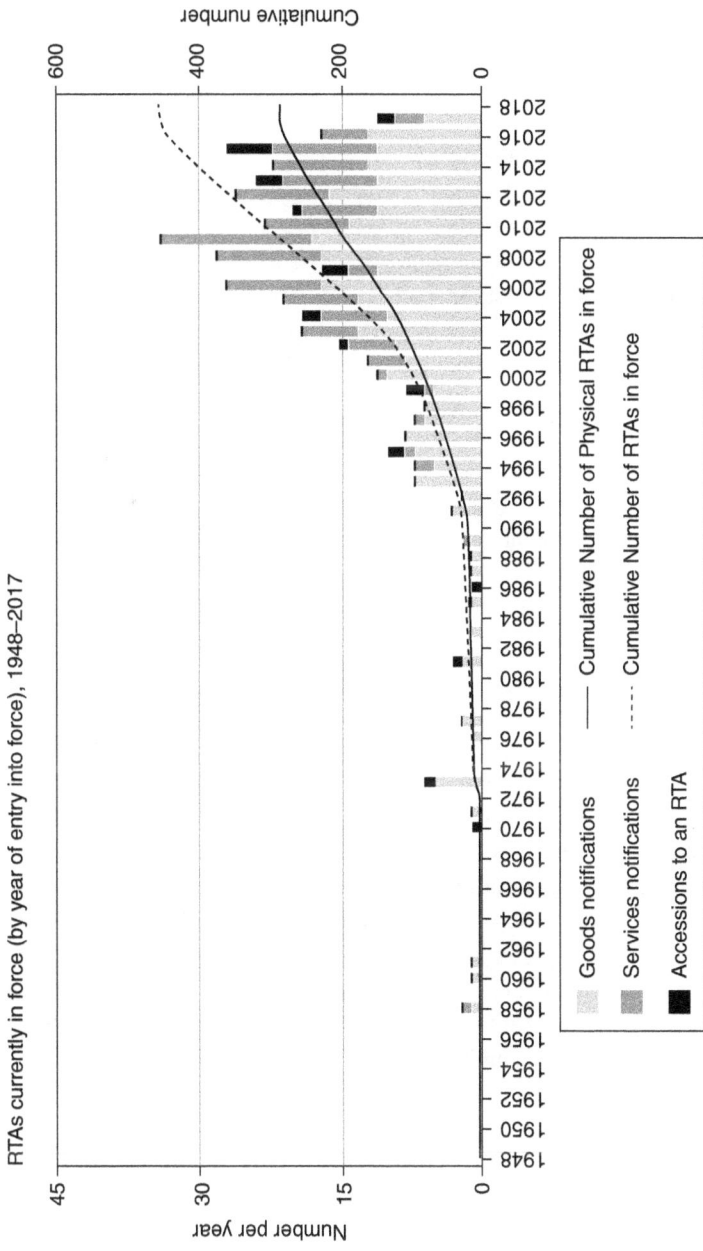

RTAs currently in force (by year of entry into force), 1948–2017

Figure 23.1 Mexican Immigrant Population in the U.S. in Decline

to curb migration from Mexico to the United States rather than increase it, the presence of numerous other factors prevented this from happening and in fact compelled the opposite to happen. Instead, post-NAFTA migration from Mexico to the United States grew as a function of (1) increased trade between the two countries *in the context of* (2) significant wealth disparity between them *coupled with* (3) the adoption by the Mexican state of neoclassical policies that independently increased economic volatility and simultaneously prevented the establishment of measures necessary to support both economic growth and stability.

Rather than coupling trade openness with measures to increase domestic capacity and to offset the immediate effect of trade-related employment losses, the Mexican government both before and after NAFTA hewed to a classically *laisser faire* set of policies that reduced its ability to do either. A number of the difficulties arising from increased exposure or vulnerability to the global economy could after all have been remedied, at least to some extent, with more robust domestic measures. The failure to adopt such measures has been a pervasive feature of the economic status quo and forms the subject of extensive critique throughout the essays in this volume. Indeed, one can say the same thing about policy in the United States, as several essays in this volume do. The difference is that, given the wage and income differential between Mexico and the United States, the absence of domestic opportunity in Mexico contributed to migration flows to the United States. As is argued elsewhere in the volume, although international economic law certainly established constraints, it did not require governments, including that of Mexico, to enact the deregulatory and defiscalizing measures that prevented them from ensuring a more equitable distribution of wealth and income gains in the era of globalization.

NAFTA's aggregate impact

An uncontested impact of NAFTA has been to augment the volume of cross-border trade in goods and services among all three partner countries. In the years since NAFTA's implementation, the value of US trade with its NAFTA partners, in terms of both imports and exports, has multiplied fivefold,[23] about twice as quickly as that of the US economy as a whole.[24] Beyond this observed increase, debates over the benefits of NAFTA have often been quite polemical. A broad swath of literature has concluded that its net effect, apart from the increased total volume of trade, is, if anything, hard to characterize.[25] From the US perspective, NAFTA did not deliver on President Clinton's initial (and mistaken) estimate of "a million jobs in the first five years"[26] or on other NAFTA

[23] M. Angeles Villarreal and Ian F. Fergusson, "NAFTA at 20: Overview and Trade Effects" (Washington, DC: Congressional Research Service, February 21, 2013), 11.

[24] The US gross domestic product increased from $6.879 trillion in 1993 to $16.155 trillion in 2012 (US current dollars), an increase of 234 percent (World Bank Development Data, data.worldbank.org).

[25] Villarreal and Fergusson, "NAFTA at 20," 1.

[26] Glenn Kessler, "The Strange Tale about Why Bill Clinton Said NAFTA Would Create 1 Million Jobs," *Washington Post*, September 21, 2018.

proponents' forecasts of hundreds of thousands of jobs.[27] The most positive contemporary assessments conclude that the overall impact of NAFTA for the United States has been "small, but positive."[28]

Whatever NAFTA's aggregate impact, all assessments of it also agree that it produced concentrated gains and losses for particular sectors. In the United States, for example, agriculture experienced a boon in its increased exports to Mexico. On the other hand, the US automobile industry experienced significant losses in conjunction with the continental vertical integration of the industry facilitated by NAFTA.[29] The more critical assessments have contended that auto-related and other manufacturing job losses produced a net loss of 200,000 US jobs in the first five years.[30]

The Mexican side of this picture reflected, to some extent, a mirror image: exports from Mexico to the United States in the auto industry grew 480 percent,[31] at the same time that US corn displaced a significant amount of local agricultural production. US critics of NAFTA saw the agreement as a giveaway to Mexico that would create a "giant sucking sound" as US jobs fled south of the border; however, the net effect of NAFTA on Mexican employment and economic growth has been just as equivocal as on the United States. Mexico's economy has remained fairly flat in the decades since NAFTA's implementation, showing an annual average growth rate of 0.9 percent—lower than the average rate of the US economy, and particularly low for a developing country.[32] The failure of the Mexican economy to take off post-NAFTA constitutes one of the factors contributing to the increase of migration to the United States.

Why didn't NAFTA job growth reduce Mexico–US migration?

For NAFTA to have performed the function predicted by the Heckscher–Ohlin substitutionist theorem, increased trade would have had to accompany an increase in economic production in Mexico, which in turn would have absorbed workers who might otherwise have migrated to the United States. The problem with this scenario, however, is that, in reality, post-NAFTA Mexico saw a net *loss* of jobs. As indicated above, overall economic production remained flat over the medium term. A further disaggregation shows that agricultural job losses outweighed job gains in manufacturing, with the latter constrained by both productivity increases and the revolving-door nature of much of the new manufacturing work. Between 1994 and 2002, for example, although the manufacturing sector gained 500,000 jobs, the agricultural sector lost 1.6 million jobs as agriculture reconsolidated into large-scale production.[33]

---

[27] Gary Hufbauer and Jeffrey J. Schott, *NAFTA: An Assessment* (Washington, DC: Institute for International Economics, 1993).

[28] Villarreal and Fergusson, "NAFTA at 20," 13.

[29] Ibid.

[30] Robert E. Scott, "Heading South: U.S.–Mexico Trade and Job Displacement after NAFTA" (report, Washington, DC, Economic Policy Institute, 2011), 7.

[31] Villarreal and Fergusson, "NAFTA at 20," 14.

[32] Weisbrot et al., "Did NAFTA Help Mexico?," 4.

[33] Audley et al., *NAFTA's Promise and Reality*, 6.

Within manufacturing, employment gains arose primarily in the maquila sector, whereas nonmaquila manufacturing had actually experienced an overall decline by the early 2000s. Moreover, employment in auto manufacturing did not greatly increase.[34] While Mexico's auto exports to the United States surged, much of the work involved relatively minimal assembly work on imported parts.[35] As a consequence, a lot of the export value had been created before the products in question reached the Mexican manufacturing stage, and assembly required fewer workers than had been predicted.

If NAFTA did not create an employment boom that diverted workers from seeking migration to the United States, did it still perform a substitution function, as standard economics would predict, by ensuring that the migration rate was less than it otherwise would have been? Perhaps NAFTA decreased migration in relative, not absolute, terms. The problem with this scenario is that migration increased significantly after NAFTA was established. In the first 10 years, migration from Mexico to the United States increased by 100 percent. What then caused the spike in migration, if it was not increased economic liberalization? To preserve the substitutionist theorem, alternate explanations have to show why migration increased, rather than decreased, as trade was increasing.

Two such explanations are typically proffered.[36] The first is that Mexico–US migration, and even the post-NAFTA migration spike, was a function of a generational population boom in Mexico that overwhelmed any contemporaneous substitution effect. The second is that, particularly in the years after NAFTA was adopted, a currency crisis, rather than increased economic liberalization generally, inflicted a dramatic economic contraction and so propelled mass emigration. The two arguments here for alternate causes are explored, and ultimately rejected, below.

Why didn't population growth account for the post-NAFTA migration increase?

The post-NAFTA increase in migration marked the tail end of "one of the largest mass migrations in modern history," in which the number of Mexican citizens present in the United States grew from fewer than 1 million in 1970 to the peak of 12.8 million in 2007.[37] High population growth rates created a "demographic bulge in the workforce through the late 1990s."[38] Some have argued that, as a consequence, population growth formed the primary cause of increased Mexico–US migration, including after NAFTA.

---

[34] Ibid., 16.

[35] Ibid.

[36] I am grateful to Gregory Shaffer for organizing a workshop in February 2018 in which I was able to present this research and discuss at length the standard trade economics view with noted trade lawyers and economists (Reconceiving Trade Agreements for Social Inclusion, UC Irvine School of Law, Irvine, CA, February 9–10, 2018).

[37] "More Mexicans Leaving Than Coming to the US," Pew Research Center, 7.

[38] Sandra Polaski, brief submitted to the Canadian Standing Senate Committee on Foreign Affairs: Mexican Employment, Productivity and Income a Decade after NAFTA (Washington, DC: Carnegie Endowment for International Peace, February 25, 2004).

However, though population growth in Mexico most likely fueled some of this migration, that factor alone does not seem to account for all of it. If the population boom was the primary driver behind migration, one would expect that Mexico–US migration would have increased at roughly the same rate as the population increased, for example, by 15 or 20 percent. Instead, migration increased at a much higher and more rapid rate. Between 1995 and 2005, migration from Mexico to the United States increased by 100 percent. During the same time frame, Mexico's population grew by about 15 percent, a rate of less than one-sixth the migration rate.[39] The working-age population increased by only about 5 percent, or about one-twentieth as quickly as Mexico–US migration.[40]

The fact that migration rates increased quickly after the adoption of NAFTA and were much higher than population growth rates undermines the argument that it was the population boom, not NAFTA, that explains migration. And if NAFTA had the substitution effect predicted by trade economists, one would have expected the migration rate to slow after NAFTA. Instead, migration increased by a much higher percentage than did the population.

Why didn't the peso crisis account for the post-NAFTA migration increase?

The Mexican economy experienced a severe shock in 1994–95 with the peso crisis. The severe contraction of the economy may well have contributed to an increase in emigration, such as the increase following the 1982 debt crisis. One might argue that this, rather than Mexico–US trade and increased economic liberalization more generally, caused increased emigration. In other words, but for the peso crisis, NAFTA would have performed the intended effect of substituting trade for migration. But the peso crisis actually created more jobs due to the increased competitiveness of the export sector, so it cannot be blamed for the increase in emigration during this period.[41] Instead,

---

[39] From 1995 to 2005, Mexico's total population increased from 94 million to 108 million, an increase of 14.8 percent. United Nations Department of Economic and Social Affairs, Population Division, World Population Prospects Database, https://population.un.org/wpp/DataQuery/. During the same time period, immigrants to the United States from Mexico increased from about 6 million to about 12 million. "More Mexicans Leaving Than Coming to the US," Pew Research Center, 7.

[40] From 1995 to 2005, Mexico's working-age population increased from 59.3 million to 62.5 million people, an increase of 5.4 percent. Organisation for Economic Co-operation and Development, Labour Force Statistics on Working-Age Population, https://data.oecd.org/pop/working-age-population.htm.

[41] The severe decline in the value of the peso, while disastrous for domestic consumption and demand, helped Mexico's export sector since Mexican products became more competitive: the peso devaluation boosted Mexican exports more than NAFTA-related tariff changes on their own would have (USITC, The Impact of Trade Agreements, publication 3621 (2003)). One might counter that export increases could not compensate for the larger drop in demand brought about by the domestic contraction related to the peso crisis. In turn, this contraction would have reduced domestic employment more than any export-related increases could offset, and in that way contributed to increased emigration. The data partially bears out this

introduction of economic liberalization between countries of such a dramatic wealth disparity as that of the United States and Mexico, coupled with the absence of domestic measures by the Mexican state that would have helped capture greater gains from this liberalization, contributed to a large outmigration as Mexican citizens sought opportunities elsewhere, especially in their trading partner to the north.

Disaggregating post-NAFTA Mexico–US migration

If, contrary to the substitutionist line, displacement resulting from NAFTA helped contribute to increased migration, one would have expected to see an increase in rural migration since one of the largest immediate effects of NAFTA was a large increase in US agricultural imports to Mexico and a concomitant displacement of Mexican agricultural production. In fact, that is precisely what happened. Rural migration to the United States more than tripled between 1995 and 2002, increasing much more quickly than the overall migration rate.[42] But the picture is more complex. There was internal migration within Mexico, some of which was a prelude to migration to the United States; migration from urban areas increased; and complex patterns of back-and-forth movement emerged. Overall, what this has meant is that undocumented Mexico–US migration in the late twentieth and early twenty-first century has taken on the following dimensions. First, and most well established, has been the movement of primarily undocumented agricultural workers from the rural areas of central western Mexico directly to the United States. Second, and more recent, has been the movement of workers from urban interior communities to the United States (some of whom have already migrated internally from rural areas). Third, the northern border region serves as a site for circular migration to the United States as individuals move back and forth.[43] In addition to their geographical dimensions, these migration patterns can also be broken out into their temporal aspects, with some migration more or less permanent in nature, some temporary and based on seasonal work, and some shaped by a transnational orientation in which "immigrants forge and sustain simultaneous multi-stranded social relations that link together their societies of origin and settlement."[44]

---

theory, but only to a very limited extent that does not change the overall picture. The peso crisis period did coincide with a temporary drop in domestic manufacturing: after 1994, non-maquiladora manufacturing did decline. However, by 1997 this decline had reversed itself, and by 1998 the domestic industry had recovered the jobs lost (though by 2003 aggregate employment had declined again to below 1998 levels). Ibid., 3. Whatever the impact of the peso crisis on domestic demand and production, the isolated effect appears to have been relatively short-lived and overtaken by other dynamics.

[42] Meré, "Rural Migration in Mexico," 5.

[43] Elizabeth Fussell, "Sources of Mexico's Migration Stream: Rural, Urban, and Border Migrants to the United States," *Social Forces* 82, no. 3 (2004): 937–67.

[44] Nina Glick Schiller, Linda Basch and Christina Szanton-Blank, "From Immigrants to Transmigrants: Theorizing Transnational Migration," in *Migration and Transnational Social Spaces*, ed. Ludger Pries (London: Ashgate, 1999), 73–105 (73).

Looking Forward: To Close Markets or to Open Borders?

It is worth stopping here to consider the political subtext of the "asymmetry as caus-ation" argument. One of the concerns with explicitly linking trade and irregular migra-tion is that it will exacerbate and feed into xenophobic tendencies, which have exposed themselves to a startling degree in current political discourse. Trade agreements would be opposed for xenophobic reasons, that is, because they would lead to increased migration from the trade counterparty. This is very strenuously not the intended effect of this ana-lysis. Rather, the intention is the opposite: not to feed into xenophobia but to challenge it. Xenophobic tendencies form a good part of what has kept migration issues off the table in these agreements. Egalitarian principles demand that powerful governments that have initiated these agreements, such as the United States in seeking NAFTA in the example above, as well as in supporting international economic regimes of liberalization more generally, should not believe they can have the proverbial cake and eat it too. The puta-tive belief of powerful governments that they can cherry-pick agreements to privilege areas of interest, such as goods and capital, and ignore others, such as migration, will, according to this argument, turn out to be unsustainable.[45]

So what is to be done? How might we imagine counteracting international economic asymmetry? Imagining possibilities for an alternate status quo requires a rather opti-mistic suspension of belief regarding the possibilities permitted by political will. The most radical measure would be to open up freedom of movement altogether—to have open trade and open borders. This would be most consistent with trade theory and argu-ably with liberal commitments.

The obvious hard constraint for open trade/open borders is politics, and in the current climate that includes clearly a very nasty strain of politics. It also includes, how-ever, an aspect that may be harder to dismiss and that is related to legitimate claims of citizenship, that is, of belonging and social membership, in which membership is neces-sarily defined by both who is included and who is excluded. Either way, politics is a major roadblock to open trade/open borders, and Brexit is, of course, one of many cautionary tales that could be invoked.

In light of this, a more piecemeal and modest approach would be to subject migra-tion to GATT-style sector-by-sector reciprocal negotiations over time. The argument would be that over a period of years this would allow for some momentum. One clear success story is the post–World War II reduction in tariffs, to the point that the weighted average is now less than 5 percent for Organisation for Economic Co-operation and Development countries.

A version of this was at some point proposed in the WTO Doha Development Agenda negotiations by India and some other countries. Dubbed the "GATS visa," this was a bid to multilateralize temporary work visas that would accompany short-term labor migra-tion (so they would be available for persons covered by sectoral Mode 4 commitments

---

[45] I use the term *putative* in an allusion to a more skeptical reading of the political motivation, which is that the production of unauthorized migration is an intended and desirable outcome for powerful interests who seek to undermine the bargaining power of available workforces.

and horizontal commitments of a WTO member under the General Agreement on Trade in Services (GATS)). Ideally the GATS visa would not only facilitate entry but also harmonize immigration and visa procedures, which obviously vary wildly across countries, and perhaps also set out some harmonized rules for wage parity conditions for hiring qualifications.

The GATS visa, however, didn't go anywhere, again running into the problem of political will, since even piecemeal negotiations require some parity or reciprocity of interests from the other side. Moreover, even if the GATS visa could be successfully implemented, it would be far from an ideal labor regime. Temporary visas are subject to their own problems with respect to exacerbating vulnerability and precarity in labor through structural features such as nonportability. Typically, employees are tied to one employer, which sharply increases the power of the employer relative to the employee. This is particularly true for low-skill sectors, but there are widespread complaints of exploitation across the board, including, for example, highly skilled information technology workers in Silicon Valley. In addition, competition to get temporary work visas has led to abuses such as debt bondage and other forms of human trafficking, again particularly in low-wage sectors.

Another version of the piecemeal approach would be stand-alone bilateral agreements, such as the array of existing bilateral labor and migration agreements. Again, political will and power differential make it more difficult for these agreements to enforce standards for worker protection, as has been noted by a number of commentators.

One could therefore ditch the piecemeal approach and go back to a more comprehensive solution, but one that extends beyond the economic analysis of migration toward a recognition of the full implications of labor migration, not just for economic production but for political and social citizenship. In some ways the 2018 Resolution by the United Nations General Assembly adopting the Global Compact on Migration, following its call in the 2016 New York Declaration on Refugees and Migrants for a "safe, orderly and comprehensive" approach to migration, seeks to do just that. The United States pulled out of the talks, of course, and the Global Compact runs the risk of the experience of the UN Convention on the Rights of Migrant Workers and Their Families, which has languished at 30-plus signatories. The UN migrant workers convention at least has entered into force as a treaty, whereas the Global Compact has no formally binding legal status.

We are returned again and again to the question of political will, in that any of these institutional or legal changes, however radical or modest, could occur only in conjunction with the political and social movement necessary to create the conditions for change. Yet at the moment the political winds appear very much to be shifting away from such possibilities.

A final alternative could therefore be considered, which would be to relinquish the notion of liberalized migration as a feature of a global liberalization project that seems now to have reached its political limits and to correct the asymmetry problem not by calling for labor migration to keep up with liberalization in goods and capital but by calling for a return across the board to a more modulated and more restricted market ideal. The "embedded liberalism" of the Keynesian era is often held up as the exemplar of an era featuring more socially desirable policy space for national governments to tailor access to their markets in keeping with their own economic and social objectives, including a relatively robust labor regime. It is worth pointing out that this was precisely the same era in which labor immigration into the United States was much lower than the decades either beforehand or afterward.

The question then arises: for those of us progressives who would support more policy space and more restrictiveness or protectiveness for states when it comes to market access for goods and capital, are we comfortable with the same approach when it comes to people? Or do people exert moral and social claims that might justify an asymmetry pointing in the opposite direction, one based not on economics but on ethics?

The case for open borders ultimately rests on a claim to universal equality. Given the disparity of wealth between the Global North and Global South, and the role that migration can play in bridging that gap, opening the borders presents the best way to ensure that, contrary to the status quo, one's destiny is not predetermined by one's birthplace. For those concerned with global economic inequality, global poverty and global development, the case seems plain.

This claim, of course, runs into an objection that it is inconsistent with the arrangement of the international community and the world order into sovereign states. The sovereigntist objection itself can draw on numerous sources of justification, including democratic theory, communitarianism and positive law. According to the sovereigntist objection, the normative claim to equality, regardless of its independent value, is bested by claims from the other side: those of citizens of the Global North to the citizenship benefits of the social contracts in which they have entered with their own governments (democratic theory); claims of cultural or historical singularity, in which national communities, including in the Global North, have morally salient reasons to preserve those communities even at the cost of excluding others (communitarianism); and claims that the legal and doctrinal principle of sovereignty, and the associated prerogative of territorial exclusion, carries its own moral weight—the morality of law itself, of the moral imperative to comply with law and of the historical pedigree behind that law (positivism).

These objections, however, can be countered, each on their own grounds. From the perspective of democratic theory, if the theory of democratic representation holds that people who are affected by governmental policies should be represented in the processes by which they are made, then foreign nationals have a democratic right to be included in the social contract when it comes to hegemonic powers such as the United States, whose governments so determine the policies and practices of their own.[46] From the perspective of communitarianism, the empirical reality of an interconnected and transnational world belies the claims to cultural purity made by communitarians.[47] One need look no further than the polyglot roots of the United States or to the history of outward

---

[46]   Arash Abizadeh, "Democratic Theory and Border Coercion: No Right to Unilaterally Control Your Own Borders," *Political Theory* 36, no. 1 (2008): 37–65.

[47]   Kwame Anthony Appiah, *Cosmopolitanism: Ethics in a World of Strangers* (New York: W. W. Norton, 2006).

expansion of the Global North to the Global South to see that this is true. This last point also speaks to the objection from positive law. The claims to the sanctity of sovereign territoriality in the Global North are belied by a long and deep history of intervention by the Global North in the political processes of the Global South.[48]

At the same time, the case for open borders should be subject to all the caveats and restraints we would attach to other forms of market-opening policy when implemented by economic regulators. The process of immigration liberalization would ideally be carefully conducted and attended by measures to account for and compensate those displaced by the process. Crucial to any such process would be a core commitment to enforcing and improving labor conditions for both citizen and migrant workers, not only through direct intervention in labor law but also by targeting background rules that affect their bargaining power and income relative to employers.[49] It is no accident that the current antiglobal and anti-immigration backlash has occurred at the same time that international and domestic income inequality reached an unprecedented high, with a massive redistribution toward the wealthiest.[50] Anti-immigration political tumult distracts from addressing how the laws and institutions that govern our economies—including from global governance—have produced such a regressive turn. Reform to migration law and policy could only sustainably occur in this more considerate context. In sum, the asymmetry in the international economic order between open markets and closed borders should be corrected, not by a retreat into nationalism but by a movement of the international economic order more closely to approximate the progressive goals of equity and equality.

---

[48] For a terrific discussion of these points, see Tendayi Achiume, "Migration as Decolonization," forthcoming in *Stanford Law Review*. For an extensive review of the political and legal theory implicated by migration and sovereignty, see Chantal Thomas, "What Does the Emerging International Law of Migration Mean for Sovereignty?," *Melbourne Journal of International Law* 14 (2013): 393–450.

[49] See Rittich and Santos (chapters 19 and 20, this volume).

[50] Thomas Piketty, *Capital in the Twenty-First Century*, trans. Arthur Goldhammer (Cambridge, MA: Harvard University Press, 2014).

INDEX